Further Under the Duvet

by the same author

Watermelon
Lucy Sullivan is Getting Married
Rachel's Holiday
Last Chance Saloon
Sushi for Beginners
Under the Duvet
Angels
The Other Side of the Story

Marian Keyes

Further Under
the Duvet

MICHAEL JOSEPH

an imprint of

PENGUIN BOOKS

MICHAEL JOSEPH

Published by the Penguin Group
Penguin Books Ltd, 80 Strand, London WC2R ORL, England
Penguin Group (USA) Inc., 375 Hudson Street, New York, New York 10014, USA
Penguin Group (Canada), 10 Alcorn Avenue, Toronto, Ontario, Canada M4V 3B2
(a division of Pearson Penguin Canada Inc.)
Penguin Ireland, 25 St Stephen's Green, Dublin 2, Ireland (a division of Penguin Books Ltd)
Penguin Group (Australia), 250 Camberwell Road,
Camberwell, Victoria 3124, Australia (a division of Pearson Australia Group Pty Ltd)
Penguin Books India Pvt Ltd, 11 Community Centre,
Panchsheel Park, New Delhi – 110 017, India
Penguin Group (NZ), cnr Airborne and Rosedale Roads, Albany,
Auckland 1310, New Zealand (a division of Pearson New Zealand Ltd)
Penguin Books (South Africa) (Pty) Ltd, 24 Sturdee Avenue,
Rosebank 2196, South Africa

Penguin Books Ltd, Registered Offices: 80 Strand, London WC2R ORL, England

www.penguin.com

First published 2005
1

Set in 12.25/15 pt Monotype Fournier
Typeset by Rowland Phototypesetting Ltd, Bury St Edmunds, Suffolk
Printed in Great Britain by Clays Ltd, St Ives plc

A CIP catalogue record for this book is available from the British Library

ISBN Hardback 0–718–14792–8
Trade paperback 0–718–14796–0

For Himself

CONTENTS

Contents

Introduction

Hello and welcome to *Further Under the Duvet*, the follow-up to *Under the Duvet*, my first volume of journalism. I say 'journalism' but the articles included here are mostly humorous autobiographical pieces about subjects like my great love of make-up and ill-health and my great fear of being trapped on a bus in a foreign country with forty Irish people (it's the *singing*). There are also a few more serious pieces about feminism, mediums and charity trips I've made to Ethiopia and Russia.

This time around, some of my short stories are also included. In fact, *all* of them seem to be, all seven of them. The thing is that I find it really hard to write short stories. (The clue is in the name: they're too *short*. I'm only really getting into my stride with the characters and the plot, when next thing, it's time to finish it. As a result I've written very few.)

Also included here is something called Mammy Walsh's Problem Page. Mammy Walsh is a character who appeared in several of my novels as a supporting character (a mother, as it happens) and over time she has developed a life of her own. In response to readers' requests, she now dispenses no-nonsense advice from my website. I am slightly worried that by giving her a platform in this book, she'll lose the run of herself entirely; she's pretty strident at the best of times.

Some of the articles in this collection have already been published and the various publications are credited at the end of each piece. Thank you to all of them, especially the wonderful Marie O'Riordan of *Marie Claire*, for permitting me to reuse the pieces.

Now, just before someone writes and asks, everything in the non-fiction pieces in this book really did happen to me (yes, even turning forty), but occasionally I've changed people's names to protect them (and sometimes me).

All my royalties from the Irish sales of the hardback will go to To Russia With Love, a wonderful charity that works with Russian orphans. And thank you very much for reading this book. I sincerely hope you enjoy it.

Marian Keyes

HANDBAGS AND GLADRAGS

The Nicest Thing That Ever Happened to Me

*I*t was like a dream come true. My friend Aoife was made editor of an Irish women's magazine; after I'd congratulated her, I said, 'Give us a job as a beauty columnist,' and she said, 'Okay.'

I stared at her and went, 'HAHAHA!' She said, 'I'm serious,' and for one brief moment the world stopped spinning on its axis.

'I'm serious,' she repeated. 'I was going to ask you but you beat me to it.' And I went home that night, thinking: I'm the luckiest person who ever lived.

The idea was that I'd have my own page in the magazine where I'd 'try and test' half a dozen or so of a particular product type and award them marks out of ten. Usually when I'm doing something new I'm nervous and I doubt my ability to do it well, but not this time – I was *born* for this. I knew my subject matter inside out. I could hold my own in any discussion on free radicals and sea kelp. I could differentiate between Stila lipglaze and Bobbi Brown lipgloss at a glance.

Aoife had said she'd contact a load of beauty PRs and tell them to send me stuff. So from the very next morning, I began to wait. All week I stood by the downstairs window, my nose pressed to the glass, waiting, waiting . . .

The days passed and no free stuff arrived and then, just

when I was starting to think it had all been a practical joke, the Lancôme lorry drew up outside. (Looking back, it was probably just the postman on his bike but it was so exciting that it took on mythical qualities.)

Himself answered the door, then placed a bulky padded envelope in my arms. With shaking hands I opened it, tipped the contents out onto my bed and nearly *puked* with excitement. I had been sent their latest night cream – expensive and fabulous – but the real prize was a selection of the forthcoming autumn cosmetics. There was a blusher, a quartet of eyeshadows, a lipstick, a bottle of nail varnish and the best bit of all: a new shade of Juicy Tube. I'll never forget it!

I made Himself play 'Lancôme Lady' with me. Sometimes he'd be the customer coming into the shop enquiring about the new season's colours and I'd be the Lancôme Lady demonstrating everything for him. Other times I'd be the customer and he'd be the woman behind the counter. We played for many happy hours. I made him. Even when he begged me to stop.

Then my sister came over to share our joy, but when she saw the Juicy Tube things threatened to turn ugly. Especially when she discovered that it wouldn't be in the shops for another six weeks. 'I'll buy it off you now,' she offered. But no amount of money could have persuaded me to part with it. 'Don't make me have to steal it,' she said gently. So I emailed the girl at Lancôme, telling her the whole sorry story, and guess what? She sent another!

Two days later, the Clinique lorry arrived, laden with goodies – lipsticks, an all-weather face cream and not just one, but *two* foundations. Shortly after that the YSL lorry drew up outside with (what seemed like) most of their new autumn range for me to try.

It was like being in love, I was dizzy, giddy, giggly and my free cosmetics were all I could think about. I arrayed them in a little basket by my bed, so they were the first things I saw when I woke up. Even when I could no longer persuade Himself to play Lancôme Lady (or Clinique Lady or YSL Lady), I played by myself. Sometimes I arranged my products by brand name and other times by body parts (all lip products in one little heap, all skincare in another, etc.).

Every Thursday Himself and myself go to my parents' house for our dinner, so this particular Thursday I gathered together all my free stuff, brought it with me and spilt it across their kitchen table to be admired. But instead of being dazzled, my mother was anxious: there had to be a catch. Then Dad came in, found the price lists and began to add up the value of all I'd been sent. (Once an accountant, always an accountant.) When he had everything totted up – it came to over three hundred euro – he could scarcely believe his own sums. 'That,' he declared, 'is shagging well ridiculous.'

The magazine was fortnightly and, with a racing imagination, I began to plan my columns. First weeks, then months ahead. I had a big, big vision for autumn through winter, with the columns as follows: new lip colours, new eye colours, protective winter face care, winter hands, then as we came nearer to Christmas, a how-to-look-like-you-don't-have-a-hangover column, a party make-up special, a gift-buying guide and, finally, an end-of-year thirty best products ever! Moving into January, of course, we'd start off with a detox special, then start focusing on nice stuff for Valentine's Day, then the new spring colours would be out . . . All this I'd already planned in September.

Novels piled up unwritten, promotional work was abandoned and friends and family were neglected, as I took up full-time residence in a delicious dreamworld of time-defying eye creams and lash-thickening mascaras. Because I'm a perfectionist (i.e. insane) I didn't want my column to be just any old beauty column, a patchjob of rehashed press releases. I wanted it to be fabulously funny and witty, and there wasn't room in my head for anything else. (Triumphs included describing Clinique's Repairwear as 'It's night cream, Jim, but not as we know it' and Origins' Gloomaway shower gel as 'Prozac in a tube'.) I wrote and rewrote constantly, cutting, adding, honing and polishing. I admit it: I was obsessed.

I had to give marks out of ten, but I was so in love with every product I got that the lowest score I could manage to give was eight. My ratings shuttled from eight to nine, passing all points in between (8.5). Occasionally, I gave ten out of ten and, I admit it, there were even times I gave eleven out of ten. Yes, and twelve. All the way up to fifteen, but *only when the product really merited it.*

Part of the job was having to bond with those all-powerful women, the beauty PRs, guardians of the freebies. I'd ring, nervous as anything, and rattle off my name and rank and finish by saying, 'So if you're interested in having your products covered, let me know.' In other words, 'Please send me free stuff. Like, *please.*'

I've never been comfortable asking for something for nothing, even though, as Aoife kept reminding me, I was offering coverage and thereby saving them a ton in advertising. And the weird thing was that there was no correlation between how fabulous the brand was and how generous they were. I had thought that the more expensive and exclusive the products, the less chance I had of getting them. But it didn't work like that at all. Truly yummy brands, brands that I had, in the past, paid good money for, like Prescriptives and Clinique, were phenomenally generous and staffed by lovely, friendly girls who didn't make me feel one bit like a greedy scuzzball. And Jo Malone, one of the most beloved and beautiful brands on the planet, sent stuff so delicious I had to lie down in a darkened room. Whereas Chanel told me to fuck off. Okay, not those words exactly, but when I explained my mission to some French wan at their press office, she said dismissively, 'We do not do zee: "tried and tested".' This was my cue to sneer, 'Oh yeah? Afraid you can't hack it, eh?' But because I saw the chance of free Chanel stuff slipping from my grasp, I kowtowed shamelessly, promising 'lovely coverage'. Alas, compromising my journalistic integrity came to nought; and nothing, not even a sample-sized eye cream, came from Chanel.

But for every knock-back, someone else came through. The day the Decléor lorry showed up, piled high with gorgeous French skincare, was another high spot, a memory I take out and polish every now and then, when I'm feeling blue.

Even when the product was all wrong for my skin type and colouring, I welcomed it anyway, then, when I'd amassed enough, had a big giveaway party for friends and family.

It was like nearly every day was my birthday. And never

knowing exactly what was going to be in the envelope was so exciting – it could be anything: a hot new perfume, night cream that I would read about in *Vogue* next month, must-have nail kits, glittery lipglosses, hideously expensive serum, or, as happened on one unhappy occasion, cold-sore ointment. Each morning saw steady increments in my adrenalin levels as I awaited the arrival of the postman. I was bad-tempered and ratty if nothing came, or, worse, a press release but no product! Talk about rubbing salt in the wound. But some of the companies used couriers so even if the postman had been, I got a rush whenever the doorbell rang. No matter who it was – chancers offering to clean our gutters, my father looking for the return of his hostess trolley – every one of my senses went on high alert as I prepared to welcome another inbound parcel and give it a happy home.

All in all, this beauty column was the nicest thing that had ever happened to me. When I was a child, I lived in pitiful hope that my father would give up his job as a civil service number-cruncher and open a sweet shop instead, so that I'd have yummy things on tap around the clock. I was now living the adult version of that dream.

Himself watched anxiously from the sidelines. 'When you say that it's the nicest thing that ever happened to you, you don't mean it's nicer than getting published?'

'Nicer!'

'Nicer than getting sober?'

'Nicer!'

'Nicer than . . . nicer than meeting me?'

'Nicer! Sorry.'

He accused me of having gone weird, of behaving like 'a

lady'. 'You take ages to get ready now,' he said. 'You used to be as fast as a man.' And yes, he had a point. I now had so much stuff to put on my face that preparing to go out took a lot longer. Once upon a time, tinted moisturizer was all I used, but now I had eye cream, day cream, skin-evener, make-up primer, concealer (both yellow and green), base, blush and powder glow. 'You look like a toffee apple,' he said.

Things came to a head a couple of days later. Almost a week had passed without anything arriving and, as I'd been pestering several PRs, I knew stuff was due but was afraid it had been nicked. It wouldn't have been the first time; a consignment of Laura Mercier's finest had disappeared only a short time before.

I was in my bedroom trying to think of another word for 'eyelash' when there was a commotion at the front door. Then Himself marched into the room, bearing a blue plastic crate crammed with padded envelopes. Loads of stuff. From lots of different companies! My ship had come in! Joyously I stretched out my arms and said, 'Gimme.' But Himself clattered the blue milk-crate yoke on the floor. 'It wasn't the normal postman. They had to bring it in a special van. This,' he yelled, 'is getting OUT OF HAND.'

He stomped from the room but soon changed his tune when one of the Jiffy bags turned out to be filled with Clinique for Men stuff. Eight different products, which he ferried off to the bathroom to try out immediately. Then he turned to me, apology stamped all over his (exfoliated, hydrated, buffed) face and said, 'Actually, I'm beginning to understand how you feel.'

Occasionally I got to put on my good clothes and meet

other beauty editors at a launch of a new product. But I soon discovered I had no clue how to behave: I was just thrilled to be in a nice hotel, having lunch, safe in the knowledge that I'd be leaving with free skincare. But the other women were like political journalists quizzing Donald Rumsfeld. They sat bolt upright, their pens poised over their pads, barking smile-free, incisive questions. 'Does this day cream have an SPF?' 'If it's so great, why does it need a serum too?' And meanest of all: 'Why should we use day creams when we can just have a botox injection?'

But suddenly, as abruptly as the dream started, it all stopped. News came that the magazine was shutting down; it had been doing well but the owner had decided to move into property speculation. Twenty people were out of a job and I was devastated. I tried to keep it in perspective – I was a spoilt brat and I wasn't like the poor misfortunates who had lost their full-time job – but all the same. Something to do with the unexpected way it had stopped, totally without warning, made me feel as though I'd had a near-death experience. We know not the minute or the hour. We should live each lipgloss as if it's our last.

Naturally, I was honour-bound to contact every beauty PR I'd been dealing with and tell them to take me off their mailing list. It killed me to do it and, between ourselves, I was hoping that a combination of my honesty and sympathy for my situation would persuade them all to keep me on anyway. 'Sure, what difference does one more goody bag make to us?' I had hoped to hear them say. But no.

For a few days after the terrible news, those magical Jiffy bags continued to arrive, like letters from beyond the grave.

They'd been sent before news of the magazine's demise had got out. And then the trickle dried up completely and, after eight delicious months, it was time to resume my life again.

Previously unpublished.

I Shop, Therefore I Am

If you like to shop there is nowhere in the world like New York. You can get everything in the whole world there. Here are some highlights from a recent trip.

First stop: Saks of Fifth Avenue

We had to run the gauntlet of the cosmetics hall before getting to the lifts at the back.

Himself took a nervous look at the over-fragrant melee – at the marauding gangs of sharp-suited types lying in wait with bottles of Nu, ready to spray us, at the white-coated skin therapists, ready to ambush us with their special offers – and looked terrified.

'Just put your head down and run,' I said. 'And whatever you do, don't make eye-contact with any of them.'

I launched myself into the fray, Himself on my heels. 'Stay low, stay low!' I urged, but the inevitable happened. 'Christ! I got got,' he yelped.

'How bad?' I asked.

He sniffed himself. 'Paul Smith for women. Not too bad.'

We kept going, while all around us voices babbled a cacophony of temptations. *Hey, gorgeous, wanna try our new spring shades? Over here, over here, spend $75 and get a free lipstick. Never mind them, what about us, our dinky travel kits* *are just in. But we're showcasing our new concealer, it'll change your LIFE . . .*

Finally we reached the lifts at the back. 'Jesus,' he said, wiping the sweat from his brow. 'It's like a Moroccan souk.'

How I got barred from Miu Miu

There are many posh shops in New York and the staff are not pleasant. At least not to me. I was given some advice by a regular: look evil and bored; waft; display no positive emotion; above all, don't make a fool of yourself.

With Himself, my sister and my friend Anne-Marie in tow, we entered Miu Miu, where the first thing I saw was my favourite pair of boots – I was actually wearing a pair – at half price. Caught up in a fifty-per-cent-off frenzy, I decided to buy a new pair but first I had to check the size of the ones I was wearing. So I straightened my leg and stuck my foot up for Himself to see what it said on my sole. As he held my ankle at face height (he's tall) I felt myself losing my balance and began that hopping, arm-windmilling thing people do – usually just before someone off stage throws in a bag of ball-bearings. My sister grabbed hold of me, but unfortunately also fell victim to the waves of unbalance, then Anne-Marie tried to reverticalize us, but she too got caught up in the vortex. We hovered between balance and falling for a few tortuous seconds then Himself intervened, but the combined weight of the three of us was too much and, in slow motion, in a tangle of limbs and coats and handbags, all four of us toppled to the floor. *Oh my God, I'm lying on the floor in Miu Miu.*

Himself refuses to go into Victoria's Secret

Just point-blank refused. He didn't even say, 'Please don't make me.' He just stood at the door, looked at the prairies of underwear within, told me no power on earth would make him go in and that was that. I told him he'd look more like a pervert hanging around outside, but nothing doing.

I was keen to see what all the fuss was about; in the ads I'd got the impression that Victoria's Secret was a class act but when I stood too close to one of the nightdresses and it crackled and stuck to me, I wasn't so sure. All the same I bought a couple of bras – one pink, one lilac. Later when I told my sister about the visit, she said in disgust, 'Oh my God. You didn't buy anything, did you?' I fessed up the colouredy bras. 'Well,' she advised, 'just don't stand in front of any naked flames.'

The psychic assistants in Bloomingdales

Anne-Marie told me the assistants in Bloomingdales were psychic and I thought she meant that they were so knowledge-able they were *almost* psychic. So Himself and myself went into Bloomingdales looking for the Eileen Fisher range and – not expecting any joy – asked an assistant if they stocked it. Without missing a beat he not only confirmed that they carried it, but gave me the exact coordinates (third floor, two-thirds of the way back, bordered by Marc Jacobs to the north, Aqua to the east and DKNY to the south). Consider-ing that Bloomingdales is the size of a small country I thought he was having a little joke at our expense, but went to the third floor anyway. When we got off the escalator, we stood for a nonplussed second, trying to find our bearings.

'Where . . . ?' I asked but got no further because a young man, about fifteen feet away from us, called, 'Go right for twenty-two feet, then at Aqua go left and you'll find Eileen Fisher on the third island.' I stared at him nervously. 'Go on,' he urged. Uncertainly, with much looking back over our shoulders at him, we followed his instructions and found that the stand was exactly where he'd said it would be, but how had he known what we were looking for? Walkie-talkies was the only thing I could come up with; perhaps the man downstairs had radioed up and told him to expect us? Or maybe Bloomingdales just send their assistants on courses to develop their psychic skills.

Being laughed at by the Clinique girl

I approached the altar of cosmetics – tier after tier of silver-cylindered loveliness – and explained my mission. I wanted brow highlighter. My sister had some, I'd admired it, she'd got it from Clinique. But the glossy-faced girl knew of no such thing and I told her I thought it was called Sugar Sugar. 'Oh! Sugar Sugar!' she said. 'Oh yeah, I remember that.' Momentarily, she was overcome with silent, shuddery mirth. 'That's a trend item.'

'What does that mean?'

'It is so, like, OVER.'

The scary woman in Prada

I love Prada. Not so much the clothes, which are for mal-nourished thirteen-year-olds, but I covet, with covety covet-ousness, the shoes and handbags. Like, I LOVE them. If I was given a choice between world peace and a Prada handbag, I'd dither. (I am not proud of this. I'm only saying.)

Anyway, in Himself and myself go to the limestone palace on Fifth Avenue and up to the second floor to look at the accessories. I want to fling myself on the floor and sob at their beauty, but Himself reminds me of the Miu Miu debacle and I manage to contain myself.

Then I saw it. The handbag. *The* handbag. *THE* handbag.

Reader, I bought it. A Russian woman called Elena was my assistant and I think it must have been the quickest bit of commission she'd ever earned. Then I was kind of getting the hang of things and decided to see about matching sandals. But they didn't have them in my size. Undaunted, Elena brought them anyway. It was no go, so she brought sandals that nearly matched, then sandals that didn't match at all. And didn't fit either. But she could not be faulted for leaving a stone unturned and, reluctantly, she let me go only when it was clear that I really wasn't going to buy anything else from her.

Downstairs I stopped and idly admired some luggage, and Elena suddenly popped up again, two inches from my nose. Somehow she'd managed to insinuate herself between me and the holdall. 'You would like to buy?' I told her no thanks, that we really were leaving, but then we noticed that there was a menswear department in the basement.

Down we went, Himself picked up a shoe and a handsome young man approached and asked if he'd like it in his size. I had just opened my mouth to reply (Himself is too scared to speak in these places) when, out of nowhere, Elena appeared, did a ten-yard skid across the floor of menswear, shoved the good-looking man to the margins with her palm over his face and arrived in front of us wearing a shark's smile, not a hair out of place. 'You would like to try?'

Nothing bad ever happens in Tiffany's

Oh, Holly Golightly, how could you! You try telling that to my credit card. See, what happened was, I had to buy a christening present for my god-daughter. But once I got into the cool gorgeous halls of Tiffany, something *happened*. I'm at a loss to describe it really, except that there were all these *beautiful things*. Pendants and bracelets and watches and earrings and little silver handmirrors and cute chunky key rings. Suddenly it made perfect sense to buy presents for everyone I knew for the rest of their lives. I decided to buy my sister a silver wedding-anniversary present. Even though she's not actually married. Or engaged. Or going out with someone. Then I wanted to buy my son a watch for his twenty-first, and it didn't seem to be any impediment whatso-*ever* that I don't have children.

Eventually I got away with the christening present, a 'piece' for my sister for Christmas (it was April) and a birthday present for Himself, five months hence. And then the wrapping began – an intricate and deeply soothing pro-cess, like watching delicate, skilled hands produce the finest origami. First they put the item in a little black velvet box, then in a duck-egg-blue suede pouch, then in a matching Tiffany box tied up with a white satin Tiffany ribbon and, finally, in a Tiffany bag. I've never seen such beautiful wrap-ping. I felt so overcome it was a bit like the part in *The Great Gatsby* when Daisy weeps, 'I've never seen such beautiful shirts.'

Out in the street, it was like waking up from the most pleasant dream. Except that I had all these duck-egg-blue carrier bags and a great dread of receiving my next credit card bill.

First published in Cara *magazine, September 2002.*

The Great Outdoors

Let's get one thing straight: I'm not an outdoorsy type. If I was offered the choice between white-water rafting and being savaged by a rabid dog, I'd be likely to tick the box marked 'dog'. The reasons for this? One, I have terrible hair. Four seconds in the rain makes it all bulk and frizz up so that I look like Sideshow Bob. Two, I am very short (five foot one) and haven't worn flat shoes since 1992. As a result my calf muscles have got so used to being held up by four-inch heels that they've shrunk to the point where if I put my heels on the floor, my toes lift up. Three, I am almost life-threateningly lazy. See? Not outdoorsy, not outdoorsy at all. So how come I'm marching along at the crack of dawn, in (almost) flat boots, a mountain looming on one side of me, an atmospherically spooky lake on the other, with hailstones pinging off my face like gravel and – the weirdest bit of all – I'm not even crying?

A little background is necessary, I think . . .

Here's how it is: I love spas. More than life itself. I've become so dependent on them that I've completely lost the ability to relax by myself. I also love my husband and I like to keep him about my person at all times, rather like a good-luck charm. But my husband – who happens to be a man – doesn't like spas, he fears and mistrusts them. So how to reconcile the two?

Enter stage left, the Delphi spa and mountain adventure centre. I already knew about the adventure centre: a hellish place featuring macho, Snickers-eating, hair-frizzing, kayaky stuff. A place where young men stood around in luminous raingear and urged each other on to fling themselves off cliff-faces. Right? But I knew less about the spa – until it started winning awards. The *Observer* included it in its 'ten of the world's best spas'. Mariella Frostrup, doyenne of spas, described it in the *Mail on Sunday* as 'a world-class spa'. Now, wait a minute – a world-class spa in Ireland? Surely some mistake. We Irish do other things well – the craic, the chat, the charm. But spas? Since when?

Well, since now. Thrilled that we had found the perfect combination – I could stagger from treatment to treatment, he could look death in the face in a variety of ways – Himself and myself set off for Delphi. It's in the west of Ireland, in Galway. Or possibly Mayo. I never managed to establish which – both are keen to claim dominion because Delphi's the kind of property which would add kudos to any county's portfolio. Either way it's one of the most beautiful places on earth. The further west we drove the more soaring the peaks became, the narrower the roads and the wilder the landscape. Silver streams hurtled down the steep-sided mountains to become noisy, fast-flowing roadside brooks. Purple shale and blue-toned limestone broke the surface of the fields and the only living beings we saw for miles were the hillside sheep, coloured luminous orange and pink.

Finally, we arrived. Delphi is in a valley, surrounded almost entirely by mountains which manage to be magnificent, without also being stern and intimidating like a head nun humbling you for not doing your homework. It's so beautiful, it's almost shocking.

The first sign that these Delphi people knew what they were doing was in the architecture. Visitors to Ireland, especially those poor Dutch and Germans who love 'the nature', get terribly upset about the rash of 'bungalowitis' which afflicts much of rural Ireland. Primrose-yellow mini-ranches aren't exactly simpatico but there was no fear of that here. It was *very* simpatico – a unique building made from glass, local wood and stone, with funny rounded roof windows so that it looks vaguely like a biggish hobbit dwelling. None of Delphi spa is actually underground, but if it was, with grass growing on the roof for hobbity cattle to graze on, you wouldn't be at all surprised. It kind of has that magical Bilbo Baggins thing going on.

We stepped out of the car to be greeted by the best smell in the world – turf smoke hanging in damp air – and in we went.

With the interior architecture it's as if they've tried to bring the outdoors indoors. Everywhere there are massive windows to maximize the views of the surrounding landscape; natural wood like beech and bog oak (no nasty orange pine) is used for flooring, doors and walls; the curving oak reception desk is supported by slabs of slate, like a mini-Stonehenge; a double-height chimney breast looks like a dry-stone round tower; everything is curved, undulating, sinuous; a stream on the property flows through the hallway, covered over with thick glass. (You can amuse yourself by jumping up and down on it to see how much weight it can take. Answer: a lot. I did it one night after my sixteen-course dinner – more of which later – and it didn't even squeak.) But it's extremely comfortable. There's no point in having all that natural stuff if it's not, otherwise I might as well just stay in a tent in the field over the road. The brochure describes Delphi's style as 'contemporary-luxury in a wilderness setting' and that sums it up beautifully.

And so to the treatments! The list contained all the usual suspects – facials, massages, wraps, etc. – with more interesting stuff like reiki, Hopi ear candles and soundwave therapy also available. But I was starting with an aromatherapy massage, or so I thought. Due to a misunderstanding on my part, I'd inadvertently booked myself a wrap and I'm not a wrap-lover. (For those who don't know, you're smeared in smelly stuff and wrapped with your arms clamped to your sides in a heated tinfoil blanket and left to sweat it out for forty minutes or so. Some people swear by them. Not me, however.) I expressed my dismay and right away the calibre of the staff became clear. Sympathetically, calmly and quickly, another treatment room was found and my massage was back on track within minutes. In fact, over the few days I was there, it seemed as though all the therapists – a mixture of Australian, British and Irish – have diplomas in advanced kindness. They were warm, intelligent and compassionate, the effect of which is priceless. Technical proficiency counts for nothing if you feel your masseur is sniggering at the state of your thighs.

Which brings me to food! Everyone knows that you get fed well at spas; the days of wringing hollow laughter out of a diet of lemon juice and lettuce leaves are long gone. But nothing had prepared us for such quality. Dinner was a four-course extravaganza featuring organic vegetables from their own garden, locally caught seafood and any number of added extras – amuse-bouches, palate-cleansing sorbets, home-made bread, etc. It was fabulous!

The following morning Himself went off to learn to surf (it was November, can you imagine!) and I put on my white robe and took up position on a lovely padded lounger yoke in the health suite and stared out dreamily at the ever-changing light on the mountains, as I waited to be called for my treatments. It's all so beautiful that at busy times the area can get a little crowded with towel-based baggsying of loungers that is positively Germanic.

The health suite also has a steam-room, a sauna and a roomy jacuzzi with more stunning views. However, because high expectations are simply resentments under construction, let me make a couple of things clear: there is no pool and no gym. Purists might recoil in horror but, frankly, I was delighted. Whenever I go to a spa I bring my trainers (after first blowing off the cobwebs) and *even as I'm packing them*, I know they won't see the inside of the gym. Nevertheless I'm always bothered by a vague, naggy guilt for the duration of my stay, so a gym-free spa was a giddy relief. The general manager explained that the Delphi ethos is to persuade people to try something different from their usual regime. Instead of forty-five minutes on an incline on the treadmill, they might try a two-hour hill walk – on a real hill.

I nodded in agreement as all this was explained to me, but I was thinking: *They'll never get me out there, think of the hair.* Instead there was a great choice of indoor activities – meditation, t'ai chi, Pilates, relaxation and yoga (hey, it's just like Parrot Cay!) – and I decided to do Pilates. Lying on the floor, in a beautiful peaceful room, doing tiny quarter-inch movements, seemed easy-peasy. Until the next morning when I found it so hard to get out of bed I thought I'd had a stroke in the night which had paralysed me. I wasn't making that mistake again so next day I went for the relaxation class because I thought it would be the usual lying on the floor imagining myself bathed in beautiful gold light. Instead we were taught new breathing techniques – prana something or other – which involved snorting like a horse over and over. The three of us in the class were high-pitched and giggly with mortification and as I left I decided I would never do a relaxation class again: it was way too stressful.

Meanwhile Himself was having the time of his life, having Snickers-eating, near-death experiences twice a day. His brushes with mortality included abseiling, rock-climbing and surfing, although he could also have tried high ropes, kayaking, water-skiing and all kinds of other terrible, terrible stuff.

The funny thing was that although I'd fully intended not getting dressed from the moment I arrived to the moment I left, the place worked its magic. It was just too beautiful not to get out and about. Local highlights include Killary, Ireland's only fjord, but instead I went to Doolough, a nearby lake overlooked by jagged peaks with an icing-sugar coating of snow along the top. It was like experiencing the Himalayas, without any pesky inoculations or jet lag, and so breathtakingly wonderful that I didn't even mind the consequent hair shame which, let's make no bones about it, was *extreme*.

First published in Cara, *February 2004.*

Fabulous, Darling

Marian visits The Shows for *Marie Claire*

11.15 a.m. Horticultural Hall, Victoria: Paul Smith

A mere half-hour late and we're off! Foghorns blare, lighthouse bells ring, the walls look like a starry night at sea – very atmospheric and exciting. Almost as exciting as my front-row seat – friends had made a special visit to my flat to admire my Row A ticket. Also to help with my wardrobe angst. Dreading gimlet-eyed fashion scorn, the look I finally decided on is 'Inconspicuous but with a Marc Jacobs bag'. It seems to be working. Well, at least I haven't noticed anyone mocking openly.

'Paul's collection (those in the know never say designers' surnames, I'm told, and I'm keen to fit in) is Nautical but Nice and there are sailor stripes, anchor motifs and double-breasted Captain Birdseye jackets. Beautiful clothes – but the models are doing the most ridiculous walks: lifting their knees high like dressage ponies or horses who are made to dance in circuses.

The catwalk is so low and close that I could reach out and touch them – in fact, reach out and *trip them up*, and suddenly I'm terrified that, with one flick of my leg, I might just do that. (The same kind of irresistible impulse I sometimes get on high buildings to fling myself off.) Luckily I'm distracted by a girl clopping lopsidedly down the catwalk in one red stocking and one shoe – a style statement? It's then I notice the single shoe at my feet, smiling up sheepishly at me. Clearly, it's fallen off, but professional that she is, the model has carried on. A dilemma ensues – should I replace the shoe on the catwalk for her to reclaim on her return or am I running the risk of causing a dressage-pony-style pile-up? Leave well alone, I decide. And then, surprisingly quickly – only fifteen minutes – it's over and I go for lunch with Marie and Liz, *Marie Claire*'s editor and fashion editor respectively.

1.45 p.m. British Fashion Council tent on the King's Road: Betty Jackson

We actually have to run – 'Betty' (see, no surname, I'm a natural at this fashion stuff) has the temerity to start just under half an hour late and by the time we get in, our seats have been given away and some poor *Marie Claire* underling is ousted to make room for me. Mind you, I can hardly be bothered – I associate 'Betty' with beige cowl-neck jumpers, boring as anything. But I'm in for a shock: once the girls start down the catwalk (still doing the same silly knee-lifts, like baby giraffes learning to walk; obviously not just a Paul Smith thing) I'm transfixed. I love these clothes. Like, *love* them. Grown-up boho in bright spring greens, faded grape and aubergine. Funky tweed suits appliquéd with flowers, soft jersey dresses and a fabulous green-leather coat that I almost leap from my seat and wrestle from the model's back. Excuse me, what's going on? But, ah! Here it is! Mr beige cowl-neck jumper, we've been expecting you. Oh and here's another. And one more – admittedly brown, this time, but what is brown, if not beige, only worse?

Fabulous, Darling

3.25 p.m. Park Lane Hotel: Temperley

A dash across town only to find they're 'running late', so we go for a cup of tea. Or at least we try. We hover at the entrance to the gilt-ridden tearoom, entirely ignored, while other fashion people bank up behind us. Finally we're led to a table, but when the waiter approaches a table of *Vogue* staff before us, Liz yells, 'We were here first.' Alas, he pays us no heed. (God, fashion is *so* bitchy.)

Then to the crammed art deco ballroom where I've never seen such a concentration of fabulous handbags. On our seats, our first goody bag of the day – Diptych shower gel – has 'disappeared'. A spare is found which Marie graciously offers to me. I accept. I have no shame.

The music starts, it's all very French – accordions and chanteuses – but right behind me is a man with a MASSIVE bunch of flowers and for the entire show all I can hear is the rustling of cellophane.

And down the black marble catwalk they come, pretty party frock after pretty party frock after pretty party frock. Lots of black and pink satin, with circles of jet beading, creating a doily effect. Soft wrap-over tops and flared ballerina skirts in belle époque prints, then comes a fresh wave of doily-covered party frocks and I realize I'm a teeny bit bored. Jaded already? (I really *am* a natural.)

Alice Temperley emerges to take her bow and for my rustling friend with the flowers, this is his moment. He surges towards the stage, but Alice skips away like a startled faun and the rustler falls back, looking foolish.

By now I'm unsettled, confused even. I'd always thought Fashion was a big joke played on ordinary people, that when

Anna Wintour leads a standing ovation of a show featuring girls wearing only snorkels and gold lamé knickers, that it's a big 'let's make fun of the non-fashion peasants' conspiracy. But so far, everything I've seen has been disappointingly *wearable*.

4.35 p.m. British Fashion Council tent on the King's Road: Gharani Strok

Now this is much more like it. The atmosphere is very buzzy, dry ice swirling, people wandering around drinking mini-Moët bottles through straws and extreme seating disarray. And I've hit goody bag paydirt! A Phillo corsage, a Filofax, a Pucci-style make-up bag filled with I Coloniali products and – prize of prizes – two Krispy Kreme doughnuts, apparently one of the most addictive substances on the planet. At a promotion in Ohio, when they wouldn't give a teenage boy any more free doughnuts (he'd already had about sixteen), he attacked the staff.

The lights dim, Shaft-style seventies music starts and the first girl clopping down the catwalk is in a sliver of glitter and a pink hooker's fur coat, followed by a girl in a bikini, a black fur coat and high knee boots. Mucho sparkly disco-wear and very Studio 54 – everything is slashed to the waist, front and back, and we see our first nipple of the day. Then our second. Then our third. It's a veritable knocker-fest with dresses 'accidentally' sliding off shoulders and down to the waist and coats being worn with nothing underneath except knickers. Almost everything is totally unwearable – *exactly* what I'd been expecting.

Afterwards, everyone is terribly sniffy about it. Someone says the clothes looked as though they'd been run up by students in some back room. All show and no substance, says someone else. Well, I thought, hugging my goody bag closer, I liked it.

6 p.m. The Mermaid Theatre, Blackfriars: Boudicca

En route, I eat a Krispy Kreme and although extremely pleasing – delicious, in fact – it doesn't plunge me into a week-long doughnut binge. Maybe after the Ohio incident they removed the addictive component?

We're now running an hour late, but never mind: I have high hopes for Boudicca. Alexander McQueen described them as 'brave'. 'Brave' usually being a euphemism for 'mental'.

When they finally let us in the smell hits me: damp earth. The stage is covered in scrubby, muddy grass and weeds (all real); it smells like a sports day. Some of the seats are in the 'field' and as I watch fashion ladies get mired by their spiky heels in the mud, I fear for the models.

And here we go! The first girl out looks as if she works with nuclear waste – wearing a baggy, black boiler-suit with a hood that covers her entire face, but in lovely floaty fabric: what Darth Vader might wear for a romantic dinner. Then comes a similar rig-out in white plastic with a beekeeper's veil, followed by a hooded sou'wester and matching over-trousers – that a mackerel fisherman would wear in a Force 8 Gale – but in a purple, metallic see-through fabric. Next, a gorgeous white fur coat except that someone has taken green gaffer tape and wound it round and round the girl's shoulders and upper body. Post-*Apocalypse* headbands, French Foreign Legion hats, Lawrence of Arabia veils, lots of glaring faces – when you can see them – and Swampy hair: very warrior girl. Clothes that will have people stuttering in disgust, 'And

I'm meant to wear that to Sainsbury's, am I?' But it's affecting and exciting and if it's toned down a little (a lot?) you wouldn't be laughed at in the street.

7.25 p.m. British Fashion Council tent on the King's Road: Clements Ribeiro

Finally get to the bottom of the models' silly walk – it's so their legs will look thin for the photographers. Well, that makes sense because they look like tree-trunks ordinarily. Er . . .

As soon as they start picking their ridiculous way down the catwalk, I'm in an agony of longing. A model with plaits swirled around her ears like two Danish pastries passes in a circus-print fifties-style shirt-waister. Then a model with hair like a brioche, wearing a tweed suit trimmed with spangles. And a model with hair like a batch loaf in a petrol-blue coat, patterned with lilac triangles. There are little felt pixie hats, net face-coverers dotted with what looks like Smarties and excellent two-toned shoes with bold, big-top stripes. (The theme is a circus one.) It's fun, cheery and knuckle-gnawingly beautiful. All too soon, it's over and everyone is off to parties – there's one at Hugo Boss, another at Fendi – but I'm exhausted from all that yearning, I have to go home and lie down.

First published in Marie Claire, *September 2004.*

My Five Top Fives

How to justify buying as many shoes as you want in five easy-to-follow steps

1) The economy is slowing down, so we've got to keep spending in order to avoid a recession.
2) As my mother always says, if you're doing a job, do it properly. If you've gone to the trouble of going out shopping, make it worth your while – never take the lazy way out by buying just one pair.
3) Your current ones might be stolen by a rabid inner-city fox, so it's vital to have a back-up pair. Several, actually.
4) Everyone needs a hobby.
5) You need to match your new bag. You can't go out in last season's ones. Honestly, do they want you to be a public laughing-stock?

As if you ever need a reason, here are my top five reasons to buy even more handbags

1) You need to match your new shoes. You can't go out with last season's one. Honestly, do they want you to be a public laughing-stock?
2) What else are you going to carry your Maltesers in?
3) A second hobby is always nice . . .

4) That rabid inner-city fox could strike again and it mightn't be shoes this time . . .

5) Beautiful handbags are works of art. It's culture, innit?

Ice cream can be found in many flavours – but these are the best!

1) Triple chocolate, chocolate chip, chocolate-coated, thigh-exploding special. (Served with chocolate sauce and anti-cellulite serum.)

2) Vanilla – the unsung hero.

3) Brown bread – strange but true!

4) Baileys – it's the one thing I miss now that I don't drink any more.

5) Strawberry – we need to eat five helpings of fruit or veg a day, what better way to do it?

So, you've met the bronzed body of your dreams, the question is, what movie to go and see. The only ones that fit the bill in this situation are:

1) *Roman Holiday* – if you don't see him wiping away a sneaky tear at the end, get rid of him.

2) *Raising Arizona* – if he says, 'Blimey, what was that all about?' also hurry him to the door.

3) *Seeking Five Metal Jacket Men Still Standing on a Thin Red Toor of Dooty* – or any other of those war movie things starring the likes of Bruce Willis smeared with photogenic soot and wearing an ivy-covered helmet. You'll be bored out of your skull, of course, but he'll think you're the coolest girl he's ever met, for suggesting it.

4) *Monsoon Wedding* – you'll both feel so uplifted afterwards that anything could happen.
5) Any porno film from the local video shop – the LAUGH you'll have!

Or if you're just going to admire the actors . . .

1) Harrison Ford. I know he's getting a little mature these days, but all the same . . . I've never really recovered from *Working Girl*, the bit where he takes his shirt off at work and all the girls cheer . . . Ahhh . . .
2) Philip Seymour Hoffman. I can't understand it. He's freckly, a bit chunky, and has perhaps a touch of the gingers, but he's such a great actor.
3) Brendan Gleason. Ditto.
4) George Clooney. I never really got him until I saw him in *O Brother, Where Art Thou?*, then everything changed. You were right, I was wrong – he's YUM.
5) Likewise Billy Bob Thornton. I couldn't see why women kept marrying him until I saw him in *The Man Who Wasn't There* and he was so understatedly brilliant in it that I'd nearly marry him myself. (Assuming he was interested, of course, and I've no reason to believe he might be. I think it might be my Giant's Causeway teeth.)

First written for Penguin Books' website, 2002.

33

Action!

*F*ilm sets are exciting places. There's the chance of clock-ing (hopefully) famous actors without their make-up on, or of seeing stars slipping into another star's caravan for sexual jiggery-pokery. There's even the opportunity to feel part of the creation of something wonderful, if you're that way inclined. But what most people don't realize is that the best thing about film sets is the on-set catering.

Food is central to the cinematic process, and the catering is as much for the massive team of techies (cameramen, sound-men, etc.) as for the actors. Long, intense days, spent under boiling-hot lights, doing the same thing over and over and over again until it's right – if they didn't get regular nosh, they'd be hitting the deck like Victorian ladies who'd been flashed at.

I happen to be furnished with this insider knowledge because when a film was made of my novel *Watermelon* and I got to visit the set, I was given the choice of – get this – *three* delicious hot lunches and when I couldn't choose between banoffi pie or apple crumble and custard for dessert, they gave me both. Then mid-afternoon, there was the mother of all tea breaks. You've never seen anything like it: hordes of techies and extras, desperate for a sugar kick, descended on the catering shed where cake and biscuits were being dispatched like famine relief at a Red Cross feeding station. The catering team were barely able to tear the cellophane off the boxes of biscuits and cakes to keep pace with demand. And such high-quality confectionery! Chocolate Swiss rolls, Battenburg, fruit cake and the big tins of chocolate bikkies that only ever normally appear at Christmas time. You know the ones I mean – they contain at least two biscuits individually covered in gold foil. (One is usually mint cream and the other orange cream, which I find a bit of a let-down, but still.)

So when news reached me that one of France's best-known film-makers (Christian Clavier) was going to make a – French – film of another of my novels (this time *Last Chance Saloon*), my first thought was not of winning the Palme d'Or at Cannes but of what I'd get fed when I visited the set. If an Irish catering crew could manage to pull off such delicious nosh, just think of what the French and their culinary skill would produce. Foie gras all the way, was the conclusion of everyone I spoke to. Boeuf bourguignon, crème brûlée, tartes Tatin, crêpes, cheeses so powerful they could almost sing and dance . . . Excited? Bien sûr!

Finally the food-filled mist dispersed and I realized what an honour it was to have a book chosen to be made into a French film. As an intellectual friend said, 'Everyone knows the French make the best films in the world.'

And although I agree, to my shame I am woefully ignorant of French film. This is because

a) I am not French
b) er . . . um . . . actually I've no other excuse.

But I've seen enough to conclude that they are mostly about beautiful pouty girls called Solange, wearing extremely red lipstick, brazenly parading around in their pelt and having sex at the drop of a chapeau (hard to believe that France was a Catholic country, how come they escaped the guilt?), while men called Serge, wearing black polo-necks, slim-fitting trousers and unfeasible sideburns, pace the bedroom, smoking millions of fags. The films always seem to be shot in extremely depressing bluish light and dialogue is sparse but meaningful. 'L'amour est mort.' 'La vie, la mort – quelle différence?' Er, oui, exactement . . .

Suddenly I was wondering why they'd picked *Last Chance Saloon*. For starters it's a comedy and I wasn't aware of many funny French films. I know those *Monsieur Hulot* yokes are classified as comedies but they're as funny as being savaged by a rabid dog. But just a minute, everyone said, what about *Amélie?* That was funny. (It was.) And *Delicatessen*, that was funny too. (It was.) And as Himself said, the French might make loads of light-hearted stuff that we never see. What do we know about what they do in the privacy of their own country?

Then, you know, once I thought about it, I realized there's a fair bit of sex in *Last Chance Saloon*. And one of the characters, Tara, smokes a lot – *and* is on an eternal quest to find genuine long-last lipstick. And although it's a comedy, it's a comedy about a young man who gets cancer. Plenty of opportunity to muse on la vie versus la mort. Yes, I was beginning to understand.

So off Himself and myself went to France (any excuse) and showed up at a massive film studio in a Parisian suburb. They'd said we could come at any time of the day but we didn't want to presume we were invited for lunch, so we calculated that the optimum arrival time would be around

4 p.m. This is the hour when workers of the world unite, by downing their tools and having a KitKat Chunky and a can of Lilt (or local equivalent).

But when we arrived, filming was still underway so, through cables and monitors and tons of people, we picked our way onto the set – and all of a sudden I nearly keeled over with shock. The actress playing Katherine looked *exactly* as I had imagined her when I wrote her: very beautiful in a pure, innocent sort of way. It was the spookiest feeling – for a moment it felt as if I had conjured her up, that she was only real because I'd imagined her. And the actress playing Tara was 'my' Tara, she totally embodied her spirit. As for the man playing the book's egomaniac actor, Lorcan Larkin, he'd had his name changed to Leo (not too many French Lorcans, I suppose) and his long red hair was now short and dark. But swaggering about in a long leather coat and cowboy boots, he managed to be both sexy and repellent, just as I'd always visualized him.

I stood in the shadows, watching the scene, and I had a second shock – I knew this! The dialogue was exactly as I had written it. (But in French.) This might seem like a total no-brainer but actually, very often, all a film adaptation has in common with the source book is the title.

The spirit of my book had been captured exactly – even the smaller characters were perfect. It was all very moving and, to my mortification, I began to cry. Luckily not in a big, shoulder-shaking extravaganza of emotion – I didn't make a complete gom of myself – just in an eye-filling, discreet-sniffy kind of way. Bad enough, though.

Then the director yelled, 'Coupe!' (no, really, she did, it was gorgeous – so *French*) and the glad-handing began. When we'd bonjoured ourselves blue in the face, the long-awaited moment finally arrived: we were offered 'refreshments'. Himself and myself exchanged a flicker. Easy now. No dribbling. No running. Act nonchalant. But to our phenomenal surprise, all there was to eat were sweets. French sweets, which meant, of course, that they were superior to any other sweets, but nothing like the gourmet's smorgasbord we'd fantasized about.

Some time later, in the back of the taxi as we drove away, Himself said, 'There's just one thing I don't understand.'

'The food?' I said. 'I know!'

'Not the food. I just don't understand how none of the girls got their kit off.' Then he thought about it further. 'You know what? None of them were even smoking!'

He was right and I was seized by a sudden, dreadful suspicion – no lovely food, no nudity, no Gauloises – had all of this been a big elaborate hoax? A reality TV con-job?

After several seconds of stricken silence, Himself said, like a drowning man clutching an armband, 'Tara's lipstick was very red, though.'

Yes, I agreed, Tara's lipstick had been very red. Extremely red. Possibly the reddest lipstick I'd ever seen.

And, at that, we cheered up and started talking about what we'd have for our dinner.

First published in Cara, *February 2004.*

Au Secours, J'ai Trente Ans is now available on DVD.

The Real Thing

You know on some crappy cable channel, there are shows where a load of swizzers stand on a stage and 'deliver' messages from the dead to the poor schmucks in the audience? The swizzers spend a lot of time with their hand cupped around their ear as they 'listen' to the other-worldly voices and they call everyone 'my love' especially when they make people cry. (Example: 'He forgives you, my love, so you must forgive yourself.')

Yes, well, I admit to a certain fascination with them. One half of me is watching with my lip curled scornfully, and the other half is thinking: but what if it's true?

Then one day, I read a review in a respected broadsheet of a live show one of these swizzer women – we'll call her

Angela – had done; they reckoned she was the real thing. They also said she did one-to-one readings and, all of a sudden, I was excited.

Research, see. I was thinking of writing about a woman who can't stop looking for answers and attends all manner of swizzers. But, handily enough, I was going through a bit of a bad patch myself and I was interested in what messages from beyond the grave Angela might have for me.

Possibly as a result of the piece in the paper, Angela was very hard to get hold of. I sent an email, which wasn't replied to for months. When she finally did get in touch, she offered me a half-hour reading over the phone in two months' time. But first I had to send a cheque for twenty-five euro – which, in all fairness, wasn't rip-off astronomical.

So I sent my cheque off, counted down the days and tried to keep a tight rein on my hope.

Over the years, on and off, I'd gone to tarot readers, as you do. (Or maybe you don't.)

I often went when I was having man trouble (most of the time). And then there were the social events, when you got in a load of Chardonnay and a tarot reader came to your house and 'did' nine or ten of you, and you all got scuttered and had a good laugh.

But recently I'd had a bad run. I'd gone to a few (again in the name of research with my personal interest add-on) and they'd been seriously crap. A tiny little voice inside me was suggesting that perhaps they'd always been bad. Maybe I'd wanted so hard to believe that I'd overcompensated for their bollocks. And indeed, years ago, I remember one who'd got so much alarmingly wrong about me that when she said, 'You've just suffered a bereavement?' I found myself agreeing that I had (although I hadn't) because I was so embarrassed for her.

Recently, when I'd asked a tarot reader about my career, she'd said, 'Don't worry about your career, love. Let your husband take care of all that. Be there to support him and maybe in a couple of years' time you can get a part-time job.'

I'd also been promised two children who'd never arrived. I'd been told I'd be moving house, which I hadn't. And a dark-haired man would deliver good news and then ask for money – as yet, no sign of him. The accumulated disappointments had stacked up on top of each other and were on the verge of toppling over into cynicism. So I really, really, *really* wanted this Angela person to be good.

But on the appointed day and hour, when I rang, she said, 'Who are you? Maureen from Dublin? Look, I can't talk to you today, I've got builders in. Bye.'

She was about to hang up, but anxiously I said, 'Wait! When *can* you talk to me?'

She said impatiently, 'Oh I dunno. Ring me on Saturday at five,' and the line went dead.

So I rang on Saturday at five and even before her answering machine clicked in, I knew she wouldn't be there. I left a message, then sent another email and after I didn't hear from her, I decided to forget it. Friends and family got heated about the twenty-five euro I'd been swizzed out of, but I let it go – maybe it would teach me not to be so stupid in future.

Life moved on, then out of the blue – perhaps seven months after the initial contact – Angela emailed, offering me a half-hour phone reading between seven and half past seven, on a Tuesday, six weeks hence.

Naturally, I was trepidatious but when I rang on the agreed date, she answered the phone and this time seemed prepared to talk to me.

'Where are you based, Maureen?'

'– Marian –'

'Is it Dublin? Because I'm coming to Dublin soon to do ten shows. Tell everyone you know. I'm doing my shows in xxxxx.' (Name of venue withheld to protect her identity, although I'm not sure why I'm bothering.) 'Do you know it?'

I admitted that yes, I knew the theatre in question.

'Whereabouts is it exactly?' she asked.

I told her the street name and she said impatiently that she knew the name of the street but whereabouts in Dublin was it precisely. Using the Brown Thomas handbag department as a reference point, I did my best to explain and she cut in, 'Is it anywhere near Heuston station?'

I admitted it was near enough.

Walking distance?

Not walking distance, I admitted.

How long would it take to get there in a taxi?

I said it would depend on traffic.

So how much would the taxi cost?

Not much, I said, feeling a little panicky. Could we close down this line of enquiry?

No, actually. She wanted to know what time the last train for Portlaoise left Heuston station. Would she be able to get the train home every night after the gig? Or would she have to stay in a B&B in Dublin? And if so how much would a B&B in Dublin cost?

I was stumped. I mean, how would I know? How often do I have reason to stay in a B&B in the town I live in? I suggested she contacted the tourist board.

It was now eight minutes past seven and we still hadn't started on my reading. Desperately trying to steer things back on track, I asked, 'How does this work? Someone will come through for me?'

She sighed as if I was being selfish and unhelpful. 'Oh aye, the reading. Let's see who we have for you.' A pause. Another sigh. 'I have your granny here.'

Surprise, surprise. That was pretty low-risk. 'Which granny?'

'She says her name is Mary. Does the name Mary mean anything to you?'

'My mother's name is Mary.'

'Ah! It's not your granny, it's your mother! Sorry, sometimes they don't make it clear.'

'My mother isn't dead.' She's at home in Monkstown, watching *Emmerdale* and eating peanut M&Ms.

'It's not Mary I'm getting anyway.' Like I'd tried to mislead her. 'I'm getting the name Margaret? Maggie? Mean anything?'

No. No.

'Bridget? Bridie?'

No. No.

'Catherine? Kate? Katie?'

No. No. Yes. My mother's mother was called Katie. Angela had finally hit paydirt on the eighth attempt. Mind you, how hard could it be to get the name of an Irish granny right? They came from an era when women's names were rationed; there were only four or five possibilities.

43

'Katie says to say hello to you.'

'Right back at her,' I said.

A pause. 'She's telling me you have relationship troubles.'

Actually, I hadn't. And, instead of trying to save Angela's blushes, I said so.

'No relationship troubles? Aren't you the lucky girl? Well, you're probably going to get them, they don't always get the timing right. Katie tells me you're thinking of moving house.'

I wasn't. And I told her so.

'Sorry, I misheard. Katie says you're thinking of changing job.'

No.

'You're worried about a family member. They have health troubles.'

No.

'*You* have health troubles.'

No. Not really. Not apart from the ear infections I got every Thursday.

'So what *are* your troubles?' But the tone of her voice said, So what are your fucking troubles?

So what were my fucking troubles? Fear of not being able to write my next book, fear that everyone would hate my current one, fear of public speaking, fear of journalists, fear of causing offence, fear of saying no, fear of looking in the mirror, fear that all the size 36 sandals would be gone before I got to the shops. You know, the *usual*. How to encapsulate it? 'Sometimes I feel like I can't cope.'

With that she took a deep breath and yelped, '*You* feel you can't cope. You'd want to try being me. I've not got a day off, not one day for the next month and a half. I'm booked solid with readings, back to back, and they're always asking me to be on TV, they're making a documentary about me – did I tell you that? – a film crew are going to follow me for a week, then I've got the shows in Dublin and I'll be on telly a lot for that and talking to journalists and being on the radio. I could tell you a thing or two about not being able to cope!'

She said it with enormous pride. She loved it. She fucking *loved* it. The giddy whirl of being a busy, in-demand medium had gone to her head.

'Book a massage, breathe deeply and spare a thought for me, girl,' was her advice.

It was now seven twenty-four. 'No one else is coming through for you. Bye now. And don't forget to tell everyone to come to my shows!'

A couple of months later she came to Dublin to do her live shows and she got a lot of publicity. I saw her on the telly; she'd done a reading for a presenter on a daytime programme and the presenter looked at the camera and intoned solemnly, 'This woman is amazing. In a world full of con-merchants, I can promise you that she is the real thing.'

Previously unpublished.

ON THE ROAD

Passport Out of Here

*M*any years ago I was living in London and about to visit New York for the first time. My sister had moved there four months previously, and I was going to spend Christmas with her. Three nights before the off I began to pack and when I looked in my 'official things' drawer for my passport, there it was – gone! Except it couldn't be. It had sat in that drawer since I'd last needed it, on a trip to Greece the previous summer. I rummaged through bills and stuff expecting it to appear and when it didn't I took the entire contents out and systematically went through each item one by one – nada. My mouth went a little dry, my heart-rate increased, but I told myself that it *was* here, I just couldn't see it – hadn't my mother always told me that I couldn't find the water in the river?

But unless it had gone invisible, it simply Was Not There and with sweaty hands I began to tear my room apart, going through every pocket of every item of clothing in my wardrobe, looking in old rucksacks and handbags, pulling books out of my bookcase, and although I stumbled across a handful of sandy drachmas and half a bag of inexplicably abandoned Maltesers (still edible, quite nice, actually), there was no passport. Then I launched an attack on the rest of the flat and late into the night I finally had to admit the inadmissible: my passport wasn't here. At this stage I was almost whimpering with terror; although my ticket to New York had put a huge dent in my meagre finances, it was non-changeable and non-refundable. If I hadn't a passport in two days' time I wouldn't be going.

I rang my mother in Ireland. There was nothing she could do but, selfish brat that I was, a trouble shared is a trouble doubled, and at least she promised to pray to St Anthony – for those not familiar with the superstitions of Catholicism, the idea is that you pray to St Anthony when you lose stuff and if it turns up you make a donation to the poor box. Under normal circumstances I poured scathing scorn on the notion but right now I was so desperate that I nearly considered doing it myself.

I went to bed in my bomb-site bedroom but I barely slept and got up again at about 5 a.m., dervishing through the silent flat, looking behind boxes of breakfast cereals, inside video cases and when I arrived at work I was a hollow-eyed manic wreck, with the taste of panic in my mouth.

I spilt the terrible story to my boss, Charlotte, and she calmly advised me to apply for a new passport.

'But it takes weeks to get a passport and I leave in two days' time!' I had to try hard not to screech.

'Ring the Irish Embassy, tell them it's an emergency and send a courier for an application form.'

Within an hour, the application form was on my desk and Charlotte helped me read through the requirements because I was so frenzied the letters kept dancing in front of my eyes. First I needed a photo so she combed my hair, dispatched me to a nearby photobooth and reminded me to smile. (The photo is still in my passport; I'm a pretty pistachio-green shade.)

Next, I needed a professional to endorse my photo and my bank manager seemed the obvious choice. However, despite the lively, almost daily correspondence that zipped from her to me, despite the audacious way she addressed me and the intimacy of her advice, she elected not to know me.

So Charlotte got on the phone and tried a magistrate she knew, but he turned out to be on holiday. Undaunted she found a nearby barrister who owed her a favour and was prepared to bend the rules and pretend that he knew me. I nipped round to him, then back to the office where Charlotte told me I could catch up on work later and pushed me out through the door, shouting, 'Go, go, go!' like I was an SAS man parachuting into enemy territory.

Then, gasping for breath, I was running through the streets of Belgravia, counting the numbers on the wedding-cake rococo mansions, looking for the Irish Embassy. I found it and panted up the steps to the fancy front door, then back down again with a flea in my ear: the passport office was round the side and in the basement. Down the rickety spiral staircase I went, burst in – and suddenly I was no longer in toney Belgravia but in a sub-post office in Athlone. It was a tiny little place, with four rows of plastic chairs cowering beneath merciless strip lighting and a serving counter with three glass hatches. I grabbed a ticket: number 792. When was my turn? I looked around for the number display and there in hellish red digital was the next number in line. It said 23. My heart almost leapt out of my chest with panic. I'd be here for ever! But no one was in sight, either in the waiting area or behind the counter . . .

Then from some hidden back room, a plumpish young man appeared, came up to one of the hatches, looked at me and declared, 'Next!'

I looked in confusion at my ticket.

'Next,' he repeated.

'But . . .' I flapped my little piece of paper.

'Oh we don't bother with that yoke.'

Fair enough. Up I stepped and blurted out the tragic tale of the missing passport, the cheap, non-refundable, non-changeable ticket, the lonely sister sitting out her first Christmas in New York, and he listened, leaning easily on his elbow, nodding in sympathy. 'I see, I see, I see. Do you have a couch?'

Nonplussed, I stopped in my tracks. What was going on? Was he trying to sell me furniture?

'See, you wouldn't credit the things that get lost down the back of a couch.'

'I looked down the back of the couch.'

'But did you *really* look?' he persisted. 'Did you put your hand in?' He undulated his hand in front of my face. 'Like this?'

Yes, I said. Yes, I did. And he muttered to himself, 'Looked down back of couch,' and appeared to tick something on a piece of paper but it was to the side of the glass and I couldn't really see it properly.

'Okay. Have you drawers?'

Excuse me?

'Desk drawers?' he elaborated. 'Some of them have a spring mechanism and you'd be amazed what gets caught in them. You really need to give them a good shake.'

I insisted that I had, although none of the drawers in my melamine chest of drawers had any kind of mechanism, but the panic was building again and threatening to choke me.

'Shook out desk drawer,' he told himself and seemed to make another tick on the piece of paper.

'Finally, have you prayed to St Anthony?' (As God is my witness, I'm not making any of this up.)

I admitted that I personally hadn't and he looked as though he was gearing up to tell me to go away and come back after I'd had a good pray, then I played my ace. My mother was praying round the clock!

'She is, is she?' He studied me carefully.

'Round the clock,' I gasped. 'I swear.'

'Right,' he sighed. 'If St Anthony has been prayed to and it hasn't turned up, then it really is lost.' An arm movement that could have been the final tick on his checklist. 'We'd better organize you a new passport, so.'

Under the glass hatch I slid in my thick bundle of documentation – the application form, photos, birth certificate (which bizarrely I had a copy of at my office) and photocopies of my plane tickets which Charlotte had suggested I bring in case they needed to be convinced of the urgency of my case. Your man picked up my photo. 'Not the most flattering of pictures,' he remarked. 'Mind you, they never are. Right, all of this is in order. All you have to do now is pay.'

'Here, here.' I thrust thirty quid at him (which Charlotte had lent me because all my spare cash was in traveller's cheques awaiting unloading in the Zara on 59th and Lexington).

'You pay at the Cashiers. That's the next hatch.' He slid the bundle of papers under the glass hatch and back to me, and I stepped three feet to my left to the next hatch, the one that said Cashier. At the same time he stepped three feet to his right. For a moment we eyed each other through the new glass and he said (and I'd say he was joking, I *hope* he was joking), 'Can I help you?'

Once again I slid the bundle of paper under the glass to him and this time he took the money.

'Come back tomorrow,' he said, 'and we'll have a new passport for you.'

The following day Charlotte once again gave me time off work to go to the Irish Embassy. When they gave me my pristine new passport I couldn't let go of it – I kept opening it and closing it and reading my name, just to make sure it was mine – and the following day I was on a plane to New York.

Previously unpublished.

Cheaper than Drugs

I know a man who denies that jet lag exists. He regularly flies halfway across the world, marches off the plane after a twenty-seven-hour flight, goes straight into the Auckland office, pausing only to brush his teeth, and immediately starts barking orders and making people redundant. (Or whatever super-macho, no-human-weakness job it is he does.) I want to sue this man. As far as I'm concerned denying jet lag is like denying that the earth is round. I am so prone to jet lag that I even get it when I haven't been on a plane: I get jet lag when the clocks go back.

(It's because I'm so in thrall to sleep. I'm grand if I get my habitual sixteen hours a night, but if anything happens to interfere with that, I'm all over the place. I am a *martyr* to my circadian rhythms.)

Naturally, I've investigated all the jet-lag 'cures': stay away from the jar on the plane; drink plenty of water; eat lightly; do a little exercise; get on to local time patterns immediately; and, most importantly, walk around in the sunlight as soon as you arrive at your faraway destination.

All nonsense, of course: as effective as giving someone a Barbie plaster for a shattered femur. I must admit I don't trust 'natural' solutions to conditions, I like chemicals. I am probably the last person in the Western world who doesn't have a homeopath and who still swears by antibiotics. I would *love* it if someone invented an anti-jet-lag drug and I couldn't care less about side effects, in fact I'd embrace them – dry mouth? Trembling? Blurred vision? Better than being fecking jet-lagged and falling asleep face downwards in my dinner at six in the evening.

But unfortunately, for some things there is no cure but time. Like a hangover or a broken heart, you just have to wait your jet lag out and try to live through it as best you can.

Of all the suggested 'cures' I think that trying to get on to local time as quickly as possible is probably the best, but doing it is so phenomenally unpleasant. Walking around on feet I can no longer feel, swimming through air that seems lit with little silvery tadpoles, the pavement lurching towards me . . . everything takes on a strange, hallucinogenic quality. (Mind you, if you're that way inclined, it'll save you a fortune in recreational drugs.)

In Australia, I had the worst ever example of this. In a pitiful attempt to recover from a twenty-four-hour flight and an eleven-hour time difference, Himself and myself thought we'd 'do a little exercise' and 'walk around in the sunlight' as soon as we arrived.

It was early evening and clutching our bottles of water ('drink plenty of water'), we staggered about on an area of greenness so verdant that we gradually realized it must be a golf course. Bumping into each other and grumpily apologizing, like we were scuttered, I suddenly saw something that stopped me so abruptly in my tracks it was as if I'd run into an invisible wall. Through the gathering gloom, about twenty feet away, I saw two kangaroos kicking the CRAP out of each other. They were balancing on their tail and laying into their sparring partner with such powerful *whump*s that I could actually *feel* the impacts. They were kicking each other so hard and fast it was as though they were doing kung-fu.

It was then that I got a bad dose of The Fear. 'Please tell me,' I clutched Himself's arm, 'please tell me that you see them too.' (He said, 'See what?' but he was only messing, thank Christ.)

However, jet lag isn't all bad. It's a great excuse to go out and get pure stotious, on the principle that if you're sick and psychotic with a hangover you won't notice the jet lag. Or if you were planning a nervous breakdown, now's your chance. You'll be feeling alienated and fearful anyway, so you might as well double up. And my own personal favourite: jet lag affords the perfect opportunity to eat guilt-free Toblerones at two in the morning. Picture it – it's pitch-black outside, a deep blanket of sleep has settled on whatever strange city you're in, and suddenly, as if you've just been plugged into the mains, you're AWAKE. You're super-awake, you've never before been this alert in your *life*. You're so firing on all cylinders that you could go on *Who Wants to be a Millionaire* and win it in fifteen minutes. And you're also hungry. Savagely so. Your poor stomach is still on home time; it had to miss its breakfast and it's not best pleased that someone wants to deprive it of its lunch as well. But deep in the bowels of the silent, sleeping hotel, the room-service lads have shut up shop and gone home and it's a long, long wait until morning.

What choice have you but to shine the luminous light of

the mini-bar into the darkened room and select an overpriced, supersized bag of M&Ms and clamber back into bed to eat yourself back to sleep.

See? Not all bad.

A version of this was first published in Abroad, *July 2004.*

Stack 'n' Fly

'*I*t is better to travel than to arrive.'

Whoever said that should get his head examined. It is NOT better to travel. To travel is AWFUL and to arrive is LOVELY.

The only time it's not entirely unbearable to travel is when you're on the Orient Express, and your daily champagne allowance would fell an elephant. Or on a cruise liner the size of a small country, and you're sailing from place to place but it doesn't feel like it, the same way you don't feel the earth turning at four million miles a day (or whatever it is).

Let's look at how awful it is to TRAVEL, will we? I won't even mention the car-clogged crawl to the airport, the dog-eat-dog scramble for parking and the overland trek from the long-stay car park to the departures hall. (All I'll say is that I've heard frequent travellers discussing the feasibility of paying homeless people to sleep in a space in the short-stay A car park, so that it'll be reserved for them for when they need it.)

Anyway . . . Arriving at Departures but already having lost the will to live, I look up at the telly monitors wondering where I should check in. But I needn't bother overexerting my neck muscles by looking *up*. All I need to do is look *in*, at the rowdy, pushing, shoving mass of humanity spilling out into the set-down area. It might look like a riot at a Red Cross feeding station but actually it's a queue. A queue filled with shrieking babies all sporting ear infections, overexcited teenage boys playfully breaking each other's limbs and greasy long-haired men wanting to check-in rocket-launchers and garden sheds.

Step right this way, Miss Keyes!

For many, many hours I shuffle, far too slowly for any movement to be visible to the naked eye, and because – through no fault of my own – I'm one of the last to check in, all the good seats are gone. I'm usually told it's not possible for the left side and right side of my body to sit together, so one half of me is in 11B and the other in 23E.

Then I proceed to security in order to be groped and to display the contents of my brain on a little table. (Okay, security checks are a very good thing; I'm just sore because recently I was relieved of one of my finest tweezers in a handbag search. Very expensive they were too, something people don't seem to realize about tweezers. They think they only cost a couple of euro, but mine cost *eighteen quid*. Sterling.)

The security check eventually comes to an end and when I've replaced my internal organs in something approximating to their correct configuration, I proceed to the gate – just in time for the delay!

Now the thing is, I expect delays, I don't even mind them (apart from when I miss my connecting flight to Mauritius). I've learnt to embrace them in a Zen kind of way: why resent them? Resenting them would be as futile as resenting the sun rising in the morning. Delays *are*.

What I mind are the delay-related lies, the massive conspiracy that every airport employee is in on – the 'Delay? What Delay?' fiction. Sometimes I try to con the check-in person by asking, all super-innocent, 'How long is the delay?' And just before they yawn and say, 'Oh, you know, the usual, about an hour and ten,' they suddenly flick me a furtive, fearful glance and go, *'Delay?* What delay?'

We're treated just like small children on a long car journey who ask their mammy, 'Are we there yet?' Instead of the mammy saying brusquely, 'It's another three hours, so just get fecking-well used to it,' she fobs them off with, 'Soon, love, soon.'

However, I would rather know the facts, unpalatable and all as they might be, because then I could quite happily go round the shops and try out lipsticks on the back of my hand, instead of sitting anxiously at the gate watching the greasy long-haired men polishing their rocket-launchers.

But when I've pleaded, 'Just tell me the truth,' the response has been, 'The truth?' Mad B-movie cackle. 'You can't HANDLE the truth.'

But no night is too long and, finally, on we get! Most planes smell a bit funny now because the airlines have 'cut back on' (euphemism for sacked) their cleaning staff, but who's complaining? God Almighty, when did a bad smell ever kill anyone? We can spray perfume on hankies and keep them clamped to our faces; it worked fine in Elizabethan times, why not now?

Anyway, so I take my seat and calmly wait to be joined by the twenty-stone person with personal-hygiene issues, who is invariably seated next to me. But once in a blue moon the unthinkable happens and the seat beside me remains empty. Other passengers flood in and sit down and still no one gets in beside me. I hardly dare let myself hope. Like, what are the chances? *No, I won't let myself think it, I won't even entertain the thought.* But then the trolley dollies start making their 'cross-check' and 'cross-hatch' noises and my hope can no longer be contained. It breaks free and goes on the rampage. Could it possibly be . . . ? Have I really been given the luxury of space and privacy and fragrant-ish air for this flight? Thank you, God, oh thank you!

And then I hear it: the faint pounding noise, which gets nearer and louder. Please, God, no, I beg. I can actually feel it now, the plane is shaking slightly with each rumble – the unmistakable sound of a twenty-stone smelly person running down the metal walkway. With a sinking heart I hear the groan of metal straining as he steps onto the plane and he makes his way directly towards me, the floor buckling and creaking with each step. After ten minutes of banging and clattering, as he tries to fit his rocket-launcher into the overhead compartment, he fights his way into his seat, gives me a gap-toothed smile and unwraps his kebab.

If only that was all I had to endure, but as airlines have also cut back on (i.e. sacked) their maintenance staff, I usually spend the flight with my table tray crashing down onto my knees every time the person in the seat in front breathes.

Eventually we reach our destination, and after we have staved off the curse of Icarus and prevented the wings from falling off by completing the ritual thirty circles over the entire city, we're allowed to land. Only to discover – why, why, why? – that we have to sit on the tarmac like a crowd

of goms because they can't find a set of steps for us. This is
the point when I start talking to myself, pretending to be the
local air-traffic control people. 'A plane, you say? Landed?
What, *here*? And you all want to get off? Steps, is it? And a
coach? And what magic wand do you expect us to wave?
Look, we'll do our best to accommodate you this once but
bear in mind this is an *airport*, we're not equipped for this
sort of thing.'

A speedy couple of hours polishes off the passport control,
the luggage carousel, the unattended luggage desk to report
the unarrived luggage and the taxi queue 'managed' by some
power-crazed weirdo who understands the laws of the universe in an entirely different way to the rest of us. Then,
after a soupçon of heavy traffic – finally, I ARRIVE!

Come in, they say, sit down, no *lie* down, on a silken
feather bed and have some nectar. Ambrosia, so? KitKat
Chunky? Wide-screen TV? Jo Malone candles? Foot-rub?
Spot of reiki? Sex with George Clooney? Just say it and you
can have it.

See, TRAVEL = horrible and ARRIVE = nice.

Surely we're all agreed on it? Apparently something like
a hundred and twelve per cent of regular travellers say that
the one thing that would transform their quality of life would
be a 'Beam me up, Scotty' machine so that they could just
arrive directly at their destination and cut out all that nasty
pesky travelling.

But in the absence of that, ladies and gentlemen, let me
introduce the unique Stack 'n' Fly System (currently pending
patent). The brainchild of seasoned traveller ... er ... me
and my friend Malcolm – this is how it works. You check

your bags in as usual, go to your gate, lie down on a stretcher, get strapped in, then a nurse comes along and administers a knock-out shot. You're totally out cold and until you arrive at your destination, you know nothing. Not delays, not kebab-man, nothing.

The seats would be removed from the planes so that several stretchers could be stacked on top of each other, not unlike the onboard catering trolleys (which, of course, there would no longer be any need for). That way there would be room for the airlines to get loads more passengers in, so everyone's happy. Instead of air-hostesses on board, we'd have a nurse who'd patrol the aisle with a hypodermic syringe, just in case someone starts to come to, too early. Fantastic, eh?

And that's just how it would work in economy. Business-class passengers would be guaranteed a deluxe service where an ambulance-style vehicle would come to their home and give them their injection right there, so they'd be spared *everything* – the drive, the check-in, the groping, the delays. Same at the other end: still unconscious, a whole stack of them and their clicky pens could be wheeled through passport control, baggage, etc., and they need know nothing until they'd ARRIVED and everyone's running around being lovely to them.

I have seen the future and it's sedated.

A version of this was first published in Abroad, *March 2004.*

Thirty-six Hours in Jo'burg

A few years ago I went on a book tour of South Africa. It was the beginning of my love affair with this magical continent. Before the work started, I had a day and a half in Johannesburg.

The thing is, Johannesburg has a terrible reputation for violence, and certainly on the drive from the airport all the houses looked like grim, blank-faced fortresses. So my publishers had installed Himself and myself in a cosy hotel in a safe suburb where we were less likely to get raped and shot. However, I'd been all geared up for African 'otherness' and almost cried at our red swirly carpet and pink, flowery room. It looked like Surrey.

Disconsolate, I switched on the telly looking for the South African *Who Wants to be a Millionaire* (I was keen to add to my collection – I'd seen it in Japanese, Czech and German) and instead I found the pan-African news and I was shot through with a deep thrill at being on this vast continent.

Because we'd come in on an overnight flight, we slept for a lot of the day, which was lucky because we were under the strictest instruction to go nowhere on our own. *Nowhere.*

Around seven that evening, just as the rose-covered walls were starting to close in, Karen, my publicity girl, sprang us and took us to an area full of bars, restaurants, music and throngs of tall, thin Xhosa and Zulu. Not a bit like Surrey. I cheered up a little. But after Karen had parked her jeep, she foraged for a rand, to give to the guys minding the cars. She muttered something about how embarrassing all this need for security was, so I told her how we have the same situation in Ireland, how they're called lock-hard men ... then I noticed something and, abruptly, I shut up. Irish lock-hard men don't carry AK-47s.

On Sunday morning I had a hair appointment. (And as the salon was actually *in* the hotel Karen was prepared to let me go without an escort.) Now, a quick word about my hair. It's thick, frizzy and unruly and only a highly skilled professional can tame it. I had a week of publicity ahead of me, kicking off with South Africa's version of *Ireland AM* very early the following morning – too early to get my hair done before it – so Karen had arranged for the hotel's hairdresser to come in specially.

He was a prissy Swiss bloke and very narky about having to work on a Sunday. But he was one of those passive-aggressive types who told me he didn't mind, it's just that Sunday is his only day off, and that if he doesn't get enough rest, he gets ill; he had a really bad throat infection there last month, he's prone to throat infections when he doesn't get enough rest; but don't get him wrong, he doesn't *mind*. So when he 'showed' me a phial of special expensive gear which mends split ends (as if!) and told me I was under no obligation to buy it, I felt obliged to buy it.

When I returned to the room, Himself leapt to his feet and, in ragged tones, told me the rose-covered walls were moving in on him again. However Karen had told us that if we wanted to go out, to call her. But I didn't want to bother her on a Sunday. (She might make me buy some stuff for my split ends.) A dilemma ensued. From our window we could see a shopping centre only fifty yards up the road; it didn't look like the sort of place you'd get raped and shot. But then I thought of the men with the AK-47s – and they were the good guys.

In the end we decided to chance it but, on the short walk, I felt as if I was in Sarajevo, in danger of being picked off by sniper fire.

The gas thing was the place looked like Donaghmede shopping centre, all small and ordinary, but there was a market on, jammers with African carvings and metalwork, bizarre-looking vegetables and smells of exotic cooking. It was intense, exciting and crammed with Bantu, Indians, even one or two whites. *Nothing* like Donaghmede. Or Sarajevo.

Everyone was lovely, no one tried to kill us and I bought an embroidered tablecloth – what was to become the inaugural tablecloth in my Tablecloths-bought-on-book-tours collection. (Funny thing is, I'm not a tablecloth kind of person. Must have been the stress.) We even had our lunch before returning to the hotel.

Giddy and elated with having cheated death, we got through a good portion of the afternoon before the walls began to close in again. We had to get out. Earlier we'd noticed a small cinema in the shopping centre and after so successfully avoiding being murdered on our previous outing, we decided to give it a whirl. All that was on was *Chocolat* and under normal circumstances we might have made fun of its tweeness, but in our fragile, dislocated states, it was exactly what we needed.

However, when we emerged from the cinema, it had started to rain. As an Irish woman, I thought I knew all there was to know about rain. But this African stuff took it to the next level: water tumbled from the sky and ricocheted off the pavements in great bucketloads.

Himself said, 'We'll be drenched.'

Drenched? We'd be concussed. And worse again, if I went out in that deluge, the narky Swiss man's work would be entirely undone in two seconds and I'd have to go on telly the following morning looking like Jack Osbourne. We waited ten anxious minutes; it got noticeably worse. The roads had become fast-flowing torrents and not a car was about.

Back in, looking for something to protect my hair. The only shop still open was the pick 'n' mix and I explained my situation to the lovely Xhosa woman. From a sheet of cellophane, she fashioned a cunning rain-hat, like a hanky knotted at four corners that English men used to wear on the beach. (The cleaning staff had got wind that a human drama was unfolding in the Sweet Factory and had gathered to snigger.) Once my head was watertight, I draped my denim jacket over it and tied the sleeves under my chin. I looked gorgeous. Not.

We could have white-water rafted home. So much rain was wrung out of our clothes, you'd swear they'd just been washed. But my hair? Well, my hair was perfect.

First published in Abroad, *September 2003.*

Being Sent to Siberia

News arrived! I was being sent to Russia! To some place called Novosibirsk.

I was extremely pleased as I'd always wanted to visit somewhere ending in 'sk'. I'd favoured Omsk, Tomsk and Murmansk, but Novosibirsk would do nicely.

But where in the vastness of Russia *was* Novosibirsk? 'We'll buy the city guide to it.' Oh how we laughed. The laughing stopped, however, when I looked it up on the internet. Himself had left the room and I nearly shouted the house down for him to come and have a look. 'Himself! HIMSELF! I've found out where it is. Novosibirsk is the capital of SiBEEEERia.'

He nearly broke his neck running and in grim silence we stood before the screen and scrolled down through the details. Average temperature in February (which was when we were going): sixteen degrees below zero. Dropping as low as minus thirty-five. 'We'll need gloves,' we concluded.

Then trying to establish the time difference was tricky. Eight hours ahead of GMT. 'Unless they have daylight-saving time?' 'D'you think they have any daylight to save?' I countered bitterly.

In the following weeks we wrung much hollow laughter from the situation by telling people at every opportunity that we were being sent to Siberia.

How to keep warm became all we talked about. We shopped for thermal underwear – quartering the average age as soon as we walked into the super-warm-knickers emporium, and passionately we debated the rights and wrongs of fur coats, a debate abruptly abandoned once we discovered how much fur coats actually cost.

Then word came. A change of plans! We weren't going to Siberia after all! Other parts of Russia instead, all quite cold too, just not as cold as Siberia. We were mortified as by then we were dining out nightly on our gulag story. Our credibility was in shreds.

Day one

Wearing an awful lot of clothes, we landed in Moscow. At immigration, I was quite annoyed at how quickly they processed us. Call itself Russia! I wanted to queue, I wanted the authentic experience.

Outside in the perishing cold with sleet in the air and dirty slush underfoot, we met Valya, who would be our guide/ minder for the trip. She was fresh-faced and blue-eyed, with blonde hair swirled over her ears. As soon as we'd said hello, she told us that her husband had just left her. God, I love Russians. *Love* them. They'd tell you *anything*. They do unhappiness with such verve, such style, such passion. As we lugged our suitcase to the car, Valya told me that she had nothing left to live for, but that she would still take care of us on the tour.

We had a driver, Boris, to take us into the centre of Moscow and he looked so unhappy it was almost comical. He had a wide clown mouth that turned down at the corners.

His girl had just left him, Valya told us. After a short conversation in Russian, she divulged it had been for a younger man. Another burst of chat. Who happened to be his brother.

I sensed a matchmaking moment coming on. 'You wouldn't consider your man, as a replacement for your husband?' I asked her.

She considered Boris, then curled her lip. 'He is not good at making the sex.'

'But how do you know?'

'It is why his girl left him. He drinks too much. He wets the bed.'

Ah, well . . .

We had only four hours in Moscow before getting the overnight train east, just enough time to see that there was a Chanel shop in Red Square (Lenin must be rotating in his grave like a great big oul kebab) and to be stopped twice by military police looking at our papers. Everyone always says how grey and grim Russia is, but in Red Square is St Basil's Cathedral, the most beautiful building I've ever seen. It's what someone might dream up on a good acid trip: turrets and spires and onion domes swirled like ice-cream cones, all decked out in magnificent carnival colours. Commissioned by Ivan the Terrible who was so pleased with it that he poked out the architect's eyes. (So he couldn't ever do a cathedral for anyone else – a real mark of respect, your man must've been thrilled.)

Over dinner, in a smoke-filled wannabe-brasserie, Valya tried to make herself heard over the ear-blistering techno, to tell us more about her husband doing a runner.

'Maybe he'll come back,' I bellowed hopefully.

'He will not,' she said, matter-of-factly, doing that lovely Russian honest/pessimistic thing. Valya was fabulous. (And just a small bit mad, as befits a woman who has just been left by her husband.) I loved her. I am always at my happiest with slightly mad people.

Then it was time to get the train. Moscow station was like a vision of hell: desperate-looking, unshaven men standing about in the perishing cold, looking for an unofficial portering gig. Everywhere were little kiosks selling drink; they were doing a brisk trade.

But to my surprise, the train came on time *and* it was gorgeous. Our sleeper carriage was like a cottage on wheels – it had two little beds, with old-fashioned, patterned blankets and chintz curtains at the windows. Wood-panelling lined the walls and it was all cosy and lovely. Just as soon as they turned off the deafening techno.

We rattled through the snowy night between two small points on this enormous land mass.

Day two

And then it was morning and we had arrived in the beautiful city of Nizhni Novgorod. (I love saying that. 'I was in Nizzzhhhhhni Novgorod, you know.' Even now, I still look for chances, however tenuous, to drop it into conversations. 'So you like chocolate, do you? Funnily enough, I had some lovely chocolate in Nizzzhhhni Novgorod.')

God, it was cold, though, the kind of cold where it hurts to breathe. Although not by local standards – they were having a heatwave. Normally, at that time of year, it was thirty below, but this was a balmy, unseasonable minus ten.

We were met by a wonderful young man called Artim, checked into our hotel, the dinkiest, cosiest, most charming place. From our bedroom window we could see children ice-skating on a frozen football pitch. I felt very far from home. In a nice way.

My first gig was a creative-writing session with some university students. Artim, Valya, Himself and myself descended into the bowels of a violet-walled nightclub, where said students slumped around, reassuringly surly and disenchanted. I beamed with pleasure. I can't be doing with those eager, puppy-eyed teenagers who are keen to learn. It's not natural.

My next engagement was a television interview. Off we all went in Artim's car, our numbers swelled further by a sweet if slightly smelly student called Pyotr, who'd developed a crush on me in the violet-walled nightclub. We were stopped twice by military police en route to the telly station.

The interviewer was a skinny, super-intense bloke who called himself Ed and wanted to talk about 'art'.

'Would you die for your art?'

Well, of course I wouldn't. But I didn't want to disappoint him, so I nodded yes, certainly, indeed'n I would.

But then he threw a curveball. 'We have just heard the tragic news that your Princess Margaret has died. Would you like to say something?'

Caught on the hop, I said the first thing that came into my head: 'They should have let her marry the man she loved. The bastards.'

This caused confusion. 'You do not love your royal family?'

'Irish, see? Not mine.'

More confusion. When the interview ended, we decided to go for a drink and Ed said he'd come too. And so would his researcher. By now, my entourage had swelled to Jennifer Lopez-size proportions.

Back in the hotel, before we went out for dinner, Himself and myself were hit by a sudden longing for coffee. Luckily we had sachets – they'd been in our little welcome packs on the train – and all we needed was boiling water, so I volunteered to try out my Russian on the hotel staff. Standing in front of the mirror, I practised a few times: a gracious smile, then 'Zdrastvuti.' (Hello.) 'Voda, pazhalsta.' (Water, please.)

Down I went, smiled at the lady and delivered the line.

'Hmmm?' she went. 'Oh! You want hot water? Would you like it here or in your room? Whichever you like, it's up to you.'

'Er, right. Up in the room, so.'

(Helpful hint for you here, which I discovered entirely by accident because I wanted to cool my coffee so I could drink it: if you want a cappuccino but you don't have access to a machine, you could try adding carbonated Russian water to your coffee. It fizzes and froths like something in a scientific experiment. Funnily enough, it doesn't seem to work with non-Russian water.)

Then we went out for dinner and were stopped about sixteen times by the military police on the way to the restaurant. I was starting to recognize some of them.

We had a lovely evening, the people were so intelligent, warm and funny, tingeing even their saddest stories with a very attractive irony. I LOVE Russians. I want to be one.

The thing about them is, in an increasingly homogeneous world, they're so *Russian*. And when the bill came, the Russians flung themselves at it, doing that thing that the Irish do, wrestling people to the ground, trying to pay for everything. See, I like that.

Day three

Met Valya on the way down for breakfast and made the mistake of asking, 'How did you sleep?' Most people would just say, 'Fine.' But Valya rendered a blow-by-blow account of her feelings. Clopping down the stairs to the breakfast room, she said, 'I am thinking about him making the sex with his new one and I cannot sleep. I smoke all night and think of him making the sex with me instead.'

Still talking loudly about making the sex, we entered a neat little dining room with white, linen, embroidered table-cloths and napkins. Everything was charmingly twee, apart from the telly blasting out techno at a level that felt like a physical assault, and the fug of cigarette smoke obscuring the sideboard of food.

That afternoon we proceeded to the town hall. Nizhni Novgorod was having an arts festival and I was the star exhibit! The place was jammers, the atmosphere was buoyant and lovely people kept appearing to practise their English on me, except Pyotr kept trying to shoo them away so he could have me to his (smelly) self.

Then it was showtime and just as I mounted the stage to start my reading, the lights flickered once, twice, then disappeared entirely. What the . . . ? It was the electricity! We were having a power cut. A lovely, authentic Russian power cut! Was it the real thing or were they just laying it on for us tourists? Oh it seemed to be the real thing, alright. Everyone was rushing around and people kept promising me, 'This never happens. *Never!*'

Enquiries were made: was it a localized thing? Just the town hall, perhaps? But no, the whole town was out. Even though it was only three in the afternoon, it was quite dark. A decision was made; I would do my reading by candlelight. But I couldn't read and hold my candle at the same time, in case I set my book on fire, so the love-struck Pyotr was on his feet offering to hold my candle. As it were. So the show went on, with Pyotr taking every opportunity to stand far too close to me. But hey, I was facing forty and flattered.

Afterwards, I fell among poets. There was a load of them in the front row, several looking like James Joyce, right down to the flattened hair, roundy glasses and sober suits. They grabbed me as I stepped off the stage and all gave me signed copies of their slender volumes. Although I couldn't understand a word they were saying, they were a right laugh.

Armed with home-printed books of Russian poetry, I returned to Valya and Himself and we watched a little drama in mime. (It ended tragically.) Then someone sang a song. (A sad one.) Then there was a stand-up comedian. (A special unfunny Russian one.)

But then there was some sort of disturbance. A kerfuffle. The poets seemed to be staging some kind of anarchic take-over. There were an awful lot of them crowding onto the small stage, looking like Kool and the Gang. Then a guitar appeared and they wouldn't stop singing.

It was a great, *great* afternoon, everyone had been so nice.

But Artim, the wonderful man who had organized it all, wouldn't take the praise. 'It's those damn poets,' he said. 'They stage a takeover every year and this year they *promised*.'

Day four

Up horribly, horribly early to catch the plane to Samara – too early even for the techno, smoke-filled breakfast.

The week before I'd been in the US and got mightily humbled for having tweezers in my hand luggage, so Himself made me promise that I had nothing dangerous on my person for this flight. Not that it mattered a damn. I could have carried a ground-to-air rocket-launcher onto the plane and no one would have minded. They'd probably have helped me lift it on.

It was a novel flying experience. Nothing was screened through any metal-detector yokes and the plane looked like a toy plane with steps that went up from under into its belly. There were no conveyor belts or chance to check in luggage: you had to carry on all your own stuff – suitcases, rocket-launchers, etc. Then, when I emerged into the body of the plane, I thought it was one of those military planes with no seats, where you sit on the metal floor waiting to parachute out over enemy territory. But, mercifully, behind a little curtain there were seats. Sort of. There were chintz curtains at the windows and no working seatbelts. Everyone was frozen, you could see the cold air when they breathed out, and they all kept their furry hats on. It was like being on a rattly old bus going between Knock and Claremorris on a wet January day. Think about that the next time you're tempted to complain about Ryanair.

And the thing was, I knew that this was the safest airline in Russia.

Nothing to eat, mind you. *Nothing to eat.* And now it was getting to me.

Between the hunger and the tiredness and the strangeness of everything and being in the grip of mad, bad PMS, I behaved very badly in Samara. I was in a right fouler and I just couldn't bury it. (I'm still so ashamed of myself. It's one of those memories that whenever it surfaces, I wish I was dead. You know those ones? Even writing about it is killing me, but it must be done.)

When we landed, our lovely driver took us on a tour of Samara. Until very recently it was a closed city. (They used to make bomber planes and other secret stuff.) It was a big banana to be allowed to visit and, in all fairness, it was beautiful and the Volga was frozen over and men were sitting fishing into little holes in the ice and it was all very atmospheric and charming, but I couldn't care less. I wanted something to eat. Instead I had to do a press conference.

After which we were finally allowed to eat something. Our host led us along a slushy, potholed street, to a pancake place, where he ushered us to the cloakroom and said, 'Here. Please to take your clothes off.' And I was too narky to even raise a smile.

Food usually does the trick with me but even after I'd eaten about fifty-six pancakes with a variety of fillings, my mood remained sour. And still remained so when we arrived at the local university, where I was to adjudicate a debate. In honour of me being a recovering jar-head, the title of the debate was: Should drugs be legalized? It was the most

one-sided debate I'd ever come across; it was clear that all
the students were horrified by drugs and it kind of annoyed
me, what with Russia being rife with alcoholism. Why worry
about keeping pot criminalized when alcohol was perfectly
legal and in the process of killing and destroying more
Russian lives than every other drug put together?

Anyway, I should have kept my mouth shut and smiled
politely, but to my great shame I couldn't. Brutally and rudely
I laid down my views, and although they gave me a box of
chocolates when I left, I could tell that they were thinking of
keeping it for themselves. Not that I blame them. Oh the
shame! The rudeness of me!

And so, finally, to our hotel, a flimsy unreassuring place
which seemed to have been bought in its entirety from Ikea.
(This is not a good thing, some of the unhappiest moments
of my life have been spent in Ikea.)

I was feeling too ashamed to go out for dinner that night,
but Valya made me. In the restaurant she was in a strangely
restless mood, drinking vodka shots and on the prowl. She
still loved her husband but she wouldn't mind making the
sex with someone else. Your man over there, in fact, she said,
pointing to a bull-necked but otherwise quite attractive
man, who had surprisingly nice shoes for a Russian. I was
thrilled. I'd taken violently agin the deserting husband and I
wanted her to hook up with someone new. Himself and
myself wished her well, left her to it and went back to our
flat-pack assembled hotel. Some unknown time that night we
were woken by an almighty crash. It sounded like a ceiling
had fallen in. We'd just drifted back to sleep when we heard
another. Then one more, this time so bad that Himself's

washbag fell off the bathroom shelf. It was Valya-related, I just *knew* it.

Great excitement next morning at breakfast, when through the haze of cigarette smoke, we saw, bobbing his head along to the techno, Valya's fella from the night before. She shoots, she scores!

Unfortunately not; it transpired that he was just another guest in the hotel. Feck!

Then Valya appeared, telling the entire room, first in English, then in Russian, that she had been so drunk the night before that she had fallen into her wardrobe. (The first crash we'd heard.) Then she told everyone that she had missed her husband so badly that she had rolled around with a pillow so much that she had fallen out of bed. (The second crash.) Twice. (The third, washbag-dislocating one.)

Day five

Flight to St Petersburg. The plane was disappointingly normal. Seatbelts and the like. I much preferred the other one.

Now St Petersburg, with its wide European-style boulevards and impressively bombastic buildings, is the Russian city that everyone gets their knickers in a twist about. And yes, it's undeniably impressive and beautiful, but actually I think I preferred the smaller, more 'Russian' towns, the ones that you mightn't normally see.

My work consisted of holding two workshops, where I met students of English so staggeringly talented they put me to shame.

Then it was my last afternoon, when I stumbled across – and I'm not joking here – one of the most beautiful shoe shops I've EVER been in. And let's face it, I've seen the inside of a few.

God, I love Russia.

PS Soon afterwards Valya met another bloke. He is excellent at making the sex.

PPS A few months after my return I was driving back from County Mayo when I realized the next town I was about to drive through was called Tulsk. Tul*sk*. See my point? It ends in 'sk'. So there's no need for me to go to Murmansk, Tomsk, Omsk, Bryansk, Gdansk or Novosibirsk. But I might anyway.

Previously unpublished.

Queen of the Earplugs

Recently, for reasons we needn't get into right now, I was on a long bus journey in foreign parts. This would have been fine, interesting even, awash with local colour, which usually consists of people carrying chickens, except that every other one of the forty passengers was Irish. We were travelling as 'a group'. And the thing about a large group of Irish people visiting a different country is that we feel the national obligation to be 'great craic' weighing heavily upon us. It's our duty to be entertaining. It's what we're famed for and we can't let those poor humourless foreigners down.

The vivacious journey began with everyone bellowing cheery insults from the front to the back of the bus. And whenever someone went into the bus's toilet, if you didn't make squirty, hissing noises, and give the poor weak-bladdered person a round of applause when they made their red-faced exit, you were regarded as a bit of a killjoy. (I say 'you' but I mean 'I'. 'I' was regarded as a bit of a killjoy.)

You see, I, despite being Irish, was miserable. The problem was the noise. I'm not good on noise at the best of times. And it was midnight and we had an eight-hour journey ahead of us and I was hoping for a sleep.

But the shouting and the 'good-humoured' slagging was

as nothing when I realized that, Christ, we were going to have a famed Irish sing-song! Someone produced a guitar. Someone always produces a guitar. And it's usually the person sitting right behind me.

Never mind that it was the dead of night and we were passing through mile after mile of deserted, freezing country-side, the Irish people sang their patriotic hearts out for those poor craic-free foreigners. We had the sad songs about having to leave Ireland – emigration themes are always popular on journeys abroad, even if it's just a day trip to Achill. And then we had the shouty, foot-stamping anthems. When the opening strains of 'The Wild Rover' started up I began eyeing the door of the speeding bus, longingly.

NO, NAY, NEVER.

One day this will all be over, I thought.

RISE UP YOUR KILT!

A time will come when I'm somewhere peaceful and quiet. A library, maybe. Or perhaps a convent, one of the ones where they've taken a vow of silence

NO, NAY, NEVER, NO MOAAAAARE!

I'll be old some day and hopefully profoundly, profoundly deaf. Mind you, they say that hearing is the last faculty to go. Just my fecking luck . . .

AND I'LL PLAAAAAAAAAAY THE WILD ROVER, NO NEVER NO MOAAAAARE.

Actually, never mind hoping that things will improve in this life, because I can't imagine it. One day, I'll be dead and buried and unable to hear anything and none of this will matter.

It was literally like being tortured. I wanted to turn around and shove my hands at the guitar player and plead with him,

'Go on, pull my fingernails out, I don't mind, do anything you want, just stop FUCKING SINGING.'

After about an hour of this hell – which seemed to last a year – they stopped for a cigarette break and, despite the freezing temperatures outside, everyone trooped off the bus and Himself went with them. (I won't say where the country was because the other passengers might recognize themselves and track me down and sing at me. Let's just say it's a part of the world where the winters are harsh and the misfortunate natives aren't much craic.)

Even Himself, despite being the most easy-going, tolerant person I've ever met, was finding this tough. He had stopped smoking about five years earlier and I was terrified that he was going to start again. I didn't blame him. After being on the dry for ten years, I was contemplating going back on the sauce. Genuinely. It was the closest I've ever come to cracking in the entire decade.

Eventually everyone got back on the bus, but there was still no sign of Himself. *He's definitely had a cigarette*, I thought, *and he's too upset to face me*. But no, here he was, climbing back on at the last second. 'I nearly didn't get back on,' he admitted. 'I was thinking I'd run away into the forest and take my chances with the wolves.'

'I'll come with you,' I said, grabbing his hand and lunging for the door, but it was too late, the bus had set off again and so had the singing.

When we'd exhausted all the Irish songs, we had a Beatles medley; then the Rock Around The Clock type ones; then something about a red rooster, where everyone had to flap their arms and make 'bokabokabok' roostery-type noises; for reasons that escaped me, 'Take Me Home, Country Road' reappeared on a loop, every ten songs; then finally we had a Rolling Stones tribute where one of the 'most hilarious' of all the (extremely hilarious) passengers took it upon himself to strut up and down the aisle, with his arse stuck out in an approximation of Mick Jagger's, while everyone else yelled, 'Go on, you good thing!'

Every song that was ever written was sung on that bus that long, long night. It was a living hell and it made me wish I was Finnish. (They're fairly taciturn, aren't they?)

Other people's noise just wears away at my nerves. I used to live in a flat where the upstairs neighbours used to decide at four in the morning that they didn't like the way their furniture was placed, and with fabulous 'let's do the show right here' spontaneity, decide to move it around there and then. And another flat where it sounded like twenty or thirty people had strapped woks to their feet in the flat above and were doing a tap-dancing marathon – the weirdest combination of clanging and thumping you've ever heard. I used to bring people home to my flat just to hear it – I could almost have sold tickets – and they always agreed that it sounded *exactly* like twenty or thirty people had strapped woks to their feet and were tap-dancing around the (wooden – oh but of course) floor.

Because I travel so much and stay in hotels (which I know sounds fabulously glam, and as a result my whingeing will elicit no sympathy), I'm constantly at the mercy of other people's rackets: next-door's telly, next-door's alarm clock (going off at five-thirty with no one to turn it off because it was set by the previous occupant who is long gone), loud conversations about vending machines held right outside my door, people upstairs having grunty, athletic sex or holding what sounds like gymnastic classes. There are times when I actually cry from the frustration of not being able to sleep. See, I don't just stay in the hotels to enjoy myself, I'm there to work. And yes, I know I get lovely room-service breakfasts and nice, free shower gel and I don't have to make my bed – which is all wonderful – but if I don't get enough sleep my eyes swell up and go all slitty and sometimes I have to have my photo taken when I'm like that, and I'm unphotogenic at the best of times. Also, without sleep, my brain gets removed and replaced with a lump of suet, which makes things a bit tricky when a journalist asks me, 'What exists in the thin line between pleasure and pain?' And, just in case you were thinking this, I'm not allowed to answer, 'How in the name of Jayzus would I know?' Oh no! I have to come up with a coherent, witty, charming, original answer or else the journalist will mock me mightily and tell her fellow country-women not to bother buying my book.

As a result, I never leave home without earplugs. But my earplugs were no match for the busload of Irish people. The 'great craic' and late-night sing-songs continued throughout the week-long trip and Himself and myself returned home in flitters, physical and emotional wrecks. My back teeth were worn to stumps from the tense grinding I'd been doing and I had so much suppressed anger I was afraid I might run amok with a tennis racket in a public place (possibly McDonald's).

Soon after we got back, we thought we'd go down to Clare, in the hope that a few days by the sea, listening to the soothing suck and rush of the waves, would glue our frayed nerves back together. But we'd have been better off staying at home and lending a hand on the Booterstown roadworks for all the good it did us.

The house we were staying in was in the middle of a terrace of other houses and no sooner had we parked the car and dragged in our bags than we realized that the sound-proofing was so bad we could almost hear the breathing of the people three doors down. But never mind breathing! They could do much better than that! For reasons best known to themselves the house on one side of us had people on perma-nent duty clattering at high speed up and down wooden stairs in stiletto heels. While the house on the other side had gone to the trouble of providing a rota of people on a twenty-four-hour door-slamming vigil. Worse still, there wasn't even a regular pattern to it, so that at least after a few non-stop hours, we'd simply get used to it – like when you live next to the railway, after a while you don't even hear the trains. But oh no. They'd go on a good fifteen-minute banging session – then abruptly stop. Gorgeous, throbbing silence would reign just long enough for me to think that maybe they'd gone out, and no sooner would I begin to exhale with relief than one supersonic crash would herald the start of the racket again.

Even late at night I was just drifting off to sleep when a mys-terious door banged so violently the windows rattled, then from the other side, a burst of hammering heels as loud as machine-gun fire had me bolt upright in the bed, my heart pounding.

'What kind of mad bastards are they?' I fumed, sleep having deserted me. 'Can't they get a proper hobby?'

After my sleep had been fractured for the third time I began to fantasize about killing them; the stairs-clatterers with their own stilettos and the door-bangers by closing their heads in their own door and giving it a good slam.

Our second night's sleep was no better than the first so we decided to call it a day and go back to Dublin early. A vein beneath my eye was starting to twitch.

'When we get home we'll clear the mice droppings out of the shed,' Himself suggested. I tried to smile and that set the jumping vein off again.

As we were dragging our bags back to the car, the stairs-clatterers were emerging from their front door, and the oddest thing was how normal they looked – a tubby man, a woman carrying a baby, and a granny-type person. They didn't look like nutters who got their kicks by non-stop pounding up and down stairs. In fact, none of them looked *capable* of the sustained physical activity that had been going on.

I gave them a curt nod, but I just couldn't find it in me to be any friendlier. As we walked to the car, the man called, 'Excuse me!'

For a moment I thought he was going to apologize, that he and his family had been in training for the forthcoming stairs-clattering championships and that they needed all the practice they could get. But instead he started complaining!

'We can hear you, constantly talking, laughing –'

Laughing? Crying, more like!

'You woke the baby twice. Can you keep the noise down?'

I looked at Himself. This was too weird. Perhaps it was time for a sing-song.

NO, NAY, NEVER, NO, NAY, NEVER NO MOAAAAARE.

Previously unpublished.

Climb Every Mountain

Recently I went on holiday to Bhutan, a small, unspoilt Buddhist kingdom in the foothills of the Himalayas. It's existed in self-imposed isolation for decades and has only recently opened for business. It's all forests, mountains, single-lane roads, sheer three-thousand-foot drops to the valley below and people in funny – compulsory – national dress. (The men have to wear argyle-patterned knee-socks and oversized dressing gowns, hitched up over a waistbelt to create a charming blouson effect. Look it up on the net if you don't believe me.)

I thought Bhutan would be fascinating, and indeed it was, but it was only after I'd arrived that I discovered the main reason people go there is to 'trek'.

Trekking. Even the word annoys me. And 'rambling' – there's another one. It's *walking* and giving it a fancy title changes nothing. The thing is, exercise and I have never really seen eye to eye. (I do yoga. About once a year.) Nor have the 'outdoors' and I. Walking the thirty yards from the car park to the shops I sometimes get an earache. So when I go on holiday, my normally sedentary lifestyle goes down several gears, until I'm practically flatlining.

But after a week of non-stop Buddhist temples, I was ready for a change and when our guide suggested 'a nice, easy walk' Himself looked at me with desperate, pleading eyes and I was persuaded.

'But you'll need flat shoes,' the guide said, looking at my boots.

'These *are* flat,' I replied. They had only two-and-a-half-inch heels, what was he talking about?

He handed me a brushed-steel and latex 'walking pole' and the three of us set off. It was a lot more uphill than I'd been led to expect, but between the fir trees, the clear blue sky, the stunning views, the blood flowing in my veins, my heart pounding in my chest (but not too much), the way the air smelt exactly like Fanta – suddenly I got it. I felt great.

We stopped at a seventh-century Buddhist monastery, where we met a monk who looked unnervingly like Graham Norton in orange panstick and a red robe. Appropriately enough he 'blessed' me with an eighteen-inch phallus, which could have come straight from Ann Summers, but apparently was some ancient artefact. It was only then that I discovered that people come from around the globe to this monastery to get pregnant. I didn't get the deluxe fertility treatment, which involves several monks, chanting and burning things, but all the same, if I get up the duff, I'll let you know.

Then we carried on through the deserted forest, passing a three-hundred-year-old stupa (holy sort-of-shrine yoke) and I nearly died of fright when I saw a small girl, nestled in one of its hollows, eating what appeared to be a pan pipe.

Finally we reached the top and the sense of achievement was indescribable.

Exhilarated, I leant on my pole, surveying the valley, feeling like Sir Edmund Hillary.

It was a moment of personal epiphany: I can be different. I can change. I will become a trekker. Or a rambler. Whichever is better. I will buy a pole. And proper flat walking boots. I would have a 'hobby', an 'interest'. Up to that point if anyone had asked me what my 'interests' were, I'd have replied, 'Handbags, KitKats, Dermot O'Leary.'

A new exciting future unrolled itself in front of me, for inspection. I'd be strong, sinewy, as thin as a whippet. (I saw myself looking a bit like Paula Radcliffe.) All my holidays would be spent heading off with a rucksack full of high-protein bars to climb the Andes and the like. I might even lose the tops of a couple of fingers to frostbite and everyone would think I was fabulous. People would ask me why I climbed the highest peaks in the world (I had mutated from being an ordinary trekker to a mountaineer) and I would reply, 'Why do dogs lick their balls? Because they can, Oprah, because they can.' And nobody would think I was vulgar.

From now on I would only wear tracksuits made out of those high-tech fabrics which can stop a speeding bullet but weigh less than a feather. I would never wear skirts except on special occasions when, although I would be lovely and slim, my calves would be bunched and enormous in my high heels and my legs would be bandy. I would look like a transvestite, exactly like Tony Curtis in *Some Like it Hot*. But I wouldn't care. The broken veins in my cheeks wouldn't matter, either. I would have a solid, cast-iron identity.

Then I got home from Bhutan and unpacked and looked at the mountain of shite arrayed on my bed – stuff I'd bought while I was away. Mesmerized, I was picking things up and wondering: *what the fuck . . . ?* Hand-woven throws which would make my home look like a social worker's. Hand-woven bags which had seemed extraordinarily charming at the time but that I wouldn't be seen dead with now. A hand-woven passport holder. Hand-woven oven gloves – back then it hadn't mattered *at all* that they weren't insulated. Funny brass things that might be door handles. Or ceremonial cups. A cowbell. Seven Buddhas of varying sizes. A prayer wheel. Awful gaudy wall hangings that you'd see in low-rent Chinese restaurants.

Why, why, *why?* What had I been thinking? I sat in my hand-woven hell and waited for sanity to return. Which it did.

It has been several weeks since my return. I have not yet purchased my walking pole.

First published in Marie Claire, *May 2005.*

HEALTH AND BEAUTY

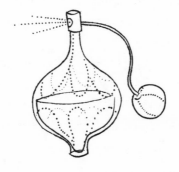

They Say You Always Remember Your First Time . . .

I was eleven years of age and a friend and I were messing around with my mother's make-up. Until that day, I'd been happy enough just trying her lipstick and eyebrow pencil, but suddenly emboldened by some strange impulse I smeared myself from hairline to jawline with foundation (orange, as was the fashion at the time) and couldn't believe the transformation. An upgraded version of me was looking back from the mirror. I looked like myself, only far, far nicer. My eyes were greener, my hair looked shinier, everything was smoother and better.

My friend, too, was astounded. 'You look . . .' She groped for the most appropriate compliment. 'You look . . . *Spanish*!' No greater praise. At the time (mid-seventies) it was what we all wanted – to obscure our shameful blue-white Irish skin beneath a see-it-from-the-moon Jaffa-style glow.

For the first time I became aware of the transforming qualities of make-up. It could rebuild me, make me a better version of me. From the word go I was enslaved.

My attitude to life has always been that if a small bit of something was good, then a big bit was even better. So right from the beginning I was a little heavy-handed in my make-up application. Luckily these were the days when Irish women wore their foundation to be noticed – the foundation, I mean, not the women. Foundation was almost regarded as an accessory in its own right, like a piece of jewellery or a tattoo. And no one had any truck with the idea of matching foundation to your skin-tone. Why would you do that? You'd end up looking exactly like yourself!

Instead, orange was the shade du jour. It was a good colour, a noble colour, a sexy colour. And just in case you weren't quite orange enough you could always give yourself an extra going-over with some coloured face powder. (Orange, of course. Or maybe pink, just for the variety.)

None for your neck, though. Necks remained as white as God had intended them to be. Back then you were *no one* if you didn't sport an orange tidemark and a matching dodgy line on your collar.

It wasn't just foundation, though; I was mad about it all – lipsticks, blushers, eyeliners, mascaras . . . I once read a magazine article asking which single beauty product you'd bring to a desert island and I tied myself in absolute knots over it. I narrowed it down to the big three: lipstick, mascara or base – but I couldn't decide which. It used to keep me awake at nights. Even now, if I've run out of normal worries, and am looking for something good to worry about, it fills the gap admirably.

The great thing about cosmetics (in my opinion, and yes, I know it's shallow; for a spirited defence, see below) is that they keep inventing new things – and I've bought them all: concealers, brow highlighters, skin primers, blending brushes, double-ended eyeliners, slanted sponges, tinted moisturizer . . . (Mind you, in my early days I thought tinted moisturizer existed to be worn beneath your foundation. For extra orangeness, like.)

My bathroom drawers are like a cosmetic museum. Clear mascara, anyone? Eyelash primer? Pillar-box red lipstick? I've stuff dating back to the early eighties: crimson eyeshadow, puce blusher, blue mascara. Plus a good few relics from the red-lipsticked, power-made-up yuppie years, and several other bits and pieces, right up to the high-tech, light-diffusing, natural-looking present. (Imagine, I have lived long enough to see Irish women match their base to their skin-tone. Truly I have lived through turbulent times.)

The love affair has never waned: make-up always makes me feel better. With it I am more confident, more articulate, more amusing. But it took far longer for me to start caring about my skin. I thought: oh skin! That old yoke! Sleep in your make-up – who cares! The important thing is that you have make-up to sleep *in*!

But somewhere along the line I changed and now I have so much skincare that to get into my bathroom you have to run at the door with your shoulder and push hard.

For me, the pleasure starts with the packaging. Ripping off the cellophane, opening the cardboard box, trying to find the instructions in English, unscrewing the lid, tearing off the tinfoil seal, then finally reaching the magic stuff within. (Yes, shallow *and* very wasteful of the earth's resources, I *know*. As I said, see spirited defence below.)

So what about the extravagant claims the skincare manufacturers make. Do I believe them? Well, yes!

And no.

Basically, it depends.

When I was a teenager, I heard a report on the radio, an exposé of face creams. (Hadn't they anything better to do exposés on? At a time when Ireland was jackknifed from corruption? I swear to God.) Anyway, they picked on a particular brand whose press release promised that their night-cream molecules would 'enter' the skin and restructure from within. The crackshot journalist concluded that this was as impossible as pushing potatoes through the holes in muslin weave. I tried not to listen, I tried not to be influenced, but it left me with a healthy dose of scepticism.

I know that nothing is going to reverse time. Apart from a deal with the devil, of course, and at the moment he's refusing to return my calls.

But, at worst, using so much night cream that I slide off my pillow, can't do me any harm. And if it's not doing me any good, it doesn't matter because I never use anything for more than a few months. Unlike po-faced French women who use the same brand from the age of fourteen until their deathbed, I'm a product slut. I love them all. If face creams were husbands, then I am Elizabeth Taylor.

The thing is that I'll try each product on its merits and I'll draw my own conclusions, and there are some products that I *know* make a difference. I've seen it with my own two (kohl-rimmed, mascara'd) eyes. It's probably not fair to single out a special few for mention when there are so many good brands, but I'm going to anyway.

Example: after using Crème de la Mer for a month, I was looking so well that I was accused of having had botox.

Example: if I have a late night and use Jo Malone's protein serum before going to sleep, instead of waking up with a face like a pair of greying, saggy y-fronts, I look like I've had my full sixteen hours.

Example: if I've been hitting the chocolate hard and look spotty and sluggish, a go of Elizabeth Arden's Peel and Reveal will sort me out.

As the whole area of beauty becomes more high-tech and sophisticated, innovative products keep appearing. New areas of the face and body come under scrutiny and suddenly a new special cream is required for them. And sometimes a cream on its own isn't enough. Sometimes you need serums too. Or finishing gear. And there are times when a little voice inside me asks: do you *really* need this inner-arm super-serum, to be worn under the ordinary serum and over the day cream? And I think: feck it! Who cares? I love it!

Which brings me to my spirited defence.

Spirited defence: yes, I admit to a certain amount of guilt, but loving beauty products is not the worst thing in the world. It's not like I'm doing cocaine, or collecting Swatch watches or shooting quails or invading Iraq.

Everyone has to have a hobby.

Previously unpublished.

Hand Upgrade

*U*ntil recently, I never took any interest in nail care, on account of never having any nails to care for – I wasn't a smoker so I had to develop *some* way of coping with stress.

Not that I didn't occasionally make the effort to grow my nails. When I was in school, the myth circulated that if you ate a cube of jelly a day you'd have fabulous long strong nails, but once I started into the jelly I could never stop at one cube; I'd always eat the entire packet, then have to face the wrath of my mammy when she went to make something to go with the custard and found I'd eaten it all.

Then the summer I was fourteen – and I don't know how it happened – all of a sudden I had a prize nail, a gorgeous elongated shapely creature on my ring finger, left hand, which I guarded and displayed like it was a Fabergé egg. I almost kept my hand in a glass case for the entire summer and charged people to look. But then September arrived and the prize nail broke and that was the end of that.

I just wasn't a nail person. All my life I've hated my hands; I'm prone to short limbs anyway and nowhere is it more pronounced than my fingers – short fingers, short, bitten, strangely shaped nails. That was just the way it was. No point wishing for things to be different.

Then, a couple of years back, I had to go to New York

for work and a 'well wisher' took me aside and told me that unless I got my nails sorted out my career in the States was so OVER. She put the fear of God into me – I mean, what the hell could I do about my bloody nails? Fake it, she advised; thanks to the miracle of science, I could get my pitiful little mismatched stubs lengthened and strengthened with all sorts of fake jiggery-pokery.

I didn't believe her because nothing ever works for me, but I went along anyway, out of curiosity, to a new nailbar. Where I spent a long, boring – *and painful* – ninety minutes: my 'well wisher' hadn't warned me that it *hurts* as they solder the fakey nails to your real, crappy nails. But it was worth it. I emerged one amazed hour and a half later with ten supermodel-style nails. Unbelievably, they didn't look remotely fake, just very, very beautiful.

And suddenly, miraculously, with my long, glam nails, I was transformed. I thought I was *IT*. It wasn't just my nails which had been enhanced, my entire *hand* had been upgraded. Even my *arms* and *shoulders* looked more elegant. I kept clattering my new nails impatiently, even when I wasn't impatient – *just because I could* . . . I became more dynamic, I spoke faster and louder and gesticulated more with my hands. To my surprise, I became slightly bitchy; I think it's easier to get away with catty comments when you've long nails. In fact, I felt it was nearly *expected* of me.

It wasn't all fun and games, of course; there are always side effects – I could no longer type, I had to use a pen to make phone calls and it took me over ten minutes to pick a safety pin off the carpet (in the end I had to kick it up with the toe of my boot and catch it mid-air). None of which seemed like a problem! Instead I thought I was fantastically glam.

And how was I going to cope when I was under stress, once I couldn't bite my nails any more? I contemplated getting false ones to bite, the way people get fake fags once they've given up smoking. Or indeed, I could take up smoking!

For the first time in my life I started buying nail varnishes; I felt as if I'd been finally let into a club that I'd always been barred from. Naturally, being me, I went a bit mental and went on an over-the-top rampage of opaques and clears and metallics and glitterys and opalescents . . .

Mistakes were made, of course. I bought one varnish which was described as plum, but in reality it was chestnut – or in other words, *brown*. I looked as though I'd got all ten of my nails caught in a door. But we live and learn. I was on a steep learning curve and I had the occasional success. Another one, which the ad said had been 'inspired by the dazzle of gemstones' was *extremely* glam: like I was wearing garnets on the ends of my fingers and I kept telling dramatic stories just so I could wave my hands around and light up the air with flashes of luminous red light. Happy days . . .

Within no time I was utterly dependent on my nails. Without them I felt like Samson without his hair – naked and devoid of power. However, nothing had prepared me for how high maintenance they were. I had to get them done every two weeks because they grew so fast – which was very odd because all my life, when I'd been depending on my real, underneath, stubby nails to grow, the little shaggers had stubbornly refused to budge. It was as bad as having to monitor the roots of my hair, only worse, because I only needed to get my roots done every three weeks. And the roots of my hair don't suddenly grow a long grey inch overnight – but breaking a nail was the work of an instant. And it happened. The first time, I was distraught at the sight of nine long, glossy talons and one short, bald, funny-shaped stub. In the olden days I'd have been first in the queue to laugh at a girl who was upset about breaking a nail. But it was all different now. I knew exactly how distressing it was and a broken nail had the same effect on me as Kryptonite on Superman. It was an important life lesson to learn: you know what, I realized, we should never judge. Not until we've walked a mile on another person's hands . . .

But eventually the maintenance began to weary me. Upkeep was a constant worry, requiring round-the-clock vigilance, and the nails seemed to grow faster and faster and break more and more often. When I got them redone the warm glow would last for about a day, then I'd chip the nail varnish or the edges would get raggy and start catching in my jumper, or my own manky ridged nails would appear underneath the glossy fake ones and I'd try to pretend it wasn't happening by painting over the join, but I'd make a right shambles of it and get polish everywhere, as far down as my first knuckle . . .

In the end the worry broke me and it just wasn't worth it. Life's too long. I'm back to my short, stubby, misshapen ones now and, contrary to what I once thought, it's not so bad. At least now, in times of high tension, I've something to gnaw on.

First published in Marie Claire, *July 2005.*

Knickers: A Vexed Area

*I*t used to be holiday brochures. Whenever I was stressed or sad I'd take to the bed with a bundle of them (expensive ones, that you sometimes have to pay a fiver for), spend many happy hours in sunny places without any pesky jet lag or coming home to find my house had been burgled while I'd been away, and without fail, I'd be restored to myself. But recently my interest has specialized: I've become obsessed with spas. I read about them incessantly and it's got so bad that I'm reluctant to go anywhere (city breaks, work trips, the post office) unless they have a spa attached. As a result I consider myself a bitteen of an expert; in fact, it could be my specialist subject on *Mastermind*. Let me share with you my hard-won knowledge.

1) *Appointment.* Vitally important, because how else will you get in and get rubbed? But beware! The bad news is that, based on my experience, there is a 58.7 per cent chance that your appointment will be gammied up. Sad but true. It must be all that essential oil in the air, softening brains and compromising concentration, but the number of times spa receptionists have lost my booking or booked me for the wrong day or for the wrong things . . . Interestingly, it happens just as much in the dear places as in

cheapo ones. In a fabulous spa on the Barrier Reef they had me booked in for everything I'd requested in my email. But they were so super-efficient that they'd done it *twice*, the two lots of treatments happening simultaneously. And they wanted to charge me for both. In the world-famous Sanctuary, when I arrived with my sister – both of us in *flitters* and gagging for a comforting touch – they had no record of us. No record AT ALL. Even though I'd given them my credit card details and rung to recon-firm – nada. (And they were fully booked, so they couldn't fit us in.) Considering that most people go to spas be-cause they're feeling frayed and fragile, this IS NOT GOOD.

2) *Sound-proofing*. Or lack thereof. Many spas have walls so thin, you can hear the people breathing in the next room. They're the good ones. In the bad ones, you can hear what the next-doors are *thinking*. In London's extraordinarily beautiful Agua Spa (I mean, it really is, it looks like an artist's impression of heaven), the treatment spaces are separated only by muslin curtains. Did you ever hear anything so stupid in all your life? While I was being reiki'd and desperately trying to relax and get my money's worth, the woman in the next space was droning on to her therapist about how hard it was to be a mother, how she'd forgotten what a good night's sleep and uncracked nipples felt like, how she was dreading sex again . . . For the entire hour I had to fight against leaping off the table, pushing aside the muslin curtain and shrieking, 'Shut up, shut up, SHUT UP!'

3) *Reflexology*. Don't be fooled: it's not the same as a foot massage. Reflexology is good for you and like most things that are good for you – leg-waxing, climbing Croagh Patrick, the truth about your dodgy boyfriend – it can hurt.

4) *Face-masks*. In most facials there comes a point when they cover your face with plaster-of-Paris-style stuff and leave it to set into a hard, scary mask, then the girl murmurs something like, 'I'll just leave you to relax on your own for a bit.' She makes it sound as though she doesn't want to leave, but that fifteen minutes of solitude is for your good. This is a complete fiction. While you are lying there blind and terrified with claustrophobia, she'll be outside having a fag and making calls on her mobile.

5) *An hour of bliss*. When they say a treatment lasts for an hour, they really mean fifty minutes. If you're lucky. Latecomers are often allowed to run over into the next person's time (mine) but when the paraffin sock is on the other foot and they start my treatment late, they finish on time.

6) *Opportunities for theft*. An unexpected bonus. You have a relaxing massage or facial, then when your treatment is finished, the rubbing-lady will withdraw, leaving you in the little room to get dressed. However, the sharp-eyed among you may have noticed that, very often, there are lots of products in the room. Trolleys and shelves groaning under the weight of special-catering-size gallon jars of lovely Decléor or Clarins or Elemis – and you are alone with them. This is an ideal opportunity for theft.

Yes, yes, it's immoral and illegal. I *know*. And smuggling them out in the pocket of your towelling robe might prove a bit of a challenge. But when we get to the next point, you'll be glad you did.

7) *Pressure to buy products.* Unfortunately it happens, although not usually in the top-end places. Nevertheless, nothing works faster to wreck your expensive buzz than being bullied into shelling out further readies when you already have a houseful of stuff you never use, or being made to feel like a stingy scuzz-ball who doesn't give a shite about her skin. However – and follow me closely here – I can provide you with the perfect defence. You can agree bitterly to buy the day cream. Oh, and eye cream. And the exfoliator. And the rehydrating mask, if they insist. Or, you can just say, 'Why would I need to buy that pitifully small 30g tube of Decléor when I'm just after nicking a gallon bottle of it from the treatment room . . . whoops!'

8) *Knickers.* A vexed area, without a doubt: to leave on or take off. If you leave them on, discomfort could mar your enjoyment, but if you take them off, there's nowhere to run, nowhere to hide – every bit of you will be on display, in all your cellulitely glory (if you're me). I know they do that trick with the towels, holding them up and sliding them out from underneath, to protect our modesty – but it would be the work of an instant for anyone to sneak a look. Many beauticians I've spoken to about this issue like to make out that they're similar to doctors, that because they're looking at bums all day long, they no

longer notice what any of them look like. Another fiction. *Of course* they're checking you out – I mean, wouldn't you? Not in a sexual way – more in a 'there but for the grace of God goes my arse' way (again, if you're me). But for the massagee, it's hard to relax and float away if you suspect your therapist is sniggering at the state of your bum. There are some places – notably the Oberoi in Mauritius where the therapists, although charming and warm, are steely professionals – where they would hardly raise a *smirk* at the sight of someone's bum. Not even mine. I have only been once; however, I dream of going back. It's a long way for a snigger-free massage, but worth it.

9) *French facials*. By this I mean a facial either received in France or administered by a French person on non-French soil. Most facials are transcendent, extremely pleasurable things (apart from the fifteen minutes lying blind and sweating with claustrophobia while your mask 'does') but the French have a totally different approach. They take skincare so seriously that their facials are almost medicinal. By this I mean painful and unpleasant. Starting with interrogation-bright lights shone on your dial so they can see just how bad everything is, followed by a drenching with scalding steam so dense and hot that you can't breathe, then, reaching a crescendo of unpleasantness, all manner of squeezage: blackheads and whiteheads and other nastinesses. Then, for a grand finale, they tell you afterwards, as if you're being convicted of a crime, that your skin is in rag order, in absolute *bits*, possibly the

worst they've ever seen and how could you have let this happen. However, this is not because they want to flog you stuff. It's because they care. (Honestly.)

10) *Face-holes*. Wonderful inventions! They've taken away the necessity, when you're lying on your stomach having back rubbage, of suffocating into your pillow. You lie face downwards, stick your face through the padded hole – and breathe normally! (I don't know how we managed before them; I suppose death or brain damage from oxygen deprivation was just the risk I ran every time I had a back massage.) There's just one thing, and I wish someone had told me the first time I used one: the mark can last for up to a week.

A version of this was first published in Abroad, *January 2004.*

Your Bad Health

*M*ost of my life, I've enjoyed bad health. I develop a bad ear infection, necessitating antibiotics, most Thursdays and I get everything that's going – every cold, every bug, every virus – and usually manage to give it my own special twist. I can take an ordinary cold and, via some cunning add-ons, like a strep throat, I can parlay it into something really dramatic and croaky-voiced.

This is due to a combination of factors:

a) I've no stamina and my immune system is like a rusting 1989 Ford Fiesta.
b) I'm neurotic and a drama queen.
c) I love going to bed with a load of magazines and having people bring me cheese on toast and not be able to complain about it because I'm *sick*, see.
d) I'm extremely suggestible. If I hear of anyone else being unwell, I start to develop their symptoms. Which is fine when it's an upset stomach or labour pains, but more of a challenge when it's a twisted testicle.

If I'm very busy and stressed and I hear that a friend or family member is in bed with the flu, I always think, 'God, the lucky yoke.' You see, I'm just thinking about the lying-in-bed-having-someone-bring-me-cheese-on-toast bit. I forget all about the feeling-atrocious bit, until it happens.

And then I'm very sorry. I don't like feeling atrocious, not one bit, and by the afternoon of the second day if I'm not starting to feel a good bit better, I get a flash of alarm and a little voice in my head says, *This isn't right* . . . This is no ordinary flu, I think. It's far worse. It could be pneumonia. Or TB. Or cholera. And if it remains undiagnosed, I might die . . . (See, told you, drama queen.)

If I try disclosing my cholera-style anxieties to Himself, he just laughs and tells me to cop on. Himself, you see, almost never gets sick. And when he does, I take it very badly. You'd think that after all the running up and down stairs, bringing toasted cheese, that he does for me, I'd be prepared to repay the favour. But actually, no. I hate it when he's not well because it doesn't fit in with the way we've shared out the characteristics between us. *I* get sick and *he* fixes things. *I* put black wine gums over my teeth and pretend to be a seventy-year-old farmer chatting up an eighteen-year-old and *he* cuts the grass. If he starts crossing over into my territory and getting viruses, there's a danger that I might have to migrate over to his and start being useful.

On the rare occasions when he does succumb to illness, I go into denial. Wait till I tell you how mean I am. We were on holiday in a lovely resort in Thailand and he got food poisoning. (It was kind of funny, we ate at street stalls in Bangkok, even Vietnam, without any harm befalling us and now in this fancy-dan resort he was after getting poisoned.) Anyway, we woke up one morning and he was sweating and grey and had terrible stomach pains, so first I said that that was what it was like every month for women and now he knew what it was like. Then I asked (sarcastically, of course) if he wanted me to get a doctor and I got the fright of my life when he said yes. Right away I knew this must be extremely serious – because men just won't go to the doctor. Even if their leg falls off, they go, 'Ah, I'm grand, I never really used it anyway.' And, if you persist, they go, 'For God's sake, leave me alone, I'm FINE. Stop BADGERING me. It's only a leg, okay?'

I belted to the reception desk and although the resort didn't have a doctor, it had a nurse. She'd be with us in ten minutes, I was promised.

Sure enough, ten minutes later the bell rang and I opened the door to find a sloe-eyed, blossom-faced babe waiting outside. The nurse.

She was like a nurse from a porn film. She wore a tiny short white outfit and a ridiculous little hat perched atop a head of long, swishy, blue-black hair. She tiptoed over to Himself, took his paw between her tiny soft hands and whispered in a gentle voice, 'I will make you better.'

He gazed at her with unblinking adoration, like she was some sort of angel, while I watched, sour-faced, from the door. She produced a dinky bag (which just looked like a stripagram prop to me) and extracted all sorts of great stuff – painkillers, antibiotics, rehydrators and detoxers, which she helped him take by holding a glass of water to his mouth and supporting his head with her tiny hand. Then, with a final soothing touch on his forehead, she floated fragrantly out, promising to return to see him later.

Three hours later, a great improvement had been wrought in him. He was thrown in bed, watching CNN and smoking moodily (this was before he gave up – smoking, that is, not being moody), looking well on his way back to full health. Then the doorbell rang. 'It's her!'

He sat bolt upright in bed, switched off the telly and waved frantically, trying to disperse the cloud of smoke. Then he rearranged himself back on his pillows, deliberately trying to look wan and pitiful.

All smiles, in she tiptoed and we had a repeat performance of the head-supporting and hand-holding and when she said she would visit again later, I got in before him. 'He's fine!'

'But –' (From him.)

'You're fine,' I told him, then turned to her. 'He's fine.'

See, I'm horrible. Could I not just have let him enjoy being sick for a while? After all, it happens so rarely. Which brings me to a very important point: there's a myth that men are stoical. But actually, men aren't stoical. Men are *healthy*. Women get sick a lot so we're quite comfortable with it. But men have no practice so when they *do* get ill, they make a right song and dance about it.

Like the time my dad went into hospital to have his hip replaced. It's a straightforward enough operation, even though it sounds gruesome as anything – the patients are conscious so they get to hear their bones being sawed. (Even writing this, I'm getting twingy stabs in my hips.) Naturally enough, before Dad went in, he wasn't exactly in the best of form and he had a good old shout at Tadhg, warning him not to drive his car while he was incarcerated. (Tadhg had only just learnt to drive and was tooling around in a rusty pile of junk, the four-wheeled version of my immune system. He'd been looking forward to taking to the roads in Dad's shiny, upmarket wheels but Dad was terrified that the boy-racer would damage them.)

Anyway, Dad had the op and it was a relief to hear that it had gone fine and he was recovering nicely. (We decided it would do him no good, no good *at all*, to know that Tadhg had found where he'd hidden the car keys and was driving the pride-and-joy all over Dublin.) But the following day, when Himself and myself went to collect Mammy Keyes to go to visit Dad, Mammy was looking ashen.

'What?'

Her words were like a staple-gun to my heart. 'Your father's after taking a terrible turn for the worse. It's very serious. He's asking for a solicitor, he wants to change his will.'

Through numb lips, all I could mumble was, 'Where will we get a solicitor?'

'What about Eileen?' Mam asked.

Eileen is my friend. She is indeed a solicitor, but she handles huge, multi-million company mergers, not some small-time will. All the same, with shaking fingers, I put a speedy call in to her – she was at a meeting – then we drove like the clappers to the hospital, rushed upstairs and raced down his corridor but when we reached Dad's room, we slowed down, then stopped. We were afraid to go in. What if he was dead already? The door was ajar, so I put my fingers on it and pushed lightly. It swung open. I swallowed hard and forced myself to go in. And there he was. Sitting up in bed. Not dead. Not even slightly.

No, instead of being dead he was tucking into a big 'dinnery' dinner – I was dimly aware of mounds of mash, some sort of chops and loads of peas.

What the . . . ?

'Dad,' I said, almost irritably. 'We thought you were dying.'

'Oh right,' he chortled, through a mouthful of mash. 'It was the painkillers.'

What about them?

He was allergic to whatever they'd given him – they'd 'upset his stomach'. But as soon as they changed the prescription, he experienced a miraculous recovery.

'Well, great,' I said. But without conviction. Himself, myself and Mammy Keyes were a little thrown and found it hard to be nice to Dad for the first few minutes. I mean, as hypochondriacs go, I'm bad, I admit it. I'm one of the worst you'll find but even *I* wouldn't confuse an upset stomach with my imminent death. For a few happy days I felt wonderfully unneurotic.

(As a PS to this story, the reason Dad was asking for a solicitor was because in a fit of deathbed enlightenment he'd decided to leave his lovely car to Tadhg; but in a gorgeous cosmic juxtaposition, hadn't Tadhg crashed the car only that very morning.)

First published in Marie Claire, *March 2005*.

Hair-brained

I have a crush on my hairdresser. I'm pitiful, I know, and you might think that this doesn't relate to you in any way, but read on . . .

I'd been going to my regular fella, Jimmy, for a long while and he did a perfectly fine job. But one day he wasn't there – one of the usual excuses: resitting his taxidermy exams/ rescuing his sister from the Moonies/running for governor of California. But, said the receptionist, they had another fella just as good, who'd do me. Immediately all my antennae were on Gom Alert.

I am the kind of person who gets fobbed off with goms, *a lot*. I have a round, trusting face, and everyone from hairdresser receptionists to airline check-in staff thinks about me, She'll never complain. Not only has she a round, trusting face, but she's overweight and shame about that keeps her self-esteem low. I can actually *see* their thought processes. And they're right – I never do complain. I simply swallow my rage and burn holes in the lining of my stomach instead.

I resigned myself to getting the worst hairdresser in the place and, sure enough, this vision approached me. Whippet-thin, dressed entirely in black, his eyes obscured with dark glasses, wearing three-foot-long winkle-pickers so pointy the last six inches were actually invisible. From visiting the salon

I knew him to see. He did his snipping and blow-drying still wearing his dark glasses and danced gracefully around his clee-yongs, like he was doing speeded-up t'ai chi. In other words, the biggest gom on the planet.

Feckin' great!

True to form, I pushed down my fury, gave my incipient ulcers another shot in the arm, and stapled a smile to my round, trusting but miserable face. Then Gomboy opened his mouth and spoke. ''Allo Marrrrrreeeeannnne. I am Chrrrrrristian.'

French! He was French! Not a gom at all! In an instant everything changed.

Before we go any further, I have to say that I'm not one of those women who go wild swoony over Frenchmen. I think I must be the wrong age. The likes of my mammy would be mad about them, but my generation laugh scornfully at their smarmy accents and clichéd, overblown compliments masquerading as charm. All I'm saying is that Christian's Rock God get-up suddenly made sense and I was relieved.

We sat knee to knee and he treated me with as much concern and tenderness as if he was giving me a cancer diagnosis. I told him how I'd like him to do my hair, then – and this is unheard of – *he did exactly what I asked for.* Even with the best hairdressers, this never happens. I blame myself. Clearly there is a gap between the vision in my head and the words I use to convey it. It doesn't work even when I bring a picture and ask for an exact recreation. But Christian, as if he had a psychic transmitter in the toe of his winkle-pickers, accessed and downloaded the file in my imagination and reproduced it precisely.

I was thrilled, but next time I needed my hair done I went to Jimmy, because you have to, see? (This is the kernel of my dilemma.) However, about a month later, Jimmy was once again MIA and hastily, before the receptionist allocated me elsewhere, I requested Christian.

Again, he was fantastic. It had become clear that if I asked him to blow-dry my hair into a perfect scale model of the Statue of Liberty, he would, no questions asked. Then – and this is where it gets good – midway through the blow-dry, he paused, removed his dark glasses (revealing beautiful dark eyes) and said, 'I 'ave 'ad you before? A monz ago, per'aps?'

I chortled that he had indeed 'had' me before and that he had a very good memory. With that, his eyes held mine in the mirror, a fraction too long and he murmured meaningfully, 'Only somezimes.'

It had been so long since someone had flirted with me that it took me a moment to realize that that was what was actually happening. As soon as I got it, though, a great redness roared up my chest, neck and face, rushing to the tips of my ears and the roots of my hair, like a damburst. It was almost audible. But he wasn't being slimy or sleazy, he was just . . . nice . . .

All of a pleasurable dither I hurried home and told Himself about the encounter. 'He made me feel beautiful.'

Over the next few days I told everyone about Christian. He was so life-enhancing that I wanted everyone I loved to do themselves a favour by experiencing the delights of his attentions. Eventually I made Himself go. He was almost crying as I dispatched him; he's afraid of hairdressers at the best of times. But when he returned – with lovely hair, I must say – he seemed quietly pleased. For the next couple of hours he spent an unprecedented amount of time looking at himself in the mirror, then suddenly exclaimed, 'I never saw it before but I'm quite good-looking, aren't I?' Shamefully he admitted, 'I prefer him to Jimmy.'

Which brings me to my problem. How do you break it off with your hairdresser? There is no etiquette in the Western world for cleanly and unequivocally ending a relationship with anyone other than a lovair. Has anyone ever sat down with a same-sex friend and said gently, 'It used to be great but, out of nowhere, you're boring as fuck. All you talk about is your children. I'm looking for someone who cares about shoes and *Big Brother*.'

Likewise, there's no mechanism for ending it with a dentist, an optician or, in my case, a hairdresser. What can you do? Give them the 'I've met someone else' speech? The 'It's not you, it's me' riff? They'd think you were mad.

My only option was subterfuge. I deliberately began to make appointments on Jimmy's days off. 'Oh Jimmy's not in then, is he not? That's a shame. Well, er, would Christian be available instead?'

The day came, of course, when Jimmy caught me. I'd been becoming more and more careless. You could almost say I wanted to be caught, that all that dishonesty and sneaking around was getting too much.

It wasn't pleasant, how could it be? Jimmy, though he hid it well, was hurt and humiliated and Christian and I were wretched with guilt.

Even now, occasionally, I still catch Jimmy watching me with wounded eyes. But Christian is officially my hairdresser, everyone knows it. All the angst and anxiety? Well, it was worth it.

First published in Cara, *December 2003.*

Mirror, Mirror

I remember the first time I discovered my face didn't fit.
I was six and had a smiley, chubby-cheeked little brother
and a toddler sister who was a dark-eyed angel, a real beauty.
A distant cousin of my mother who was about to get married
met us and decided my exquisite sister would make an ador-
able addition to her wedding party. Train-bearer, perhaps, or
mini-bridesmaid. However, on account of not being exquisite,
I wasn't required. Until the distant cousin discovered that my
sister was not only beautiful but dangerously strong-willed
(they often seem to go together. Does plainness make us
meek?) and mightn't be relied upon to march up the aisle at
the appropriate time. So a token position was created for me
(flower girl, as I recall, although what I really was was a
bouncer) to be on hand to keep my baby sister under control.
Of course I should have told them to get lost. But hey, I was
six, there was a long dress involved, my hair was going to
be 'up', I got to carry flowers . . .

This episode, although terribly upsetting, didn't come as
a complete shock. Even before then I'd always hated having
my photograph taken and used to make horrific faces for the
camera on the questionable pretext that if I made myself
super-ugly they wouldn't notice the ordinary, workaday
ugliness lurking beneath.

God only knows where such neurosis comes from. I've been over my life with a fine-tooth comb, searching for trauma, for that one moment when I began to hate myself and, to my great disappointment, I've found nothing at all. I had a stable, perfectly ordinary upbringing and whatever notions I've developed about my appearance I've got to take responsibility for myself.

I carried this self-hatred through my teenage years (aarrghh!) and into adulthood, where it sometimes got easier but never went away. Okay, it's not all my fault. We live in look-tastic times and are bombarded with unreachable standards of beauty. Unformed adolescent girls are used to sell clothes to thirty-something women. Images of models are photographically enhanced so their skin is inhumanly translucent and their bodies drastically elongated and thinned down. Indeed, Cindy Crawford was quoted recently as saying, 'Some mornings even I don't wake up looking like Cindy Crawford.' On my good days I know none of it is real but, even on my best days, I can't help trying. Or at least having the decency to feel wretched when I fail dismally.

I've never met a woman who was entirely happy with her appearance, there always seems to be at least one thing they'd change, but – and it shocks me to admit it – I like almost nothing about mine. Not that I waste time raging against it, at least not all the time – just when I've PMT, or need to buy an outfit for a wedding, or meet someone I was in school with who's had three children but is still a size ten . . .

Over the years I've done enough therapy and picked up enough pop-psychology to know that none of this is about what I look like, but how I feel about myself. I've learnt that most 'ugliness' is in the head, that even people who objectively speaking are dazzlingly beautiful have it, but actually there are tons of things that really *are* wrong with me. Kicking off with – tricky ears. People sometimes complain of having big, sticky-out ears. In fact a good friend of mine (a babe, always was, always will be) had a spell of Sellotaping her ears to her head every night for about a month when she was twelve. Then she stopped, coming to her senses at the same time as she ran out of Sellotape. But I don't have sticky-out ears. No, it's worse. I have sticky-out *ear*.

That's right, just the one. The other ear is small and neat and flat against my head. I discovered the disparity when I was fourteen and examining myself in the mirror (I was a teenager, I did little else). Suddenly the horror dawned. *Where did my other ear go?*

As a result I can't have short hair or wear my hair off my face because my great aural lopsidery becomes laughably obvious. In fact, during another intense teenage inspection, I discovered that my entire face is asymmetrical. I can often get away with it in real life if I keep talking animatedly and never let my face settle into stillness. But in photographs, when I'm frozen in place, the horrible truth becomes evident and I look like something Picasso painted in his cubist period. (And I'm not looking for your pity here but in my line of work I have to get my picture taken *a lot* and I can't tell you how many hours of my life have been wasted with photographers faffing about with lighting and lenses and angles, but no matter how much they faff the end result is always that I end up looking like Dora Maar.)

And that's just from the neck up. Don't get me started on

the rest. My body is a battleground and there are a couple of 'friends' that I'm trying to avoid seeing because the first thing they always do is 'weigh' me, with a scathing, gimlet-eyed once-over. Bad enough for me to judge myself, but I'm not going to take it from someone else. (I've a feeling this is a good thing, a sign of maturity.) Believe me, I *know* when I'm putting on weight – it usually coincides with me breathing. The thing is, I'm in a double bind because I eat sweets when I'm anxious and unhappy but when I'm at peace I don't go to the gym. The result? Ever increasing girth where shopping for clothes becomes a torment. I love clothes, especially the ones the unformed sixteen-year-olds try to flog me, but I return from shopping trips in a blind fury, shamed and embarrassed at how strange I look in the merchandise. The only time I come home happy is when I've inadvertently tried on things in shops with mirrors that lean forward and knock ten pounds off my silhouette. Idiot that I am, I believe what I see – until I try the stuff on in front of my own un-forgivably upright mirror. (For some time now I've wanted to start a Name-and-Shame campaign of those swizz-merchant shops. Is anybody with me? Let's storm the changing rooms!)

Misery with how I look is a bit like a flu. I can carry on happily for quite a while without feeling any symptoms, then it can hit like a ton of bricks. A couple of years ago I was suddenly assailed with my old trouble and a friend suggested I try hypnotism; she herself had gone and emerged one blissful hour later, floating with confidence, self-regard and inner peace. I couldn't make an appointment fast enough. But mine was a different therapist and when I arrived at her office, instead of lying me on a couch and telling me I felt sleepy, she sat me on a chair and asked me about my relationship with my father. Anxiously I told her I was here about the hypnotism, the instant fix, not another bout of therapy. Whereupon she told me there was no instant fix and that until she knew all about me, she couldn't help me. At that point I almost wept, then got up to leave, so sulkily she agreed to try a bit of hypnotism. Still sitting in the chair, I closed my eyes, while she intoned, 'You are going down, down, deeper and down. Down, down, deeper and down. Downdowndeeperanddown.' At that point, I snapped my eyes open and it took everything in my power not to leap to my feet playing my air-guitar, singing that Status Quo song. ('Down, down, deeper 'n' down. Ner-ner-ner-ner!' Shake those shaggy dos, baby!)

Anyway, the hypnotism didn't work and, paradoxically, this whole business has got easier as I've got older. And not just because I feel that once I'm old people won't care what I look like, that they'll be far more interested in my personality. (Mind you, I'm sometimes tempted to lie about my age and say that I'm older than I am. If I tell people I'm fifty-two instead of thirty-nine, they'll think I look great. They might even say, 'You know, her figure isn't bad for a woman in her fifties.' See, context is *everything*.)

The stuffing has definitely been knocked out of my inner demons; maybe it's all the therapy I did or perhaps I'm finally growing up. After all, obsession with one's appearance is embarrassingly adolescent, and actually gets quite boring after a while. Not to mention time-consuming; frankly, these days I'm too busy to free up the time to hate myself.

Constant exposure to my limitations has brought me to

the point where I can see photos of myself, observe idly, 'Christ, I look horrific,' and move on. Instead I've got quite adept at focusing on the good in me. (Examples thereof: I often buy *The Big Issue*; I am kind to animals even though I'm afraid of them; I have never hit a photographer and I wish Cindy Crawford well.)

Most important, though, is a point my mother once made to me when I'd subjected her to a mad, energetic rant about my hairy legs. She listened patiently, nodded sympathetically, then answered, 'At least you have legs.' She's right, of course.

First published in Woman and Home, *May 2003.*

Faking It

The nicest bit of news I got in recent years was that we're not allowed to sunbathe any more. I never enjoyed it; the *boredom* of lying there with sweat running into my hair and I couldn't even talk to the people I was with because they were devoted sun-lovers who believed that conversation cancels out the action of the sun's rays. Anyway, sunbathing never worked for me. I seem to be the only person in the world who has different types of skin on different parts of the body, and this is how I took the sun: feet – golden; stomach – mahogany; shins – Germolene pink; face – bluey-white with an overlay of freckles. The cherry on the cake: my Red Nose Day nose. At the end of two weeks in the sun I looked like a patchwork quilt.

But now, courtesy of the hole in the ozone layer, I'm off the hook. (You see, it's not all bad news, this ecological disaster stuff.) And this is where fake tans come in. (Except we're not really allowed to call it 'fake' any more. 'Self' tanning or 'sunless' tanning is what it's about.) However, it's not always plain sailing. Let's consider the following.

What do you hate the most?

a) the horrific smell

b) the curse of the orange paw
c) the tie-dyed effect on your heels
d) the hour of 'Riverdancing' in your pelt, as you wait to dry
e) the indelible brown stains on your clothes and sheets
f) all of the above

If I may come back to the horrific smell. The first time I ever 'did' myself, I went to bed, only to wake in terror in the middle of the night, wondering what the unspeakable stink was. Could it be the devil? Wasn't he supposed to be preceded by dreadful, poo-type smells? Quaking with fear, I peeped over the covers, expecting to see coal-red eyes and a thick, forked tail, only to discover that the choking stench was none other than my freshly tanned self. In recent years, the cosmetic companies have been working hard on diluting the ferocious pong and now some brands even claim to have 'a pleasant fragrance'. Yes, indeed they *do* have a pleasant fragrance. But mark me well here, that's *as well as*, that's *in addition to*, the extremely *un*pleasant fragrance that is the hallmark of all self-tanners.

I have made every fake-tan mistake in the book.

Elementary mistake number one: I was in a mad hurry for a colour and decided that one thick layer would do just as well as several thin layers. Forty shades of orange ensued and I couldn't leave the house for a week.

Elementary mistake number two: Believing the claims of swizzy salespeople who care only about their commission and don't give a damn about your tan. I won't shame them by naming them, but I was persuaded by a flamboyant queen in

Los Angeles to shell out plenty on his brand. He used it himself, he told me, for 'baking and browning'. (Himself, that is.) Convinced by his Tangoesque visage, I duly coughed up, but all I got was a mild dose of the streaks and the orangest palms I've ever seen; if I'd held them upwards, they could have been seen from outer space. I learnt two important lessons from this tragic encounter. One, I discovered surgical gloves. Not only will they save you from the curse of the orange paw, but you can have an *ER* moment when you snap them on. Two, the same brand doesn't work the same way for everyone.

Elementary mistake number three: I decided to do it properly. I'd do wafer-thin layers and leave plenty of time to dry between applications. The only thing is, I got a little obsessive about it and it kind of took over my life. I'd apply a layer, then do some free-style dancing in my pelt waiting for it to dry, then I'd apply another layer and do some more dancing around my room, and when the colour still hadn't come yet, I'd apply another layer. At some point, the end product of a tan no longer seemed to matter so much, it was simply the doing it that became important (which is how self-help gurus are always telling us to live our lives.)

So there I was, having a lovely time dancing and humming and thinking lovely thoughts, I'd even enlisted a floaty red scarf to waft about over my head, when Himself walked into the room and yelped, 'Jesus Christ!' I thought it was the free-style dancing and stopped abruptly, a little mortified by the scarf. 'Look at yourself,' he urged. 'Look!'

So I looked and instead of the radiant golden hue I'd been expecting, I was a nasty Eurotrash mahogany, which I was prepared to bet went all the way down to my internal organs. Again I couldn't leave the house for a week. I mean, no one wants to be humiliated in the street by strangers shouting, 'Who's been drinking the fake tan, then?'

Elementary mistake number four: The mud and how it works. In the deliriously happy days of doing my make-up column, I was invited to have the mud done. So I showed up at a hotel room, stripped off and hopped up onto the table, where a lovely girl smeared me with smelly mud, then got a big loofah and rubbed some of the mud off, then told me to get up and get dressed.

When I pointed out that I was still covered in smelly mud, she said, yes of course I was, that was how it worked, everyone knew that, but I'd be able to wash it off in the morning.

'Obviously you're going to look manky for the evening,' she said. 'But tomorrow morning, after your shower, you'll have a fabulous tan.'

'Grand, grand,' I said.

She seemed to pick up on a little anxiety from me. 'You hadn't planned to go out tonight, had you?'

'No, not really.' Just for my mother's birthday.

'Probably best if you leave off your boots and tights. They'll only interfere with the tan. You can drive in your bare feet.'

I looked out into the March night, it was pelting rain and freezing cold. 'Okay.'

So off I went. And as luck would have it, the police were doing random checks on the Booterstown road. I rolled down my window and watched the copper's face recoil as the smell hit him.

'Licence, please.'

I handed it over, but the smell was clearly alarming him, so he had a low muttered consultation with his colleague, and the net result was that they asked me to get out of the car. In my bare feet. I tried to explain about the fake tan, but they just ordered me to open my boot – presumably to show them that I had no smelly dead bodies in there.

They kept me for ages, searching in their rule book to see if they could bring me in on anything. I wasn't obviously breaking any laws, but they were very suspicious.

In the end they let me go and when I arrived at the restaurant to celebrate my mammy's birthday, I caused a bit of a stir. As if the smell wasn't making me unpopular enough, bits of the mud were going black and green and falling off my face into my dinner. I looked like a burns victim.

Mind you, it's important to say that the following morning, when I'd washed off the muck, I had a rich, deep, smooth beautiful tan. And isn't that what it's all about?

First published in Marie Claire, *Septmeber 2005.*

Once Were Worriers

I worry, therefore I am, and in my ongoing quest to bring it to heel, I have given many things a go: reiki, craniosacral therapy, hypnotherapy, yoga and angel channelling.

None of them really helped, certainly not for any length of time, although, mind you, the reiki did generate a response. As I left the clinic, I felt a surge of rage that nearly knocked me into the street and into the path of a passing Saab. Perhaps an unlocking of decades-old rage had occurred? Or was I just feeling super-swizzed at having handed over eighty nicker for someone to lie me on a table in the dark and mutter at my head and feet? Who can tell?

Anyway, recently, three separate people suggested I try meditation.

One of them was a feathery-strokery, away-with-the-fairies reflexologist who told me I should think of myself as a golden egg (er, why?), so naturally I immediately discounted his advice. But one of the others was one of the most beautiful human beings I know – we'll call her Judy. (It's her name.) She's been meditating for years.

And the third was a specialist who was treating me for TMJ – some jaw condition that I'd brought about by constantly clenching my jaw, because of anxiety.

Being advised by three such disparate people gave me

pause for thought; suddenly I began to like the idea of me being someone who meditated, and instantly started trying out different versions of myself where I would be asked, 'Marian, how come you're so calm?' And I'd say, 'Oh, well, I meditate, see? Meditation is part of my life. But not in a beardy, sandal-wearing weird way, as you can see.'

I would smile in a wry, knowing way. I would be invited to lots of charity lunches. I would still wear very high shoes and lipgloss.

Then I discovered that the recommended amount of time to meditate was twenty minutes, twice a day and I reacted with outrage. Twenty minutes! Twice a day? Where would I get twenty minutes twice a day? I'm really busy!

And never mind the fact that I can quite happily while away twenty minutes studying my shin, poised with a tweezer, on the search for ingrowing hairs. (TMI?) (Too much information?) If not, let me continue. Those smooth-limbed women (lucky cahs) who've never had their legs waxed won't know what I mean but the sourcing and extraction of ingrowing hairs is life's consolation prize for the hairy-legged woman. The sense of satisfaction is incomparable.

Anyway, I compromised by agreeing to try one lot of meditation a day. Committing to two daily sessions would be akin to buying a full set of golf clubs before I'd had my first golf lesson. (Or so I told myself.)

So how did I go about it? First, I needed something to tell me when my twenty minutes were up, so my Shaunie the Sheep kitchen timer was called into active service. Then, apparently, you have to say a mantra. The most famous is 'Om'. But how do you say it? Like, 'Om, om, om, om, om,

om, om, om, om, om . . .'? Ad infinitum. Like the sound of
soldiers' feet marching across a parade ground. Or would it
be more like an 'Aaaaaaaaaaaaaauuuuuuuuuuuuuoooooo-
ooooooommmmmmmmmmmm'? Which made me feel very
anxious, as if I was having to hold my breath under water.
How long did I have to say one 'Om' for? When would I be
allowed to stop and start the next one?

I consulted the lovely Judy who told me you needn't
bother with 'Om' if it's not working out for you. If you
prefer you can simply meditate in time with your breathing.
Or count to four, then start back at one again. Or there are
several Aramaic and Sanskrit mantras doing the rounds.

I selected a four-syllable Aramaic word and every day I
say to Himself, 'I won't be available for the next twenty
minutes. I'll be meditating.' And I think I'm *it*.

Off I go and I sit on my special chair in my special room
(spare bedroom) and light my special candle (Jo Malone
Lime) and twist Shaunie's head round to twenty minutes – it
feels like wringing a turkey's neck – and think, God, I'm
great! Right then, now for a bit of meditating! Okay, off we
go. Okay, meditate, meditate, *meditate* . . . Oh Christ! I never
rang that woman back about the insoles. I'll do it as soon as
I'm finished this. Although, what did her message say? That
she'd be out of the office this morning? Right, I'll try her this
afternoon, if I remember. Oh God, I'm meant to be meditating. Concentrate, concentrate. Okay, I'm concentrating.
What are we getting for dinner tonight? That salad can't be
in the full of its health, we bought it on Monday . . .

And if I go more than three seconds without thinking of
something I have to do (or eat), I suddenly think, 'Look!

Look at me. I'm meditating! I'm actually meditating.' And then, of course, I'm not.

It might look easy, you might think that all you have to do is sit in a chair and close your eyes for twenty minutes, but this meditation is actually very hard. And long! As Shaunie's poor gormless face clicks his way back to health, every meditation minute is like a Northern Line minute.

Nevertheless, three months down the line, I am still doing it. I think I might actually be a small bit calmer. It's all a little alarming – if I stop being anxious, who will I be?

First published in Marie Claire, *February 2005.*

WOMAN TO WOMAN

Man Power

When I first met Himself he had a very good job – company car, pension plan, grudging respect from his staff – the lot. I, on the other hand, was badly paid and devoid of ambition. Then I got a couple of books published and confounded all expectations by starting to earn more than he did. As soon as I could, I gave up my day job in order to write full-time and discovered that my writing had so much associated admin that I needed a full-time PA/dogsbody/ kind person to hold my hand and tell me I'm not crap. Himself has a degree from Cambridge, can do hard sums in his head and knows the meaning of ataraxy. But he became that full-time PA/dogsbody/kind person to hold my hand and tell me I'm not crap and resigned from his job, waving goodbye to the car, the money, the grudging respect. Soon his days were an undizzying round of phone answering and five o'clock dashes down the road to catch the last post. In short, I ruined his life.

Our situation isn't such an unusual one: since time immemorial, one clever spouse has given up their ambitions to run the home and facilitate the career of their perhaps less clever, but higher-earning partner. But until recently it was nearly always the women who made the sacrifice – not necessarily without justified, cat's-arse-faced resentment, but it has been done.

Look at Hollywood: how many stories have we heard of women who put their own ambitions on hold in order to support their actor husband through the lean years? (Only to be abandoned as soon as the money begins to roll in. 'Thanks a million for working three crappy jobs while I went to auditions. I'm off now with that anorexic one with the fake knockers and bee-stung lips over there, but hey, I'll always speak fondly of you in *People* interviews.')

And are things any better in the non-Hollywood world? Not very often. Now and then, when they've had a few drinks, their team has won and they're generally in a benign humour, men will let a woman or two into the higher strata of the workplace. Just for the novelty value, of course. Sort of like getting a pet. And in case you're thinking I'm overstating things, just take a look at the business-class section on any plane: you'd break your neck on all the grey-suited testosterone swilling around in there.

But, the odd time, the very, very odd time it happens that women are more successful than their male partners; even to the point where men take over the role of stay-at-home wives and become househusbands.

And men don't like it; at least that's the perceived wisdom. The rule states that men are the hunter-gatherers and if their spouse has some spare time to help out with the berry picking, then well and good, but they must never forget who the *real* providers are or else they'll up and punish us by becoming sulky and impotent.

I asked my brother Niall how he'd feel about being a 'home-maker' and he said he'd love it: he'd get to play golf and party while someone else went to work, shouldered the stress and provided the readies. But when I put it to him that he'd be responsible for childcare and making dinners, he disappeared behind his newspaper, muttering, 'Feck that.'

The funny thing is that when people promise that they'll stick with their spouse 'for richer, for poorer' it's the 'for poorer' part that causes the worry. No one thinks for a minute that the 'for richer' bit could be a problem.

I know a writer who got an advance that was described as 'life-altering'. Sadly it proved to be just that because about six months later her husband legged it. But who is to say that the dosh was the reason he went? To be quite honest she has more than a touch of the Madeleine Bassets (super-drippy girl from P.G. Wodehouse novels) and if I was married to her I'd have gone too. (All that talk of when an angel cries it makes a new star, it's enough to make anyone run.)

I know another writer who got a big enough advance to keep her family in i-Pods and skiing holidays for several years, but her husband has continued to work all the hours God sends, and she sees less of him now than she ever did.

Anyway, when Himself changed his role to being my PA, I knew how important it was to preserve his dignity. So shortly into our new arrangement a concerned friend took me aside and suggested that next time I wanted Himself to bring me something to eat, perhaps I shouldn't pound the bedroom floor with a thick stick and yell down the stairs, 'Oi! More Percy Pigs up here. On the double!'

But I can't stop other things. Like the way that Himself gets called Mr Keyes (it's not his name; that's my dad). In fact, some people can't even get his first name right: in the last few months Himself (aka Tony) has been John, Tom

and Joe. Even his profession is misrepresented: in one magazine article he was described as a psychiatrist (which he may
be, having to deal with me on a daily basis, but not in a
professional capacity) and in another he was 'a dentist'. And
the thing is, he doesn't stomp around in a big, mad, hairy
rage, shrieking at me to write to the editor, demanding a
retraction. He doesn't care because he knows who he is. (I'm
making him sound like a saint here and definitely running
the risk of being hit with the Curse of the Smug Girl. Now
it's almost certain that in two weeks' time he'll be caught
down some dark alley getting a handjob from a transsexual.)

But what's gas is that *women* aren't always comfortable
with Himself's lowly status. Female journalists often ask him
what he 'does' and he answers proudly, 'Dogsbody.' And, lo
and behold, when the piece comes out he is described not as
my 'dogsbody' or even my 'colleague', but as my 'Manager'.

What's that all about?

While we're on the subject, the tension created by disproportionate female success goes into overdrive when children
appear. I know a couple where the woman is a hugely
successful lawyer and her partner installs kitchens. Recently
their baby was hospitalized and the man point-blank refused
to take time off work. He actually said – can you believe
this? – 'I can't let my boss down.' A bizarre conviction
persists that sick children are the responsibility of women.
Even when both partners work it's nearly always the women
who get up in the middle of the night when the children puke
all over their Beatrix Potter pyjamas.

Despite our best efforts, Himself and myself don't have
children and at this stage it doesn't look too likely that we

will. But in the early halcyon days of our 'trying' we entertained wild notions of having at least five. Three girls, two boys. I accepted that I would have to be the one to be pregnant for nine months – that this was one thing he couldn't do for me – but the plan was that he'd take up the reins of childcare as soon as the head was engaged.

I would return to work immediately, operating out of some far-flung – or sound-proofed, if the house wasn't big enough to have far-flung bits – corner of the house, while he got on with being a mum. We joked that I would appear only occasionally, when all five of my offspring would be cleaned up and presented for inspection, and I would walk among them, like Prince Charles meeting and greeting the staff at a ball-bearings factory. Now and then I would stoop graciously and enquire, 'And which one of my issue are you?' When I had swanned away, one of the children would enquire plaintively, 'Daddy, who was that funny lady?' And he would reply, 'That was your mummy. *You* remember, you met her that other time.'

Anyway, the babies never arrived but I'm sure that no matter how sound-proofed the room, I would sense if my children were crying and would be unable to stop myself rushing to them. Another writer I know is in exactly that situation. She works at home and her husband takes care of the children, but she can't stop herself from interfering whenever they're in distress. Maternal instinct or control freakery? Either way it's an issue.

So there we are. Recently a (female) journalist described Himself as 'the perfect man' and it's not because she slept with him – at least I don't think it's that – but because he has so graciously assumed the supportive role in our set-up. I can't deny that I'm deeply grateful and full of admiration for him but – and all due respect to him – women have been doing this sort of thing for ever. Clearly, men who are willing to play second fiddle to their more successful female partners are still regarded as exciting novelties – and here's the tricky bit – by women as much as by men.

I know it's still in its early days but women are never going to convince men that the situation is no big deal if they persist in metaphorically carrying men on their shoulders through the cheering streets every time they earn less than their partners and don't sulk or become impotent because of it. If we act like it's the norm, perhaps it'll become the norm . . .

First published in the Guardian, *September 2002.*

December

All I'm saying is, it made sense at the time. Getting married on 29 December mightn't strike everyone as the smartest move, but hear me out. I was living in London but getting married in Ireland; lots of my Irish guests were also living in London but would be in Dublin for Christmas. I'd be saving them an extra trip.

And being Ireland, the chances were that the weather would be as nice in December as it would be in August. Unfortunately, however, that was not to be and two days before the wedding, the day most of the British guests (including my husband-to-be, i.e. Himself) were flying in, the weather took a turn for the very ferocious. All flights from the UK were delayed and the first little seedlings of fear sprouted in my stomach: It's a sign. He won't be coming. I'll be jilted at the altar.

I'd never been one of those women who'd hankered after a white wedding, planning the dress, the bridesmaids, the ring, etc. If ever I thought of a traditional wedding the only image that came to mind was of me and my father in a white Rolls-Royce, circling the block again and again as we waited for a groom who was already halfway to Rio. Every time we neared the church, some usher would yell, 'Go round again! Give it one more go!'

Then Himself rang to say that his flight had landed in Dublin but he was going to wait at the airport for his best man, Guy, who was due in shortly on another flight. But time passed and he didn't appear and I couldn't ring him because nine years ago only gobshites had a mobile. My hysteria built and gathered momentum, especially as we were having the church rehearsal that evening.

'It's a sign,' I announced. 'He's not going to marry me.'

'He's in the country,' everyone kept saying loudly at me. 'Of course he's going to marry you.'

'Right now,' I said, 'he's probably buying a one-way ticket to Rio.'

Himself rang again to say that Guy's flight had been badly delayed but was expected to land any minute and they'd both see us soon. But they still hadn't arrived by the time we were leaving for the rehearsal. Then the doorbell rang and I nearly puked with relief. But it wasn't him, it was my friends Laura and Bruce who, when they saw the tearful, highly strung state of me, decided to come along to the church with us.

In the car, in a thin hysterical voice, I outlined my position. 'It was stupid me thinking I'd ever land a lovely man like Himself. All my relationships are disasters and, with my history, I'm the ideal person to be jilted. I have "jiltee" written all over me. Of course, we'll laugh about it one day, it'll make a great story: two days before my wedding my fiancé ran away to Rio.'

'What's this obsession with Rio?' I heard someone mutter.

'I bet right now,' I continued, 'he's boarding the flight to Rio.'

'There are no direct flights to Rio from Dublin,' my dad said, like this was a comfort.

In the church my mother gave me a small yellow and blue capsule – some member of the Valium family – and I 'married' Bruce.

Right at the end of the 'ceremony', Himself strode into the church like a movie star, his hair all windswept, his coat covered with hail, and took me in his arms.

'You didn't go to Rio,' I said, in wonder.

'The flights were full,' he said.

However, the great thing about having a meltdown two days before my wedding meant that on the day itself, I was astonishingly calm; I'd got it all out of my system. I went to my local hairdresser's to have my complicated flower-woven updo done. (I know that nowadays make-up artists and manicurists come to the bride's home to beautify her, but nine years ago it was more of a DIY job.)

My hair took a very long time, longer than I'd expected and yet I was serenity itself. Even when Mrs Benson, mother of my friend Suzanne, and guest at my wedding, stuck her head under my dryer and said, in confusion, 'It *is* today, isn't it? Because if it is, you're getting married in an hour.'

When I emerged from the hairdresser's I was all set to get a taxi but, like a magical coach, my local bus, the 46A, drew up right in front of me. I boarded it, was let off my fare and alighted at my home stop ten minutes later, the congratulations of the other passengers still ringing in my ears.

I got home at 1.50, I was getting married at 2.30, I was still calm. My sisters – my two bridesmaids – were hysterical, fighting for mirror space. Quietly, without bothering anyone, I got myself dressed, and did my make-up. I helped my sister with her zip, then, after much thundering up and down the stairs, suddenly everyone was gone from the house and it was quiet and calm and it was just me and Dad, and the fancy car was waiting outside and one of us said, 'We might as well go, so.'

The ceremony and the getting married and all that was lovely. It was only afterwards, when we had to go outside for photos, that the weather, once again, became an issue. It was indescribably cold, so cold that I wondered if it might snow – which would look lovely in the photos – but a friend of my father said, 'It's too cold to snow.' Then several other men joined in, looking at the sky and opining, 'Ah, too cold to snow, I'd say.' Which strikes me as one of the most bizarre statements I've ever heard.

My dress was made of thin satin and, months earlier, when I'd been getting it designed, I had toyed vaguely with getting a white fur-like capelet and muff, then decided not to bother, certain that love would keep me warm. But I was wrong. I've never been so cold in my life. In the end I had to beg the photographer to call a halt to the outdoor pictures of Himself and myself.

And the group shot on the steps of the church shows an incomplete line-up of our guests because the photographer took so long fiddling with light and perspective that several of them went back into the church to warm up and missed it all.

After the wedding, when several of the guests had to return to the UK, the weather – already atrocious – took a turn for the worse. The car ferry was able to leave Dún Laoghaire but was unable to dock at Holyhead and several of our guests, including my parents-in-law, had to spend twenty-four hours trapped on the high seas. Finally they were permitted onto dry land, and my exhausted parents-in-law got into their car and made for home. However, less than a mile from their village, their car skidded on a patch of ice and they ended up in a ditch, lucky to be alive.

June for the next one, definitely.

First published in Brides Magazine, *December 2004.*

The F Word

*T*he 'F' word. The bad 'F' word. I don't mean 'feck'. I don't even mean 'fuck'. I mean 'feminism.'

I came of age just after the so-called sexual revolution and the message I picked up was that all the hard work had been done and that now everyone was lovely and equal. The world belonged to women. Men would be our lackeys and provide zipless fucks on demand and we would stalk through the boardrooms of the land in our sheer tights and red lipstick. (Well, actually, I never thought *I* could, but I thought other women could if they wanted.)

But funnily enough, the last thing I wanted to be called was a feminist: feminists were shrill, hairy-legged harridans who couldn't get a boyfriend. And they were buzz-wreckers. I felt guilty for wearing high shoes – a tiny invisible feminist sat on my shoulder, mocking, 'Look at you, pandering to men; see how your high heels make you walk with a wiggle' – when actually it was only because I was five foot one and wanted to see the number of my bus over people's heads.

My relationship with men, fraught at the best of times, was further complicated because I half-expected to be investigated by the Boyfriend Police, in order to check I was treating myself with enough respect. Whenever I was heartbroken over a man, I was braced against the Wicked Feminist Witch of the West bursting into my tear-sodden bedroom in her dungarees and Doc Martens and saying, 'Hah! That's what you get for hanging around with men. You should have joined the women's collective and none of this would have happened. No more than you deserve, *girlie*.'

The enemy had been reconfigured – no longer men, but the women who'd fought for us. Obviously, a certain amount of revisionism happens after every revolution, but how could I have been so naïve? The only thing that stops me from dying of shame is that I wasn't the only woman who ever said, 'Of course I believe in equality for women but, like, I wouldn't call myself a *feminist*.'

It took a mortifyingly long time for it to dawn on me that actually all the hard work had *not* been done and that now everyone was *not* lovely and equal. Not even slightly. It happened one afternoon when I was fighting through a throng of grey suits in the business-class section of a plane. Suddenly I wondered: where are all the women in their red lipstick and sheer tights? Nowhere to be seen. (Because they were stuck in the office, providing secretarial back-up, drinking cup-a-soup, painting the run in their sheer tights with nail varnish because they couldn't afford to buy new ones.)

In the meantime a new word had been invented for women like me – 'post-feminists'. I wasn't really sure what it meant but when I looked around I saw that we went to the gym a lot, we bought plenty of shoes and most of us still had crappy, badly paid jobs – but apparently it was our fault now, not the system's.

Not true, of course: the glass ceiling really exists. And as well as equality in the workplace, we're still waiting for affordable childcare, recognition of the value of work done by home-makers, humane treatment by the courts of rape victims (why are so many judges such senile old misogynists?), a focus on domestic violence . . . the list goes on.

But most of us haven't the energy to be active feminists: we're knackered, holding down demanding jobs, getting our roots done, fighting low-level depression, trying to do Pilates, doing school runs if we have children or agonizing about when the best time to have a baby would be, if we haven't.

We don't have it all. We're too busy doing it all, to have it all.

Meanwhile, on the feminist frontlines, not only has the war not been won, but our gains are at risk. For example, that God-botherer George Bush is committed to working towards making abortion illegal again in the US. And where Dubya leads (actually I shouldn't even call him that; calling him by his nickname is only encouraging him) his mate Holy Tone mightn't be far behind.

What feminism needs is a make-over, along the lines of the New Labour one (but without losing the core ideology, of course).

For example, did you know you can be a feminist and

a) wear pink,
b) have sex with men,
c) enjoy a good laugh?

Amazing, no? As long as you believe you're entitled to the same rights as everyone else (i.e. men) you're a feminist. See, that's not so bad, is it? In the words of that bard and visionary, Adam Ant: There's nothing to be scared of.

First published in Marie Claire, *April 2005.*

FRIENDS AND FAMILY

You'll be hearing a bit about my family in this part, so to avoid confusion, here's a brief introduction.

I'm the eldest of five and I've had the extreme good sense to pick siblings who live abroad. (So we can visit them and have a lovely time.)

I've, very cleverly, bagged a brother (Niall) who lives in Prague. Niall is married to Ljiljana, aka *The Most Fabulous Woman On The Planet*^{TM}. (She can make a fabulous three-course meal for six people from two mouldy tomatoes in the bottom of the fridge. She also speaks three languages fluently, is beautiful, kind and very funny.)

Niall and Lilers have two children, Ema and Luka. They are so very fantastic that Himself and myself (who have not been blessed with babas of our own) have offered large sums of cash to buy them. To our chagrin they keep refusing, so now we are considering plan B – reporting Niall and Lilers to the Praguish social services, accusing them of being bad parents, so Himself and myself will get custody! Ingenious, no?

Next in line is my sister (Caitríona) who lives in New York and is also very fabulous. She looks like a model, yet she can fix a broken ballcock. She is also the funniest person I've ever met.

The youngest are the twins Rita-Anne and Tadhg (pronounced Tyge) who are very, very nice – don't get me wrong. I just can't *help feeling they're being a little unreasonable, still insisting on living in Dublin, no matter how many times I mention that I've heard that house prices are very low in the Seychelles.*

Now to my mammy. Mammy Keyes is a legend; she is nearly as funny as Caitríona. She prays for Himself and myself and doesn't mind that we're dirty atheists who don't deserve it. She also cooks for us. Every Thursday we go for our dinner and one week we get spaghetti bolognese, the next week we get chicken casserole, the next week we get spaghetti bolognese, the next week we get chicken casserole, the next week ... Even when we're out of the country, the pattern continues clicking away without us and on our return we just slot straight back in. It's wonderful, a fixed point in an uncertain world.

My dad is very kind. If I'm ever coming to visit on a Tuesday or Friday afternoon, he includes me in the Telly Bingo tickets. Sometimes he also buys me a bar of chocolate to heighten my enjoyment. He is very proud of my success, even though he never reads my books. Thing is, see, he read my first, which had a sex scene in it and as a result we couldn't make eye-contact for the next six months, so now we've come to a lovely, tacit agreement: he won't read my books and I won't mind. Nevertheless, he knows everything there is to know about publishing. He used to be an accountant so he brings his keen mathematical brain to analyse my career. He knows how I'm doing, how many books I've sold, what my market share is, how my rivals are selling, who is due a book out that will knock me off my perch ...

He's very, very loyal. Sometimes I go into my local bookshop only to discover that an entire wall is devoted to face-outs of my books. Supportive and all as the shop are to me, I get a bad feeling. 'Is he ...?' I ask the manager. 'Was he ...?'

'*Yes,*' *she se*ʒ, '*your dad was in again.*'
'*Sorry,*' *I sigh,* '*I'll have a word.*'

Finally, I am married to Himself, who is beyond description.

Big Night Out

I never win anything. Nothing. Not raffles, or scratchcards, or poker, or penny cascades, or the lotto. Nothing. And even though many, many lovely things have happened to me in my life, at heart I consider myself to be an extremely unlucky person. I can't shake the feeling that there's only so much good fortune in the world to go round and if someone else is getting it, it leaves even less for me. Take Telly Bingo, for example. It's on every Tuesday and Friday on the telly (the clue is in the name), Mam and Dad are devoted to it and if I'm over visiting them, I'm devoted to it too. But I've never won anything: not a 'Full House'; not a 'Four Corners'; not even a single line (you can get *up to* 12 euro in prize money for that).

I always start off in fabulous form, my pen poised over the card, frothy and giddy with hope. It could be me, I tell myself. I've as much chance as the next person. But as the minutes pass and the balls are called and I've only ticked off three numbers and the computerized scoreboard yoke is telling me there are fifteen people in County Monaghan needing only one more number to win the jackpot, I slip deeper and deeper into a depression. Why does nothing nice ever happen to me? Why is it always other people? Why has God got it in for me? And even though I'm usually supposed to be staying at my parents for the whole afternoon, as soon as the final ball is called, I find myself sloping off home and when Himself opens the front door, surprised to see me back so early, he takes in my gloomy aspect and says, 'Oh no! Not the Telly Bingo! Stay away from it!'

And yet the hope always returns. So when I heard about Dad's golf club's Christmas fundraiser bingo night, I couldn't wait to go. Apparently there would be ten rounds of bingo and, according to Mam, *loads* of prizes. I quizzed her on them. 'Poinsettias, Christmas crackers, bottles of Jameson, boxes of biscuits, teddy bears.'

'Christmas hampers?'

'Sometimes.'

Surely, if there were that many prizes to go round, I had a chance of winning *something*?

Seven of us signed up: Himself and myself, my parents, Rita-Anne, Tadhg's girlfriend, Susan, and Mam's friend Ann Carty. Although kick-off wasn't until 8 p.m., Dad made us arrive at the golf club at seven-thirty. Mind you, we considered ourselves lucky he hadn't made us get there at a quarter to five – if a journey takes twenty minutes, Dad prefers to allow an hour and three-quarters just to be on the safe side. All the same, at seven-thirty trade at the golf club was already brisk. Books of bingo cards were rapidly changing hands and raffle tickets were being hustled. People were flooding in, baggsying tables, buying drinks and glad-handing all over the place. Funnily enough I'd expected all the golf people to be in their funny Rupert the Bear trousers and dodgy Pringle jumpers, but they were in civvies so they seemed quite normal. From what I could gather from all the people my mother kept introducing me to, a lot of the golf people were also bridge people. Clearly quite a competitive bunch. My heart sank slightly.

And then I noticed the table of prizes! I suspected it would be bad form to check them out – I should have been thinking about the socialness of the occasion, or the charity the night was in aid of – but I was *dying* to see what I might win. I had high hopes for a hamper. Himself and myself had kept ourselves awake the previous night making a wish-list of all the lovely things you'd find in the perfect hamper: a cheeseboard, a bottle of port, a Christmas pudding, a jar of brandy butter, crystallized fruit, a 200g bag of Percy Pigs . . .

I went up with Susan to check out the prizes and Susan was *fantastically* scornful. (Because the golf club didn't let Tadhg wear jeans or baseball caps she'd thought of the place as intimidatingly posh, so she'd expected their prizes to also be posh. Nothing like a bit of disappointment to release the bile.) Poking fun at the ranks of poinsettias, she said they were like *The Day of the Triffids* – with several all lined up together, they looked quite menacing, almost alive. But the bitterest of her bile was reserved for the boxes of Rover biscuits. I had never heard of them (and God knows, if anyone knows about biscuits, it's me), but Susan assured me they were horrible. So horrible that she'd thought they didn't even make them any more. Someone must have had them in their attic for the last fifteen years and donated them, she said. In fact, someone must have died and their house was being sold and the Rover biscuits must have been found when the attic was being cleared out before the new people moved in, she suggested. Or else someone had won them for the last twenty years and kept redonating them. I'm very suggestible and although I thought the prizes were lovely (boxes of Roses and non-dodgy, non-Rover biscuits) the more Susan mocked, the more I joined in. Not only am I very immature but something about being in a place where lots of my parents' friends were present had made me revert to teenage brattery.

When we returned to the table, I leant over and quietly told Mam, 'Susan says the prizes are crap.'

Mam hissed back, 'It's for charity, keep your voice down. And there's loads of vouchers for turkeys, it's just that the turkeys aren't here and you can't see them, but they're very good prizes.'

Then, on another table, I spotted the raffle prizes – different to the bingo prizes. And I could see a hamper! Already I was pulling Susan to her feet. This I had to see.

'Sit down,' Mam begged. 'Let it alone, be good.'

But we were up and pushing through the noisy throng and the first thing I saw behind the cellophane was a jar of supermarket-brand jam, then a jar of Nescafé. 'Look – Branston pickle,' Susan choked and clutched me. 'Jacob's crackers,' I riposted. 'A lovely Christmas hamper, total value two euro twenty.' We convulsed quietly, then across the room, I caught Mam's eye and abruptly my mirth dissolved. And in all fairness, in a second layer behind the first extremely poor one, there was a bottle of Smirnoff, a bottle of port, smoked salmon and a white envelope which must have been one of the famed turkey vouchers. No bag of those much-loved delicacies, Percy Pigs, mind . . .

Shortly after eight, the games began. A hush fell and balls were called and numbers were ticked and brows were furrowed and concentration was high. Win, I urged myself. Go on, win. But in no time at all, a woman at another table called, 'Check!' – which meant 'Bingo' although I don't know why we weren't allowed to shout 'Bingo' – and her card was ferried away to be verified. Amazingly, she was wrong! Everyone (not just at our table, *everyone*) exchanged small, mean-spirited smirks and someone at the other end of the room yelled, 'Swizzer!' Mam elbowed me and scolded, 'Stop that!'

Flustered and red-faced, the woman denied charges of trying to pull a fast one, bleating some makey-upey story about wearing the wrong glasses and not being able to see the numbers properly. No one believed her, of course, then the games resumed. However, a short time later another woman called, 'Check!' and this one really had won. Her prizes were brought to her table (a poinsettia, a box of Roses, a Beanie Baby and a bottle of wine), everyone clapped graciously and I clapped too, but the downward slide in me had begun. Already the night was losing its lustre. Already everyone looked luckier than me.

A new game began and obediently I ticked numbers, musing on how terrible it was to be constitutionally unlucky and wondering what it felt like to be a golden girl who won everything. Then I noticed that I needed only three more numbers for a full card. Yeah well, what was the point getting excited? Millions of people would beat me to it. Then I ticked another, and saw I needed only two more. Then, out of nowhere, all I needed was *one* number: sixty-five. Which was when the caller said, 'Retirement age.' *Retirement age?* But wasn't that . . . ? 'Sixty-five!' he called. 'Sixty-five.'

Sixty-five! Christ! I'd won! 'Check!' I called, while everyone at the table looked up from their cards in surprise. What was I doing winning something? That wasn't right.

'Stop your messing,' Dad said anxiously. 'They know me here.'

They were afraid it was going to be just like the lady with the wrong glasses all over again and I can't say I wasn't anxious that I was about to make a prize gom of myself, but my card was checked – and found to be correct! Next thing two ladies were moving through the tables, bringing me my prizes – two bottles of wine, a box of biscuits (not the Rover ones), a poinsettia and a box of Terry's chocolates. Everyone clapped me warmly and I smiled graciously around the room, savouring the moment, one of the pleasantest of my life to date. 'Just call me Lucky,' I murmured.

Off we went again but before the ticking recommenced in earnest, I warned the rest of our table, 'That's all our luck used up now, okay? We might as well go home.'

'Feck off,' someone whispered softly and although I looked sharply at all of them, I couldn't establish who it was.

It was very soothing, ticking numbers, now that I'd won something. All the anxiety was gone, I was calm and at peace. Tick. Nice and easy. And another tick. Not a bother. And another tick. And then I noticed something very odd. I had only two numbers left to go. Then one: thirty-seven. 'Thiiiirrrrrrteeeee,' the caller said, and my heart nearly stopped, 'six,' he finished. 'Thirty-six.'

Ah okay. 'And the next one up from that,' he said. *The next one up from thirty-six?* But wasn't that . . . ? 'Thirty-seven!'

'Um, lookit,' I said to the others. 'I've won again.'

'I'm warning you.' Dad glared.

But I had won! My card was full. 'Um, check,' I called apologetically. A roomful of faces turned to me, their delight kind of freezing and fading when they saw it was me. Again.

'Didn't she win already?' Murmurry voices wafted towards me from the furthest reaches. 'Isn't that the same girl as last time?' 'How did she win again?' 'Something's not right.'

But my card was verified and found to be correct. My prizes arrived – two more bottles of wine and another poinsettia and, just like the previous time, I received them with a gracious three-sixty smile. But nothing happened.

'They didn't clap,' I said quietly to Himself.

'You're lucky they didn't boo,' he replied.

Then the fuss died down, another game started, other people won, we clapped enthusiastically when they were presented with their prizes – basically we all moved on with our lives. Until about four cards later, Rita-Anne suddenly appeared to be in distress. 'Oh Christ,' she whimpered. 'I've only one number to go. Twenty-one.'

Dad stared at her aghast, like she'd done it on purpose, just in time to hear the caller shout, 'Key to the door, twenty-one!'

There was a stricken moment, when we had a panicky silent eye-conference. What should we do? Pretend it hadn't happened and let someone else win? But as Rita-Anne later admitted, she was just too competitive. 'Check!' she called.

This time the news was greeted with a nasty little oh-yeah?-style laugh. In fairness, though, when Rita-Anne was presented with her prizes – two more bottles of wine, a side of smoked salmon, a box of Roses, a box of biscuits (not Rover) and another poinsettia – they did clap – even if it was a *slow* handclap.

Blushing furiously, she put her poinsettia on the floor beside the others; in numbers of two or more they really did look sort of nasty, as though they were about to take over the world. Stressed and mortified, Rita-Anne wanted to open the box of Roses, but I persuaded her not to – we were unpopular enough without enjoying the fruits of our ridiculous luck under all their noses.

Then a new game started up and Dad whispered hoarsely around the table, 'Don't fecking win any more!'

We promised we wouldn't and Mam said anxiously, 'I hope they won't do us over in the car park later. I'd like to take one of them poinsettias home.'

We got through the rest of the night without winning anything else – although it came terrifyingly close a couple of times – and enough other people won to almost obscure our disproportionate luck. Then it was time for the end-of-night raffle and the man called out, 'It's a pale blue ticket, number seventy-five. Number seventy-five. Anyone? Anyone at all?'

Susan suddenly noticed something on the table in front of her. 'Oh Jesus,' she said. 'That's me.'

Previously unpublished.

Villa-itis

Villa-itis. n. *The fear, while trapped with your entire family in a villa just outside Cannes, of running out of bread.*

It started even before we left. About a week before the off my mother rang me and she sounded anxious.

'You know when we're in that house in the south of France? Shouldn't we organize some sort of kitty?'

This baffled me because the one thing you can say about my family is that we pay our way. In fact, it can almost get ugly. There were going to be ten adults and two children in the house for the week and everyone was going to be trying their hardest not just to 'stand their round' grocerically speaking, but to be the first to do so. I reminded Mammy Keyes of this but she refused to be mollified. 'What if I come down for my breakfast and someone's eaten all my bread and I can't make toast?'

Then I understood. She didn't mean a kitty, she meant self-determination over food. Kind of understandable: my family are all adults now, used to living on our own or with a small number of other people, whom we can monitor, hawk-eyed, to make sure they stay away from our bread. Suddenly we were going to be thrust into a situation with

164

several other hungry people and it would be a hard job to track them all.

But what was Mammy K proposing? Everyone getting a shelf in the French fridge for their own food, like in a flatshare? Even putting little notes on things? 'Tadhg's butter. It's been weighed!' Or (when in Rome) 'Les Müller Corners de Marian. Ne touchez pas!'

I tried to jolly her along with talk that it would all work itself out. But clearly she wasn't convinced because a rumour reached me that, along with her sundresses, sandals, sun-cream, etc., she was planning to bring a sliced pan in her suitcase. Allegedly (according to my source) she would keep said bread under lock and key for the week, only opening the vault once a day, to retrieve two slices to carry downstairs for her breakfast toast. She would swagger past all the hungry hordes who were too proud or too foolish to think ahead like she had, saunter into the kitchen, approach the toaster and make toast. When I confronted her, she would neither confirm nor deny it. But when I made mention of my nephew Luka's fondness for OPT (Other People's Toast – it is as ambrosia to him, rendered unbearably delicious by the fact of belonging to someone else) and that she wouldn't be able to resist giving it to him, because no one can refuse him anything ever, I could see her doing mental calculations, to see if she would have enough slices to bring down an extra one each day for Luka. Evidently the sums added up because her brow cleared and the serene 'I've got my own bread' expression resumed residence on her face.

Anyway, on a Saturday in early September, twelve of us

descended on a beautiful house just outside Cannes. We came from all three corners of the globe – Prague, where my brother lives with his wife, Ljiljana, and their two children, New York where my sister Caitríona lives and Dublin where the rest of us reside.

We got through the first night's dinner without any mention of bread because the caretaker had prepared us a dinner so delicious that we were distracted. Then the following morning, Himself and myself saddled up to go to *le supermarché* to buy supplies for the twelve of us. Everyone had special requests – goat's cheese, drinking chocolate, Special K bars, blackcurrant Winders (that was me) – but even in these carb-phobic times, bread was the one common thread. It was what everyone wanted. It made sense: we were self-catering and as (apart from Ljiljana) we're not the kind of family who 'rustles' things up – blanching peppers and making our own balsamic vinegar dressing and preparing a 'delicious, light lunch' in fifteen minutes – bread was vital. We could make cheese sangwidges. We could make hang sangwidges. We could make cheese *and* hang sangwidges. Sure, you wouldn't even need a plate. Leaving for le supermarché, I was badly jostled at the front door as everyone insisted on giving me money to pay for le shopping. (*'I'll* get it.' 'No, *I'll* get it.' 'Je . . . moi . . . le . . . ah feck it, I'll get it.') Festooned with banknotes like an Afghan bride, I left. (Is it Afghan I'm thinking of? Maybe it's Uzbek? Or Armenian?) Just before the car turned out onto the road an upstairs window opened and a disembodied voice called, 'Get some bread!'

We bought four loaves, which seemed like enough for one

day – after all we would be going to le supermarché or even la boulangerie *chaque jour*. Then we came home and a lovely, casual day unfolded. People sunbathed, swam, shoved each other off lilos and wandered in and out of the kitchen for their lunch sangwidges whenever they felt like it. (Me? I usually like my lunch around 10.45.)

But sometime in the early afternoon, Dad rushed out of the kitchen, stood at the top of the steps that descended to the garden and, like a general returning with news of an unexpected and dreadful defeat in battle, wailed at the prone bodies by the pool, 'All the bread is gone!'

I was mortified! It had been my responsibility to buy enough bread and I hadn't. Dad assembled a pitiful repast of Special K bars, goat's cheese and blackcurrant Winders and although he made the best of it, he was obviously upset.

But later, in the admittedly large kitchen, I stumbled across an almost full baguette hidden beneath a tea towel. Further investigation revealed another loaf – hello? – in the bread-bin. And half a brioche on the draining board.

But the damage – or *damage* – had been done. We were all in the grip of a hysteria, a terror of running out.

The following day more people went on the official trip to le supermarché and bought *five* loaves. Then Niall and Tadhg arrived home from golf bearing several eight-foot-long baguettes. Five minutes later Dad appeared – he'd been missing all morning – apparently he'd walked the three kilometres into the centre of Cannes and he too was laden with bread.

We had far too much, but it still wasn't enough. It was as though we had become blind to what was really there and the acquisition was the only thing that was important. (Some kind of metaphor about life there, if I could only be arsed to pursue it.)

The following day the situation reached its high-water mark. I wasn't there (in the spa in Hotel Martinez, another story) but apparently Dad did a reprise of his general returning with news of defeat act. There was NO BREAD!

Ljiljana, demonstrating she is more than worthy of her title, The Most Fabulous Woman On The Planet^{TM}, offered to *bake* bread. For some reason she happened to have a packet of bread-mix about her person. And I returned, reeking of lavender oil, to the bizarre sight of Ljiljana, in a kitchen that seemed to be heaving with bread, *baking bread.*

I have since discovered that it's not just that my family are insane, although of course they are, but that this fear of running out is a 'villa thing'. A syndrome that has something to do with displacement and temporary lack of domestic autonomy. My friend Shoshana went to a villa in Spain with her family and experienced an almost identical situation with bread. People were actually hoarding the stuff, she said, even though they had so much bread they had run out of cupboard space and had taken to stacking it on the floor. Then one day she and her mother went on a trip to Gibraltar and discovered the local branch of Marks and Spencer. Despite being surrounded by Marks and Spencers at home, they got very excited. (This is a holiday feature for me, too – shops that I can visit any time I like at home suddenly seem Aladdin's Caves of wondrousness.) What could be nicer, they thought, than to buy Marks and Spencer sandwiches for everyone? All of a doodah they hurried home and exclaimed, 'M&S sangers all round!' The others stretched to see over the uneaten columns of bread and gave grateful thanks that now there was something to eat for lunch.

A version of this was first published in Cara, *August 2004.*

Life Begins

I was never very good at birthdays. On my eighteenth I was wretched at the speed at which my life was slipping through my fingers. Again on my twenty-sixth. And as for when I turned thirty, I was so distraught I might as well have been two *thousand* and thirty.

The problem was that, like most people, my image of myself is frozen in time at some young age (I'm nineteen) and I'm still deciding what I'll do when I leave school. I still feel 'young' – although I admit that genuine 'young' people would find such sentiments risible. But, in my defence, I vaguely covet Hello Kitty toasters, I get complicated highlights, and when they launched KitKat Chunky, I was genuinely excited.

So on that reckoning, my fortieth birthday – traditionally regarded as the gateway to a twilit half-life of elasticated waistbands and gardening – should have been a total blood-bath. Next stop death . . .

But not any more!

Because forty isn't what it used to be. Forty – just in case you hadn't heard – is the new thirty. Several friends 'crossed over' this year and most of them look and behave like women ten years their junior. (Vitamins? Positive attitude? Botox? Whatever it is, it works.) One recommended smoking after several abstinent years because forty felt so young! Another got engaged – her first time; as she said with magnificent hauteur, 'Getting engaged is a big deal. Not something you want to rush into.'

Forty had been rehabilitated and, actually, so had I. From thirty-one onwards, having brokered a fragile peace with myself, birthdays had been less of an angst-fest, and as my big day neared I was swaggering about, boasting that being forty wouldn't bother me at all. I might even – perish the thought – have said, 'Age? Hah! Merely a number.' (Mind you, I'd been in training, mentally preparing myself, since turning thirty-seven.) But clearly I was only showing off because on the morning itself the realization hit me like a sack of wet sand falling from a height – I was FORTY, I was *ancient*. How had all this time passed without my noticing? Where had my life gone?

If it hadn't been for my family and my presents waiting for me downstairs, I would probably still be in bed now, staring at the ceiling, paralysed with despair.

The only thing that helped was my appearance. The previous day as a thirty-something I'd despaired over how I looked, but now that I was *in my forties* I found myself thinking, actually, I'm not that bad.

Then the hiccup passed and it was business as usual and I realized how disappointed I was – all my life I've been waiting for that glorious moment when I arrive at the top of the mountain and finally become an adult. In that instant I would suddenly be able to ask taxi drivers to turn down their ear-drum-hurting Def Leppard tapes and to tell my hairdresser that he doesn't blow-dry my fringe properly and to ask him to go over it again without feeling wretched with guilt. I had hung a lot of hope on the idea that turning forty would miraculously effect this change; but nope, I was still a nineteen-year-old trapped in a forty-year-old body, way too fond of Claire's Accessories and still getting spots.

Then something happened . . .

It was this. I've always dreaded confrontation. Even when I've been in the right and I should have hotly defended myself, I've swallowed back the words, destroying the lining of my stomach and giving my incipient ulcer a shot in the arm.

But about a week after my big day, I was talking to an old friend; someone I'm very fond of, except for her obsession with weight. It wouldn't be so bad if it was just her own, but she's very fixated on others', scornful when they put it on and jealous when they lose it. Whenever we meet, I can actually feel her *weighing* me but I've never confronted her, because that's just not what I do. Anyway, she was talking about how she'd knocked the Twixes on the head and how thin and powerful she was feeling, when suddenly, without warning, a red mist descended and, from far away, almost like I was listening to someone else, I heard myself telling her off. I listened attentively. I believe I told her that she was entirely wrong to judge people on their tubbiness instead of qualities like kindness, generosity and sense of humour. (I said 'people' but, of course, I really meant me.)

Then the mist cleared and although we were both a little puzzled, I thought no more of it. Until, two weeks later, when it happened again! Another beloved friend, a mother of three little boys, has become such a baby bore, I would rather be trapped in a lift with Osama Bin Laden than with her. She has the uncanny ability to turn any topic of conversation – parking permits, cirrhosis of the liver, aardvarks – back to her children. (Can I say at this juncture that I know tons of mothers and no one else is as bad as this.) It's *exhausting* maintaining a fixed smile, saying, 'Really? So he tried to open a letter that *could* have been your parking permit. Well, er, lucky it wasn't!' Before I knew what was happening the red mist had descended again and I heard myself asking if we could talk about something other than her children, just for ten minutes.

It was only when I got 'red-misted' for a third, then a fourth, time that I noticed the pattern and somehow intuited it had something to do with my great age. Could it be . . . ? Was it possible . . . ? I was finally an adult!

Three of the bust-ups have healed beautifully but the fourth, the mother of the three boys, hasn't forgiven me. She says it's not her fault that I haven't had children and she wants to know what she's meant to do with her babies? Hide them in a drawer? I'm sad but I will live with it. (More adult stuff, it's wonderful!) It's taken me forty years to discover that I can have confrontations – and survive. I have great hope for the lining of my stomach as I move into my fifth decade.

Now fifty, that's *really* old . . .

First published in Woman and Home, *February 2004.*

Big Air

One of the things about being a writer is having to do research. Some research is lovely (spending two months in Los Angeles), some research is tedious (looking up stuff on the internet) and some research is . . . er . . . interesting. Like attending the final of the first Irish air-guitar-playing championship. The winner would go on to represent Ireland in the world championship in Finland.

Believing that there would be safety in numbers, I trawled amongst friends and family, looking for people to come with me. Almost everyone laughed scornfully and told me to shag off, except for my father, who was apoplectic with disbelief at the ridiculousness of it all. 'No one plays air-guitar in public, it's the sort of thing you do in the privacy of your own home. In front of a mirror?' He checked with Tadhg. 'With a tennis racket? Amn't I right?'

'Yes, well, these lads are doing it in public,' I said.

'Gobshites,' Tadhg said, still crimson from the tennis racket dig.

'Ah, the poor craythurs,' my mother said, always one to support the underdog. 'I'll come with you.' But when she discovered there would be no seats, just standing only, she quickly retracted her acceptance of the invitation.

The only person I could get to accompany me, other than Himself (who had no choice), was my friend Eileen, who is a lawyer with a sense of adventure.

And so to clothing. It doesn't matter what I'm going to – a funeral, an anti-war protest, an air-guitar championship – I agonize over what to wear. All I want to do is fit in. But as I reckoned the rest of the audience at this yoke would be 'airing' along with their betters on the stage, I expected the look to be back-combed hair, headbands, spandex pants and eyeliner.

The eyeliner I could do, the rest I hadn't a hope with, so (as usual) I decided to dress from head to toe in black, black being the safest if you don't want to stand out like a middle-aged sore thumb. But in a sudden burst of defiance, I decided to not even try. Let them laugh! So I wore a pink cardigan. (Mind you, not just any pink cardigan but a really beautiful one from Club Monaco. Sorry, a quick digression here to tell my Club Monaco story. Last time I was going on a book tour in the US, it was decided that my New York reading would not be in a book store, but in Club Monaco, combining books and fashion. It would be a fun night, clothes could be bought at a discount and I would wear Club Monaco clothes for the evening, which I could then keep. When news of this got out, several people said accusingly, You have the best job in the world. Shakily I agreed, but I was in the horrors because, for me, clothes shopping is a soul-destroying exercise in damage limitation. I'm so short and tubby that almost nothing looks nice on me and I feared a terrible humiliation awaited me in New York. The guilt, too, was corrosive: I didn't deserve my job because through my own short, fat fault, I couldn't partake of the perks.

In the run-up to the tour I used to wake in the middle of the night paralysed with fear: *What if nothing in Club Monaco fits me? How mortified will I be? On a scale of one to suicidal?*

But as it happened, my fear was entirely unfounded. On my first morning in New York, I showed up at Club Monaco the minute they opened, only to discover that they had tons of stuff that looked lovely on me – gorgeous tops and jackets and skirts and bags and, yes, fabulous pink cardigans. I wear mine with pride.)

Then I saw Himself's get-up and I felt a flicker of fear. He was in jeans, a dark T-shirt and a shortie denim jacket. See, Himself, in his youth, was an air-guitar supremo, with a grand head of curly, shoulder-length hair, all the better to twist his neck in 360-degree rotations with. The hair is now a distant memory but, looking at the clothing he'd chosen, I sensed that long-dormant air-guitar-playing tendencies had been resuscitated. He denied any such thing, said he was merely 'trying not to embarrass' me. Muttered that at least he wasn't wearing a pink cardigan.

We called into Eileen's office where she quickly finished up a multi-million-dollar merger (I like to think) and rose to her feet, smoothing down her cream-coloured suit.

'Are you going dressed like that?' Himself asked anxiously.

'At least I'm not wearing a pink cardigan,' she replied.

On the short walk to the venue, I discovered that Eileen and I had diametrically opposed expectations of the night, when she said, 'I wonder how bald air-guitar people manage.'

In astonishment, I said, 'None of them will be bald, they'll all have hair, loads of it. And white spandex catsuits, and tons of make-up.'

But Eileen insisted they'd be in baggy Metallica T-shirts and dirty jeans and I wondered where she was getting her information from.

Three abreast we sauntered towards the entrance, where the bouncer checked out Eileen in her expensive, well-cut solicitor threads and asked, 'Are you sure you want to go in, love? You do know what's going on in there?'

She said she did, but he wouldn't let up and eventually she said, 'I'm the mother of one of the competitors.'

This seemed to reassure him, until his gaze moved to my pink cardigan and the anxious look was back.

'And so am I,' I added.

Then we were in and between the ultra-violet light and Led Zeppelin on the sound system, Himself looked suddenly wistful. I suspect that if he could be anyone, it would be Robert Plant circa 1971. Indeed, I was plunged into my own trip down memory lane, to when I was fourteen and Lynyrd Skynyrd and Deep Purple were on the playlist at the disco I went to.

Contrary to expectations, as we battled to the bar, the audience looked really normal: no leopardskin, no big hair. It dawned on me that they were probably family and friends, there to support. Or to laugh. I needn't have worried at all about my clothes.

With – unusually for us – impeccable timing, we'd just got our drinks when the MC appeared on the stage to kick things off. She was a girl and she looked good, like a proper rock chick, with lurex tights, short skirt, knee boots and dreadful heavy curtains of rib-length hair.

And we were off! The first competitor was a tiny bloke in

a Metallica T-shirt and dirty jeans. Although he wasn't bald, his hair was short. Eileen gave me a smug smile. Twiddling at his tummy, he roamed back and forth along an invisible eighteen-inch line and his USP was putting his foot up on the speaker and giving the devil's horns salute. He was astonishingly poor. I could have done better myself.

'Jesus Christ,' Eileen muttered, utterly appalled. 'We'll be shamed in Finland if they're all as bad as him.'

To our intense, patriotic relief the second bloke was much better. In an AC/DC schoolboy rig-out, with a peaked cap over a black nylon wig, he did the kneeling-down-and-leaning-back-and-making-agonized-faces thing. Then he lay on his back, twirling around, nearly knocking over a microphone, and for a grand finale he smashed up his air-guitar. But Eileen took agin him because she said he spent a lot of his time playing the air-*drums*. Or at least the air-guitar to the drum beat. And as she, quite correctly, pointed out, it was an air-*guitar* competition. You can see how she got to be a high-powered lawyer.

Contestant number three, *I* took agin. It was his clothes: big roundy shades, short curly hair, headband and beads, altogether too flower power for my liking. 'Are these people taking it seriously at all?' I asked. Meladdo's chosen song was something by Led Zeppelin and beside me I felt Himself twitching.

By then a pipe to the side of the stage had started to wheeze asthmatically, pumping dry ice onto the stage in irregular bursts. Just in time for Smell Gibson, another tiny little bloke. He was bare-chested, decorated with red streaks of blood-style paint and although his hair wasn't very long, it had lots of static electricity. He was great! Much struttage and lepping and he brought his dazzling display to a close with a crowd-pleasing baring of his tiny buttocks. Fantastic energy.

After that virtuoso display, number five could only be a disappointment, and indeed he was – dressed as a priest and his chosen music was Led Zeppelin's 'Houses of the Holy'. An out-of-work stand-up comedian, we concluded, and he wouldn't be going to Finland if we had anything to do with it. (In all fairness, his facial expressions were probably the best of the night – he did an excellent duck-mouth – but it simply wasn't enough.)

Number six was a girl! The only competitor of the night with long hair. I'll repeat that: *the only competitor of the night with long hair*. A disgrace. She wore a short skirt and diamond-patterned tights from Marks and Spencer; I recognized them because I have a pair myself. Her chosen music was some thrash metal yoke that I'm too old to recognize, and in the middle of it the strobe lighting suddenly came on, which made her look better than she was. But it wouldn't have mattered how good she was: rock chicks should not wear tights from Marks and Spencer.

Contestant number seven was yet another minute bloke, in jeans and T-shirt, who did a Chuck Berry-style, extended-leg hopping back and forth across the stage.

Then things picked up a bit when the MC promised that contestant number eight was wearing a catsuit. About bloody time; I was mortified that I'd so misled Eileen about what the contestants would be wearing. However, it was the wrong sort of catsuit. It wasn't crotch-clinging spandex but a cat *costume*. Without a head, admittedly, but furry and with a tail, which your man twirled a lot. Again I despaired that no one was taking this seriously enough. I mean, national pride was at stake.

In keeping with the animal theme his song was Led Zeppelin's 'Black Dog'. Beside me I could feel Himself straining at the bit. He was only dying to lep on the stage and show these whippersnappers what was what.

Number nine was a tall bloke with short hair, sunglasses, spiky leather bracelets and a denim jacket with the sleeves hacked off. He wasn't too bad.

But number ten! Please! Another girl, playing to ZZ Top's 'Bad Girl'. This one was in jeans, T-shirt, short hair, no make-up and – God Almighty – glasses. Not shades, or statement glasses but swotty, short-sighted-person's glasses. She was – and God knows I don't enjoy being cruel – but she was piss-poor.

'And these people came through regional heats?' Himself asked, in amazement. 'How bad must the others have been?'

That concluded the first round and everyone trooped downstairs and outside for a cigarette. On the stairs we passed a bloke on his mobile saying, 'Mammy? Can you hear me? They've just done the first round, the free-form round, and he did very well.'

Half an hour later we all trooped back in for the second round – where the competitors had to play along to a mandatory song, which happened to be 'Smoke on the Water'. Marvellous stuff.

Again, Smell Gibson surpassed himself and when it came to the voting, my hopes for him were high.

Competitors are apparently judged on 'originality, ability to be taken over by the music, stage charisma, technique, artistic impression and big air'. However, if I had my way, they'd be judged on 'knottiness of their back-combed hair, quantity of eyeliner used, agonizedness of facial expressions, angle of thrusting crotches and shininess of spandex'.

But never mind! Because Smell Gibson, great hope of our glorious republic, won!

And with that, I started to hustle Himself and Eileen towards the exit. 'Go quickly,' I urged.

You see, the ideology of the Finnish bloke who was the original organizer of the air-guitar competition is that air-guitar can contribute to world peace. He reckons that if everyone plays air-guitar at the same time, soldiers will have to lay down their weapons, crime will have to stop and all viruses and bacteria will be paralysed by the collective air-guitar energy.

In homage to that worthy sentiment, tonight's show would be closed by everyone – audience and all – playing their air-guitars. Now, I've nothing against world peace, nothing at all, but I couldn't take any risks with Himself: if the music 'took' him, he'd be up on that stage, banging his head, doing huge circles with his 'playing' arm and making faces like he'd just been kicked in the nads.

Before the music had even started, we had left the building and the three of us slipped away quietly into the night.

Previously unpublished.

Eyes Wide Shut

A few years ago a plethora of Keyeses went to visit Niall and co in Prague for Christmas, hoping for snow, handmade wooden toys and a merciful break from turkey. (Carp is their thing, apparently.) Unfortunately there wasn't room for everyone to stay in Niall's apartment (all mittel-European charm and atmosphere, with lovely, funny windows and strange names like Skvorecky and Havranova on the doorbell). Never mind, we sez, a hotel will do – only to discover that an alarming number of Prague hotels were closed over Christmas.

Eventually, and in a bit of a panic, we found a place – Hotel Praha – on the internet. They claimed they'd be happy to take us. But strangely, it wasn't in any guide books and although it was a mere five minutes' walk from Niall's apartment, he'd never heard of it. God only knew what it was like, but what choice did we have?

I'll admit it: from the off, the omens weren't good. First the flight from Dublin to London was massively delayed and we were terrified we'd miss our connection. The second we landed in London, we had to do an undignified, sweaty, inter-terminal trolley dash, with some of the older and more infirm members of our party crouched amongst the bags, holding on to the trolley edges for dear life. In the nick of time, the *nick* of time – that's what they kept telling us – we made the flight, the door slamming behind us the minute we wheezed aboard – and then . . . we went nowhere! We sat for what felt like days on the runway – at the very point at which it dawned on us how terribly, slaveringly hungry we were. We hadn't eaten all day and wouldn't be getting anything until the plane took off, if it ever did, and if it hadn't been for my mother's emergency stash of peanut M&Ms, we'd have started eating each other, like in that film about the plane crash in the Andes.

Worse was to come. When we landed in Prague, my bag, with all my Christmas presents in it, hadn't made the journey. (I have extremely bad luggage karma. In a past life I must have been a baggage handler who nicked loads of stuff out of unlocked suitcases.) I'm so used to losing bags at this stage that I don't bother waiting at the luggage carousel any more; I go straight to the lost luggage desk and start filling out the forms.

The rest of my family, complete with their luggage – lucky bastards – went on ahead, and when I'd filled in enough missing-bag documents to satisfy Czech bureaucracy, Himself and myself finally arrived at Hotel Praha. Now, at this point, it's important to remember I've had a long stressful day, all I've had to eat is seven peanut M&Ms and my bag with all my lovingly purchased presents has disappeared and I'm fully convinced I'll never see them again.

'Welcome to Hotel Praha!' the super-cheery desk-man said. 'You are very late. Very, very late. So we have put you in a special room!' Naturally enough, the day having gone so badly, I presumed he meant a six-foot-square windowless box and I prepared to vault over the counter to savage him. But I paused mid-crouch when he continued, 'When Tom Cruise was making *Mission Impossible* in Prague he stayed in the same suite for six weeks! Nicole cooked him dinner there!'

I narrowed my eyes at him. Taking the piss, was he? But what if . . . could there be a chance that maybe . . . he wasn't . . . ? Cautiously I accepted my key, gave him an I'll-be-back-if-I-need-to look and made for our 'special room'.

And your man wasn't joking. Our room was very special – it was *enormous*, far bigger than our house in Dublin. It took ten minutes to walk from one end of the sitting room to the other (I'm exaggerating only slightly), it had four bathrooms, a dining table that seated twelve, an office and a massive balcony which overlooked Prague castle. (All the rooms have the same view.) And so what if I occasionally got an electric shock when I touched anything metal, and did it matter that the bathroom doors were constructed in such a way that if you closed the door while still holding the handle (and how else are you to do it?) your fingers became painfully trapped?

It was costing us eighty dollars a night. Forty dollars each. For nothing. My parents and siblings came to ooh and aah and I swaggered about, delighted with the sudden change in my fortunes.

'Now aren't you glad your bag got lost?' Mam asked. 'Come on, we've to go down for our carp. Listen, are they telling the truth about Tom Cruise?'

Hard to know but over the next few days enough staff swore blind that Tom really did stay in that selfsame room and that Nicole really did visit him there, to convince me. As it happened, one of my Christmas presents was a velvet eye-mask (to aid restful sleep on bright summer mornings) but it came in very handy as a prop as Himself and myself pretended to be Tom and Nicole in *Eyes Wide Shut*. Oh *hours* of fun.

In the daylight we got a better look at the hotel and it was *gas*. Finished in 1981, it was the Czech attempt at late-seventies luxe. They were showing off – look at our most excellent, Vestern-style hotel, see how well the Soviet system is vorking for us hard-vorking Czechs – and many of the big names stayed there: Brezhnev, Andropov, Ceausescu.

No expense was spared in its interior: every single wall and door is clad in walnut and the scale of the place is *massive*. There's a swimming pool, tennis courts, a beauty salon and expansive gardens. Even a skitless [sic] alley. (Badly crap, mind you.)

The outside is text-book Czech modernist architecture – mucho, mucho concrete, but it is curved and graceful; from the air it would look like a giant 'S' shape.

And it wasn't just the architecture that was central European, and time-warped: the room-service menu listed ten different breakfasts, as follows. (I *love* this.) Breakfast # 1: 50 g of domestic cheese and 50 g of cold meat. Breakfast # 2: 100 g of domestic cheese. Breakfast # 3: 100 g of cold meat. And so on. Such precision dates from Soviet times when the fear of being swizzed was high. You could bring your own personal weighing scales just to check that the room-service boy hadn't helped himself to a 5 g corner of your cheese en route from the kitchen. (Of course you pay a premium for having your

100 g of cheese delivered to your room – a whopping two euro will be added to your bill.)

However, the charming staff are not Soviet-style and are more than prepared to go 'off menu'. I've requested – and been given – a non-menu yoghurt. And another time, a fruit salad. And another time, a banana.

However, the 'orange' 'juice' is authentically terrifying. It's a long way from an orange that their 'orange' 'juice' was reared: syrup-thick and Day-Glo, like undiluted Miwadi. And the mini-bar is charmingly bereft of produce – a couple of bottles of local beer and some dodgy-looking, chemical-filled soft drinks is all you'll get.

On account of Ema and Luka, Himself and myself go to Prague a lot and now we always stay at the Praha – although sadly we've never had the Tom Cruise suite again, but even the ordinary rooms have character and space.

For ages, we seemed to be the only people there. Although there are four floors, we were only ever put on the first, leading us to suspect that the other three floors were covered in dust-sheets, like a hotel version of Miss Havisham, waiting for the visitors to return. And then, lo and behold, they did! On a recent visit the Germans had arrived, busloads of them. Filming something. A fashion show, perhaps. Or . . . or . . . maybe a porn film. Lots of busty blonde women running around in see-through tops and beardy men in leather trousers filming them.

Then another time we went – how bizarre is this? – the Galway choral society were doing a concert. Luka and Ema were wheeled along to experience the Irish side of their heritage and Luka was evidently very moved because during a sixteen-part harmony of 'Danny Boy' he lunged at the front row of warblers with his plastic knight's sword we'd bought for him in Ikea (yes, they have IKEA in Prague) and had to be hauled off.

I love the Praha. It's a kind of memorial to a Soviet past and the staff are welcoming and incredibly obliging and, without wishing to slag the Czechs, that's not always the case. (Sometimes in Prague I'm in terrible danger of becoming the irritating kind of person who says, 'Cheer up, love, it might never happen.') It's also far enough from the town centre that if you don't want stag parties gawking their guts up outside your room every night, the Praha's your man.

Okay, it's not in the middle of town and if you need to be in staggering distance of your hotel, it's not for you. But if you're not afraid of a tram ride and you'd like to see a little remainder of Prague's recent past, you might give it a whirl. Honest to God, they're so nice. Tell them I sent you.

A version of this was first published in Abroad, *May 2004.*

Viva La Resolution?

*T*he world is divided into two types of people: those who love New Year's Eve and those who hate it. Those who love it celebrate it by going to parties, wearing glittery deely boppers, joyously doing the conga, shouting, 'TEN, NINE, EIGHT . . .' with gusto, kissing everyone in sight and generally feeling full of hope for the forthcoming year. The other kind – and they can be perfectly sociable for the other 364 nights of the year – find that New Year's Eve plunges them into a black despair. I, to my shame, belong in the latter gang.

I can't really articulate what happens to me, but when everyone else is looking forward, I look backwards. Old mortifications present themselves for inspection and I feel like a big, fat failure. It's like the stock-taking I do every birthday, only somehow far, far worse. So great is my gloom, I feel that if a tinselly deely bopper was placed on my head, it would instantly tarnish and the last thing I want to do, as one year clicks over into a new one, is triumphantly blow a paper bugle, then snog my dentist.

What makes things even harder is the scorn the deely bopper gang pour on my discomfort and their utter disbelief that I might prefer to stay at home and watch *Billy Elliot*. 'But it's the best night of the whole year! Don't be so mad.

Here,' they say, handing me a gaudily coloured tube, 'open that when we're all yelling, "Happy New Year". It shoots streamers everywhere.'

As time has passed, I have met others of my kind, a small secret band. We all suffer from Extreme New Year's Eve Fear (ENYEF – pronounced 'Enough!') and our greatest challenge was the mother of all New Year's Eves: the Millennium. I knew our angst would be magnified two thousandfold and suddenly I had a great idea for how we'd get through that night. I'd provide a safe house! All clocks would be hidden, so we'd have no idea when the dreaded midnight was upon us. We'd have Audrey Hepburn films, duvets, mashed potato, warm baths and every other cocooning device imaginable.

But somehow the deely bopper gang got wind of the gathering and they were totally unable to understand that *this was not a party*. Before I knew it, crates of champagne were being ferried in and the house was being draped with shiny red 'Happy New Millennium' banners and special one-off deely boppers – they had '2000' written on them – were being distributed as guests arrived. It was a nightmare!

And if New Year's Eve is upon us, can New Year's Day be far behind?

New Year's Day always feels to me like the day after the world has ended. It has a shocked, stunned air to it; people shakily emerge as though they're coming round from a blow to the head. We look at all the crappy presents received and given and remember that shameful business with the trifle on Christmas Day (no one else wanted any, I only meant to take one spoonful, etc., etc.) and think, 'What *happened*?'

After the utter excess of Christmas, the pendulum swings the other way so that the most commonly asked question on New Year's Day (after 'Have you any Nurofen?' and 'Er, any idea how I got home last night?') is, of course, 'What are your New Year's Resolutions?'

Because I have always overdone everything (not my fault, I was born without a 'stop' button), I completely understand the urge to purge and refashion myself. Until recently my entire life has been Operation Fresh Start. Most Mondays, I'd think: this is the week when I'll grab my life by the throat and bend its will to mine. I will lose that half-stone, I will cease my buying frenzy of lovely Jo Malone scented candles, I will learn Serbo-Croat (or something).

Therefore, I'm the perfect candidate for New Year's Resolutions. And I've always made *tons* of them. I've spent much of my life living in some faraway Utopian future, where I am svelte, a restrained shopper and fully conversant in most major European languages. Everything will be lovely when that happens but until then my life kind of goes on hold.

Every New Year's Day I am full of steely resolve: this is the year when I'll really change. But sooner or later – and it's usually sooner – I buckle and start eating, shopping and speaking English again. Naturally I end up feeling wretched with guilt and self-hatred.

So this year my New Year's Resolution is not to make any New Year's Resolutions. Life is tough enough for all of us without overloading ourselves with guilt trying to achieve some perfect (and frankly unattainable) state. The facts are: I will not lose that half-stone (and just between us, it's more like a stone now) – if it was going to happen it would have happened by now; everyone in Europe speaks English; and what's the harm in having a couple of scented candles about the place?

Forgive me (no, really, please do, I'm slightly mortified by this) for a Trisha-esque platitude, but life is what happens while we're waiting for it to be perfect enough to live it.

Happy New Year.

First published in Marie Claire, *January 2005.*

Hurling Insults

'Yiz dirty culchies, yiz muck savages!' The jeers rained down on our heads. Himself and myself were going to Croke Park, to the hurling quarter-final between Clare and Galway and our route took us through a part of inner-city Dublin where they have to make their own entertainment. Ten-year-old boys with the wizened faces of old men, smoked and leant over the balconies of their flats, partaking of the ancient jackeen sport of culchie-mocking.

Seeing as I was born in Limerick, they were within their rights, but Himself was born in England, of English parents, from a long line of English people. People who didn't know better might call him English. However, he's Irish. He's a transnational – an Irishman trapped in an Englishman's body – and since he moved here seven years ago, his assimilation process is almost complete. He has learnt Irish, he drinks Guinness – and he loves the GAA. His football team is Dublin, but his hurling team is Clare. (Long story, my mother's from there, we spend a lot of time there, a great attachment to the place and the people, etc., etc.)

He was thrilled with the abuse. 'Imagine,' he said, 'not only do they think I'm Irish, they think I'm a culchie!'

Just to copper-fasten the situation, he threw his head back and roared, 'Hould yeer whisht, ye little pups!'

Right then, hurling.

When I lived in London, and English people would compliment hurling and say what a great, fast, exciting game it was, I always said, 'Oh God, yes, it's fantastic.' Then I'd change the subject quickly so that I wouldn't have to admit that I'd never actually been to a game. In fairness, I always swore that I'd love to go, but that was only because I never really thought I'd have to.

However, when it transpired that Clare were playing Galway in the All-Ireland quarter-final, plans were fashioned, on a night out with friends, Paul and Aoife, for the four of us to attend. I thought it was just a load of drunken codswallop, but before I knew it, the tickets were bought: we were going.

It caught me on the hop; I don't really 'do' sport. (Just so there's no misunderstanding, I don't *do* it either.) Sitting in the cold, on hard benches, watching my side lose isn't my idea of a fun afternoon. Not when there are shops to go round or snoozes to catch up on. I don't think Aoife was too happy either – when the four of us took our seats, she gave me a brave smile. Under interrogation she denied that she was there under sufferance, but that is only because she is as gracious as she is glamorous. However, it was evident that Himself and Paul were absolutely thrilled to be there and let forth random bellows of 'Come on the Banner.'

Then the players ran onto the pitch and suddenly everyone sat up and paid attention. While English Premier League footballers look more and more like male models, these lads looked as if they'd just had the crap beaten out of them; tough, butty men with head bandages and pale, freckled legs, they wouldn't have known sculpting gel from a hole in the ground. They were the real thing.

Then some brass band started playing the national anthem and we all rose to our feet. I couldn't actually remember the last time I'd heard it, but something about it and the sight of the pale-thighed players, there to cover their county in glory, and all the people who had travelled to support them and endure the abuse from the flats, really stirred me.

Suddenly I was remembering a different Ireland, the Ireland of my childhood, when we were a small, unfashionable backwater, when Michael O'Hare's speedy commentary ruled the Sunday afternoon airwaves, when we were a rawer, less sophisticated nation, before we'd been enveloped in a membrane of sleekness.

It reminded me that we are – or at least were – a rural nation, where the local was more important than the global, where bad blood could endure for generations because someone had kicked someone else's donkey.

We've always had a strong sense of who we are. However, in recent decades, the troughs and peaks of our uniqueness have been flattened out. But at the risk of sounding like a Mick Supremacist, on that particular day, for those few minutes, I felt immersed in a concentration of Mickness and I thought, God, I love being Irish. Frankly, I was quite overcome.

And so to the game.

We had great seats, practically on the pitch. It being July, the weather was ferocious. A fizzy mist had hung in the air all day and as the match began in earnest, so did the rain. Aoife and I sat huddled beneath my umbrella, worrying about our hair. The rain, she said, made hers frizz up until she looked like a member of the Jackson Five. I'll see your Jackson Five, I said, and I'll raise you a Sideshow Bob.

Clare were slated to lose and I just couldn't bear to see it happen. Also the way the players hold the sliothar on their sticks while they run like the clappers makes me incredibly anxious: I'm always waiting for it to fall off. Between these dual anxieties, I averted my eyes and talked to Aoife about hair products while the unequal battle was fought on the pitch.

When the wind changed direction and began blowing the rain directly into our faces, we stoically stayed where we were. It was only when we were actually being blinded by the precipitation that we moved out of our allocated seats and under cover, where we found ourselves in the thick of our enemies, the Galway fans. A rosy-cheeked family of Galway supporters directly behind us were eating hang sang-widges out of tinfoil and drinking tea out of flasks. Bord Failte plants? Or maybe not . . .

And before we knew it, it was half-time — and that's a great thing about Gaelic games, each half is only thirty-five minutes, barely long enough to get bored.

Time to be refreshed; we made for the confectionery stall. Paul wanted Himself to have a thoroughly Irish experience, involving Tayto, Colleen sweets (remember them?) and red lemonade. But I will always remember that day as the first day I had Crunchie Nuggets. I'll never forget seeing them there on the stall in their golden bag; the breath literally left my body. What a great idea. I mean, what *inspiration*. Such vision! Until then I had thought that nothing could top KitKat Chunky in the sweetmeat reinvention stakes, but it just goes to show how wrong a person can be.

However, the glow of the Crunchie Nuggets wore off when I realized I had to go to the loo. I'd been dreading it because I feared the GAA mightn't hold with toilets. Especially a ladies'. Why would you need a ladies'? Sure, women don't come to matches! They're too busy at home, not taking contraception, kneeling on frozen peas and rearing their eighteen children. And as for the lads, well they can do it anywhere. But there was a ladies'! And instead of it being three skanky cubicles, two of them filthy and overflowing, while 800 desperate women queued out of the door and down the stairs, there was a plethora of clean and empty facilities.

When the second half started, the atmosphere shifted. The thing was that Clare had been leading at the end of the first half. I'd been in denial about it because I suspect I'm a hex: as soon as the gods know I'm supporting a team, they make them lose.

But suddenly Galway were anxious and the swagger and bluster that had characterized their supporters at the start of the game was absent.

Every time Clare had a free, a Galwegian youth (he was aged about twelve) from the hang sangwidge family behind us, yelled, 'Miss it!' And every time Galway had one, he'd yell, 'Don't waste it, ye goms, don't waste it!' I found such passion very charming, especially in one so young.

It was impossible not to get caught up in the excitement. I had a knot in my stomach and all talk of hair products was abandoned as I gnawed my nails and watched the pitch.

Both teams were scoring hand over fist. Unlike soccer, in GAA, people score all the time so that results that look like foregone conclusions suddenly aren't. With a minute to go, both scores were level; it was going to be a draw. Then Colin Lynch (Clare player) got the sliothar over the bar and twenty seconds later, the final whistle blew: Clare had won.

Himself leapt to his feet, kissed Paul, did a one-man Mexican wave, pulled his T-shirt over his face and bellowed, 'Galway, Galway, what's the score, Galway, what's the SCORE?' With the superstition that characterizes fans, he decided that I must be a good-luck charm and I'd have to go to all the Clare matches.

'Settle down,' I said, 'and have a Crunchie Nugget.'

First published in The Croke Park Annual, *2005.*

Black Out

*I*t must be something to do with getting older, because out of the blue my tolerance has declined, to all kinds of things: painkillers, late nights, people who sit too close to me on the bus and – the weirdest one yet – sunlight. Not the sunlight you get lying on a beach while lackeys bring you free fruit-based beverages, but the sunlight that pours, like an invading army, into my bedroom every summer morning at 4 a.m.

Either I wake up at 4 a.m., the room as bright as day, and can't get back to sleep without wearing sunglasses. Or else I manage to sleep all the way through to about six and wake with my forehead pleated with frowns, my back teeth clamped together, my head pounding and every muscle tensed, in a grim attempt to keep myself asleep, despite the transcendental quality of the morning light.

And it's not as if I don't have a blind. I do. A fine, canvas one. I'd thought it was quite sturdy but lately the light has been making mincemeat of it. It might as well not be there. But that's not the worst bit. Oh no, the worst bit is the thin break between the edge of the blind and the wall. Tiny – but deadly. A razor-thin line of acid-bright light slices through and burns me right on the retinas, so I've big yellow balls in front of my vision for the first four hours of being awake and can't see properly and mistake my athlete's foot cream for toothpaste and gravy powder for coffee and all kinds of other miserable-making things.

The weird thing is that I've been living in my house and sleeping in my bedroom for six years, without ever even *noticing* the big yellow ball in the sky so I can't understand why now, all of a sudden, it's a problette. It's not as if someone has shifted the earth slightly on its axis or moved my bedroom window a few degrees to the east (or have they? Could I be on some reality TV show?) so, reluctantly, I've admitted that it's got to be me.

It wasn't always like this, of course. I remember being young and tolerant. Holidays, backpacking in Greece, waking up in curtainless rooms so bright it was like being in the headbeam of a search helicopter flying over a prison riot, and my response was always, 'Oh look, sunlight, lovely!' In my twenties I spent many happy, curtain-free years in rented flats and it never occurred to me to buy 'window treatments'. Far more important things to spend my money on. Like haircuts. And drink. And cute fur-backed notebooks.

But those happy days are gone and I can no longer take the light so I decided that a black-out blind was the answer. I'd experienced the delights of one in London and, really, I cannot tell you. The room was as dark as a coal-hole even though the sun was splitting the stones outside. A vampire would have pronounced it satisfactory. Not only could no light penetrate the fabric but (my favourite bit) the blind was actually *fitted to the window*, like a painting in a frame, so that I need never again experience my old trouble – the sneaky line of ninja light which pan-fries my retinas every morning.

Full of hope, I rang a blinds' specialist. Their ad went something like, 'Blinds, blinds, blinds! You name 'em, we've got 'em. Your blinds are our command!' Promising, no?

Er, no.

I said to the young man (young man? See how old I'm getting?), 'I'm looking for proper black-out blinds. Do you do them?'

'Indeed, we do.' Said with great confidence.

'You do? That's great. You mean you do the actual black-out blinds that are fitted to a frame in the window?'

There was a pause. It was as if I'd said, 'I was watching this documentary, I think it was called *Star Trek*. And they had this great machine on it, where you could, like, travel vast distances in a few short moments. I'm pretty sure it was called a Beam-me-up-Scotty. Do you stock them?'

Gently, but unable to hide his amusement, the young man said, 'There's no such thing.'

'There is, I saw one in London – '

'There's no such thing,' he repeated, this time a little more firmly. Then he changed tack. 'Unless it's a Velux window you're looking for. Are you?'

'No, just a normal window.'

'Ah right. Then there's no such thing.' He almost added, 'Keep taking the psychotropic medicine,' then hung up. And I just knew that right away he was going to turn to his colleagues and chortle, 'You won't *believe* what I've just been asked.'

I tried somewhere else. Then somewhere else. Each conversation began encouragingly. Yes, they could indeed do black-out blinds. Until I explained I didn't just want some crappy roller-blind with black stuff stuck to the back, and then it all fell apart.

By the fifth place, I'd become a little stroppy (tolerance shot to pieces 'cos of my advancing years, see) and asked the girl why they claimed to do every kind of blind when clearly they didn't. And she answered, all indignant, 'But we do. We do blinds for the roofs of conservatories!' As though that was some sort of huge breakthrough. (Is it? Maybe it is. Not having a conservatory, I wouldn't know.)

It was a black day, I have to admit. I was very discouraged. Suddenly I took agin Ireland. I didn't want to live in some crappy backwater, where they thought blinds on the roofs of conservatories counted as progress. I was going to move to London. Or New York. Or anywhere where I could live in freedom and buy proper black-out blinds.

Then – oh isn't it always darkest just before the dawn? – my friend Eileen's fella gave me a number and I shelved my emigration plans. A man came to measure the window. My proper black-out blind is being fitted in a couple of weeks. I'm beside myself.

First published in Cara, *October 2003.*

We Really Must Get Together This Year

*I*t's not that I hate Christmas – as the season of unlimited chocolate, how could I? And, of course, the presents are nice. Not to mention the trifle on Christmas Day. And it's always cheery to see over-refreshed businessmen wearing big, mad, red antlers, swaying on the train home, oblivious to their head gear.

But, as my mother (devout church-goer) often reminds me, Christmas isn't just about selection boxes and shower gel/body lotion sets of Trésor. No indeed, she's absolutely right; Christmas is about hard bloody work.

I'm not even talking about having to get up before dawn on the big day to stuff turkeys and peel eight thousand potatoes. (Due to an excellent arrangement I have with my mother, we are both in denial about me being an adult. She's the mother, she does the cooking and she has never actually eaten something I've made. Never. Mind you, most people wouldn't.)

No. What kills me about Christmas is having to send cards. What is it about this particular task that makes me want to end my life? Sadness that there are so many people I don't see any more? To my shame, it's more the sheer life-sapping tedium of it all. Especially when people have long addresses. (The worst offenders are those with house names: Traveller's Rest, Formentera Revisited, etc. It's just a waste! A waste of ink, a waste of space and a waste of an extra ten precious seconds of my time!)

I consider my list, an accumulation of dozens and dozens of people whom I think of fondly but haven't seen for fifteen years and no longer have anything in common with, and a terrible lassitude overtakes me. I wish for a small but harmless domestic explosion, anything to get out of doing it. I could explain next year. 'Sorry I sent no card last year but our clothes horse blew up. We were picking knickers off the hedges well into the new year!'

Then there's the challenge of trying to remember the names of people's partners. If they're still with them, that is. Because although I might be dying to ask, Are you still with that weird bloke with the rabbit fixation and the beard that looks like pubic hair? I just can't. I'm supposed to know. And what if they'd had children? A vague half-memory surfaces of being sent a photo of a squashed-looking new-born with a card saying, The world welcomes baby Agatha. Or was it baby Tariq? Or Christ! ... Was it a dog this lot got? However, in such murky circumstances, I've found that a catch-all 'Hope you and the gang are well' usually suffices.

Far trickier is getting the tone right – to convey a message of warm-hearted goodwill so that they'll smile when they open the card and say, 'Aww look, one from Marian. Isn't she lovely?' BUT – and it's a very big but – without being so pally that they'll spontaneously lift the phone and arrange a night out after not having seen me for over a decade.

And so I get to thinking guiltily: this year, would it be so bad if I didn't ...? Who'd miss a card from me when everyone gets so many ...?

And that's it! The decision is made! With a light heart I tell Himself, 'I'm not sending Christmas cards this year. Life is too short.'

'Fine,' he says, 'you've enough on your plate.' I study him carefully to see if he's being sarcastic and I can't be sure, so I go away. Which is when I start thinking: but I really like so-and-so, I want to stay in touch with her, not to actually *see* her, of course, but I wouldn't like us to lose touch. But if I send one to her and don't send one to her sister, then her sister will think I've snubbed her, which indeed I will have, but I wouldn't like her to think I had . . .

The house is filled with Himself's nonreproachfulness. Just because he's sitting at a table methodically inscribing cards to everyone he's ever met doesn't mean he's judging me for not sending any.

Nevertheless, my guilt builds and builds.

Some people get around the hell of card-writing by sending what they insist on calling 'a round robin letter', typed in fake handwriting text – *like this*. They usually begin 'Hello, valued friend.' Or rather, *Hello, valued friend*. And then they tell you about all the fabulous things they've done over the past year, with a load of people you've never heard of. *Back in June, Lacey, Cain and I did a Jin Shin Jyutsu workshop! We're still walking funny!* And I'm thinking: who's Lacey? Who's Cain? What's Jin Shin Jyutsu? These letters always end with something like, *Love, light and blessings to your loved ones and you*, the subtext being 'whoever the hell you are'.

Obviously, it's an idea . . . I could knock something up on the computer, lash out a hundred copies and send them off. Mind you, I'd still have to write the bloody envelopes, never having mastered the printed label thing. That still wouldn't get around the long address, Traveller's Rest-type problem.

Anyway they're kind of creepy and too impersonal and . . . and . . . *American*. Despite my objection to doing Christmas cards, I still prefer to handwrite a personal message. Even if it's the same one on each card. Even if it's always 'We really' – with the 'really' underlined – 'must get together *this* year.'

Then the post yields up the first card of the season, saying 'We really' – with the 'really' underlined – 'must get together *this* year.' And I like the person it's from – although not enough to see them, of course – so I think, I'll just send one back to them. Then the next day five cards arrive, and I'm fond of these people too, so I dash off five 'Really' – with the 'really' underlined – 'must get together *this* year's. And then I'm thinking of all the people I haven't sent cards to and the torment is bad. And anyway, the next day the post brings an avalanche of 'We <u>really</u> must get together *this* year's and I buckle.

I walk into the room where Himself is sitting, innocently watching telly or whatever, and yell at him, 'OKAY THEN, I'll WRITE THE BLOODY THINGS. HAPPY NOW?'

Previously unpublished.

Season of Goodwill (and chocolate)

*C*hristmas comes but once a year and when it comes it brings good cheer. Or in my case, it brings The Fear – because this year, THEY'RE COMING TO ME. Lots of them. Thirteen, in fact. Unlucky for some ... Well, for anyone who might have to eat something I've cooked. I inhabit a fantasy world where there's always a delicious, nutritious casserole simmering away on the hob, so that if anyone pops in unexpectedly I can feed them up and when they – oh so reluctantly – have to leave they get a little goody-bag of my home-made rosemary focaccia to take with them. (In this fantasy I also have Nigella's hair, I'm dressed in a floaty Marni rig, I'm barefoot and sporting several groovy earth-mother toe-rings on my Chanel-painted toes.)

However, reality – that old killjoy – goes like this:

a) I live on convenience foods and Vivioptal and I have to go to my mammy's every Thursday so I get one hot home-cooked meal a week.
b) I wouldn't know one end of a casserole from another.
c) The word 'giblets' makes me dizzy.
d) I tried wearing a toe-ring on my second toe but it managed to trap a nerve, sending shooting pains all the way up my leg and into my back.

See, we all have our gifts and cooking isn't one of mine. But it's not just the thought of sticking my hand up inside a turkey that I dread, it's the coordination involved in preparing a meal – having to have everything ready at the same time gives me a knot in my stomach. I stopped having dinner parties (of convenience foods and Vivioptal, of course) when I realized that even making toast and coffee stresses me; trying to boil the kettle to coincide with the toast popping out of the toaster made me anxious and uneasy.

But for Christmas dinner, I'll be expected to produce turkey, ham, roast spuds, mashed spuds, parsnips, carrots, brusslers, peas, stuffing, bread sauce, gravy – all of them to be hot and edible *at the same time*. It makes me want to crouch in a corner and whimper.

So I'm back again to the eternal question, the one that has plagued me all my life: How Do Other People Do It? How come they were given life's rule book and I missed out? Where was I when God was dispensing capability and cop-on? Looking at shoes, probably.

For a while there I seemed to be getting the hang of this adult lark – I learnt to drive, I got a kidney donor card – but this Christmas business has plunged me back into horribly familiar confusion. Someone (a proper grown-up) advised me that lists were the key to coordination, and briefly that dissipated the dreadful disquiet – I like making lists and I like crossing things off when they're done. (Sometimes I make lists and include a few of the things I've already done, just so I can cross them off and get that warm glow.) But no amount of lists will teach me to cook, so I've taken the bold decision that I'm going to get absolutely *everything* from the turkey to the trifle pre-prepared. I know, I know, it's lazy and extravagant and yes, I feel like a failure. (No change there.) But it's the only option I've got if I want the thirteen of us sitting down to an edible Christmas dinner.

Which brings me to my next problem: *sitting down*. On what exactly? I have four kitchen chairs. Which leaves me nine short, if I've done my sums right. I have two low little pouff yokes, on which the taller guests can sit and rest their chins on the table and there's a step-ladder which converts into a chair. It's extremely unstable in chair form (and also in step-ladder form actually) but it'll have to do. The rest of us will just have to stand. Or maybe we can do it in rotas because I'm after realizing I don't have enough plates either. Dear God . . .

To my shame, it's only now that I understand just how hard my parents worked at Christmas time. There they were, racing around a steam-filled kitchen, preparing all this delicious food, while myself and my siblings were, to a man, thrun in front of Christmas *Top of the Pops*, ploughing through tins of Roses. Having trouble imagining such a thing? Well, let me help. Think of a crèche. Think of the pit of brightly coloured balls that the children roll around in. Well, instead of the brightly coloured balls, think of chocolates.

However, let's not lose sight of what Christmas is really about, because Christmas isn't just about eating yourself sick, Christmas is about something far more important. I'm talking of course of presents! And this is where I come into my own. At the best of times I'm an excellent spender of money; shopping, buying nice things, running up debt – I'm second to none. But I especially love buying presents. It's an opportunity to buy lovely things without the consequent guilt and, instead of feeling like a spendthrift, I feel like a generous, giving person.

Unlike most people (and every other area of my life) I buy my Christmas gifts MONTHS in advance. Contrary to what you might think this is not good.

a) Everyone hates me when I announce at the end of October that I've bought all my Christmas presents. Their faces go all cat's-bum sour and someone usually says, 'Well! Aren't you little Miss Organized?' and you can tell they mean it as an insult.

b) It doesn't save any time at all. The face cream that my mother said she liked, well didn't she only go out and buy it herself in the second week of November? The green cushions I bought to go in my sister's bedroom suddenly became *de trop* when she spent the October bank holiday weekend redecorating and going very much for a pink theme.

c) If I've bought something particularly lovely, I hop around like someone dying to go to the loo, desperate to give it to the recipient there and then. Two years ago I buckled and did just that with a good friend, giving her her Christmas present in early Nov. So when she gave me *my* present several weeks later I didn't understand her expectant face – until she complained to my sister that I'd become very stingy all of a sudden. She'd *forgotten* and it nearly ruined our friendship.

So when you're racing around the shops at four-thirty on Christmas Eve, you're probably just as well off.

Happy Christmas!

First published in the RTE Guide, *December 2002.*

BUT SERIOUSLY

Beyond My Wildest Dreams

In the first volume of Under the Duvet, *I wrote an account of my alcoholism, up to the point where I stopped drinking. But so many people contacted me, wanting to know what happened next, how I came to start writing, etc., that I decided to write the next instalment. Then I began to worry about those readers who didn't know my drinking story: what kind of sense would my recovery make to them? So, to cover all bases, I've written the whole thing in its entirety. My apologies to those who already know all about my adventures on the sauce – just skip it and get to the 'what happened next' bit.*

For as far back as I can remember there was always something wrong. Despite being brought up in an ordinary, loving middle-class family, all my life I sensed I was missing a piece of myself. It knocked me off balance; I was for ever out of step with the rest of the world and I never felt 'normal'. Instead I watched other people being effortlessly 'normal' and tried to copy them, like a foreigner blending in by aping local customs.

The eldest of five, I was a skinny little girl, who was constantly anxious and terrified of just about everything – dogs, boys, being late for school, having to play rounders, having my photo taken (I hated myself, I thought I was the ugliest thing on the planet). Most painful of all was my desperation to be liked – I was an emotional shape-shifter with no sense of self and my unspoken offer to everyone was: tell me who you want me to be and I will be it. Not that such magnanimity worked; frantic though I was to have a best friend, I always seemed to be a grim hanger-on in a triangle with two other girls who were proper friends.

People often ask if something had 'happened' to me. But nothing did – I think I was born this way. Which is to say I think I was born an alcoholic. An alcoholic-in-waiting.

So when, in my teens, I had my first drink, the world shifted on its axis and I fell in love. Giddy, soaring with relief, I *loved* the way alcohol made me feel and suddenly I felt how I thought everyone else felt all of the time. Now I get it, I thought. This is the missing piece of me, my saviour.

Although it took some years before I became physically addicted, emotionally I was in thrall from the word go and throughout the rest of my teens I drank whenever I could. Mind you, it wasn't often – funds didn't run to it – but when I did drink, I drank to get drunk. Chasing oblivion, trying to escape myself – I thought that was what everyone did.

Right from the start, I was waking up with razor blades of dread in my stomach, dying at the memory of something I'd said or done the night before, praying it was only a dream. Shamefaced morning-after phone calls became a feature of my life, a feature that would continue for sixteen years.

But despite all that, I was a conscientious student (too much of a scaredy-cat not to be) and when I left school I went to university and got a law degree. Something I should have been proud of, but I wasn't; as soon as something was associated with me, it became tainted and when everyone else in my class went off to become high-powered lawyers, I showed what a free spirit I was by going to London and becoming a waitress.

Bizarre? Certainly. The act of a person with no self-esteem? Without a doubt. But this was Ireland in the mid-eighties, concepts such as 'self-esteem' hadn't yet been invented.

Eventually I ended up getting a job in a small accounts office, where I radiated resentment for every second of the eight years I was there. Part of my job description was to give out petty cash and I behaved as if it was my own money I was giving away. Clearly I wasn't fulfilled but, where a normal person would just go and get another job, when it came to doing good things for myself, I was paralysed. Besides, I wasn't interested in a career (so I told myself; I told myself this a lot, especially when my flatmates got pay rises and promotions). I was interested in Having A Good Time. And for a long time it was a lot of fun; I was in London, I was young, free and single, there were bars and clubs and parties, there was always someone up for A Good Time and alcohol was a punctuation point to every aspect of my life. Sorrows to drown? Have a drink! Celebrating? Have a drink! Neighbour's dog has died? Have a drink!

All social events were simply excuses to facilitate drinking. There are many, many plays whose second half I haven't seen; I'd get someone in a headlock at the interval and persuade them that it would be much more fun just to stay at the bar.

I drank fast. But so did everyone else. Like most alcoholics,

I'd tried (subconsciously) to surround myself with people who drank as much as I did, so that my drinking wouldn't stand out. In the name of Having A Good Time, there were many nights when I couldn't remember how I'd got home, I'd started waking up covered with unidentifiable bruises (or men), frequently I was too sick to go to work, but I honestly thought that was how it was for everyone.

All the boxes in my life were ticked: I had flatmates, gym membership, a hair-serum obsession, food issues, boyfriends. Okay, so my relationships never worked out. But wasn't that all part of it too? Nights in with my flatmates, drinking Chardonnay, bemoaning the crapness of men.

However, around my late twenties, things started to go very wrong. My behaviour when drunk had started to become ever more extreme and unpredictable; I'd be aggressive or maudlin or in dancing-on-tables, drink-spilling high spirits. I could never tell in advance who I was going to be, but they were all horrible people I didn't recognize.

'I'm sorry' became my most overused phrase and most Monday mornings began with me making fervent promises to my flatmates and my friends and my colleagues and, most of all, myself that I'd never drink again. This was *it*: no more drinking. I'd start going to the gym again, eating healthily, maybe even do a nightclass in something. But sooner or later – and it started to become sooner and sooner – I'd cave in and have a drink and then I was back on the merry-go-round. Once I started I couldn't stop. And once I stopped, I couldn't stay stopped.

Around then the people I had partied with for years began to behave strangely – starting to get married, buy new couches, have children; in short, settling down. Everything was changing and it frightened me – especially as they'd begun to use the word 'alcoholic' about me. Defensively, I bristled that just because I hadn't bought a new couch didn't give them any right to call me an alcoholic. And I really didn't think I was: denial is a massive component of the condition, always one step ahead of me, obscuring the truth, growing as the disease grew, always slightly bigger.

I simply didn't think it was possible for a young woman in her twenties, with a job and a flat and nice shoes, to be an alcoholic. Alcoholics were other people, marginalized people, who had involuntary dreadlocks and shouted at invisible enemies in the street.

But when my friends continued to insist that I was an alcoholic and that I needed help, I cut off contact. I stopped going out and began to drink on my own where there was no one to judge me, and thus began my final descent into full-blown alcoholism. Every weekend I drank around the clock, even waking in the middle of the night to drink. But weekends were starting on Thursday or even Wednesday and spilling over into Monday and Tuesday; I had become – although I wouldn't have known the phrase – a binge drinker.

More and more I was sick and missing work, I'd all but stopped eating and washing myself. I would wake up in the half-light, not knowing if it was dawn or dusk and thoughts of suicide surrounded me like wraiths. Wretched with depression and paranoia, I found the world was a hostile place and I hated leaving my flat because I felt everyone in the street was staring at me. (Which, in fairness, they probably were. I wasn't big on personal grooming at the time.)

At this stage I was down to one flatmate and she'd stopped coming home, too afraid of the state she'd find me in. Occasionally I rang my sister in New York, slurring that I was going to kill myself. Self-centred beyond belief, I was prepared to lose everything; I'd hitched my star to alcohol, my best friend, my lover and I would go wherever it took me.

Incredibly, thanks to a concerned, understanding boss, I still had a job, but other than that, my life was like a blank piece of white paper which was folding in on itself, halving itself again, then again, so that there was almost nothing left.

My depression got blacker and bleaker, my suicidal thoughts got more and more graphic. I used to pray to a God that I didn't believe in that I wouldn't wake up in the morning. And when I did wake, it was as though the jaws of hell had opened.

Throughout this time, I was desperately grateful for alcohol. It seemed like the only good thing in my life, all that stood between me and total misery. I never made the connection that I was miserable because of alcohol.

Then one afternoon, in September 1993, two weeks after I'd turned thirty, when I should have been at work, but instead was at home waiting out the aftermath of yet another binge, killing time until the shaking, nausea and terror had passed, I read a short story in a magazine. It was funny and quirky and something in me responded, 'I'd like to do that.' (People often ask me who wrote the short story, but I don't know, I didn't keep it. I had no clue that a life-altering shift was taking place.)

It was very out of character for me to feel like doing anything other than drinking, but I hunted around my bare little flat, found an A4 notepad and a pen, then sat down and, without stopping from start to finish, wrote a short story. (A sweet little piece about an angel who loses a bet and comes to earth. I was ridiculously proud of it.)

I'd had no idea that I wanted to write but, in retrospect, the timing made sense: my life had become reduced to almost nothing, it was as if I was standing on a piece of land that was getting smaller and smaller, eroded by alcohol, and the crisis had cracked open something buried deep inside me in a last-ditch attempt to stop me disappearing entirely. (Not a route I would recommend for any aspiring writers, but we get what we get.)

Over the next four months I wrote four more short stories, all of them a reflection of my state of mind at the time. One was about a woman who has died and hasn't yet realized; she wanders around in her own life wondering why no one can see her. Another was about a credit card who falls in love with his owner.

I was thrilled with them. I wasn't one of those secretive writers who would die if anyone stumbled across their work – I was practically stopping strangers in the street and pressing my pages on them. But even the writing wasn't enough to stop the drinking and in January 1994, I crashed and burnt quite spectacularly. After a suicide attempt I ended up in a rehabilitation centre in Ireland, being treated for chronic alcoholism.

A case of mistaken identity, I thought. No way was I an alcoholic. Although appalled at the turn my 'life' had taken,

I must admit I was almost excited at the thought of seeing lots of alcoholics up-close in captivity. And there was always the chance there might be a famous face or two.

But rehab was nothing like I expected; after being there for about ten days, the cogs suddenly clicked into place and I was nearly blinded by what I saw. Looking back over my life, it was clear that everything bad in it had been a result of alcohol abuse and every time I had had a drink it had lit an inferno which had annihilated all in its path. The game was up and the only way forward was a life without alcohol. *How had this happened? To me? How would I survive?* The grief was intense. It was like the end of a huge passionate love affair and I raged against it.

And then, six weeks later, I was out. The sun was too bright, noises were too loud, even getting on a bus was frightening. It was as if I was doing everything for the first time and I felt as vulnerable and as raw as a newborn.

But, amazingly, I didn't want to drink. The appalling compulsion which used to sweep over me and frogmarch me into the off-licence, had gone. And there was something else – a tiny glimmer of pride. (A first-time visitor in my life.) I'd had enough of being other people's unpaid floorshow.

I returned to London where, thanks to the extreme generosity of my boss and my colleagues, I still had a job. I also had my flat and being able to slot back into those familiar things was a big help. All my energy was needed to get through a normal day. I was told in the treatment centre that when I had bonded with alcohol in my teens, my emotional development had stopped. It meant that every time I had a disappointment or a row with someone, I didn't live through it and mature from the experience; instead I sidestepped it, either by drinking immediately or by reminding myself that I'd be able to drink at some later stage.

Now that there was no escape, for the first time ever I was having to live life on life's terms. I went to twelve-step meetings, I ate a lot of chocolate, I disappeared into shopping and sleep and Jacqueline Susann novels, but I didn't drink.

And I began writing again. I'd been terrified that I wouldn't be able to write if I wasn't drinking. (That whole tormented artist thing; I'd really liked that version of myself.) But no alcohol was required: someone at a meeting promised me it was perfectly possible to still be a tormented artist without the drink.

Full of positivity I decided I'd send my short stories off to a small Irish publisher, accompanied by a letter saying I'd started work on a novel. However, there was no novel — they took way too long to write, I'd decided. The instant gratification of short stories was far more *me*. But the publishers wrote back; they wanted to see my alleged novel.

I was mortified. In a blind panic, I started to write. I had no plot or character, all I had, was the desire to avoid being caught out in a lie. In under a week, I managed four chapters and, still trying to catch my breath, posted them off. A couple of weeks later they replied — they were offering me a three-book deal.

Six months earlier I'd tried to kill myself; now I had a publishing deal. How weird was that? For the first time ever I had to celebrate without alcohol. (I bought a pair of shoes instead. Nearly as enjoyable.)

But fantasies of being able to waltz out of my day job and into a life of glamour were unfounded. My advance was an un-life-altering six-hundred quid a book, so I fitted my writing around work, writing morning and evening.

In September 1995, my first novel (*Watermelon*) was published in Ireland and did very well. People talked about how funny it was. Even about sad things. In fact, *especially* about the sad things. But I also got a couple of bad reviews, which totally knocked me off balance. I had no coping mechanisms for such public humiliation and immediately – like every time I got upset – I was desperate to drink. But I didn't. Instead I went to bed with two slices of Marks and Spencer chocolate cheesecake and waited for the shame to pass. (A solution which works well to this day.)

In the meantime I'd started work on my second novel, a cheery little comedy about depression. And I'd met a man. A very different kind of man from the ones I'd pursued while I was drinking. Even now I'm afraid to talk about how great he is in case I get nobbled by the Curse of the Smug Girl.

Then in September 1996, things moved up several gears. One afternoon I was at work, trying to balance the sales ledger, when a fax whined out of the machine beside me. It was for me, but it wasn't a copy of an invoice or some other work thing; it was from my agent, saying that a big UK publishing house had just offered lots of money (ten times my annual salary, as it transpired) to publish me. I sat at my desk, my hands shaking, hitting the wrong buttons on my calculator – I still had to balance the sales ledger – wondering if it could be true.

It was and shortly afterwards foreign rights were sold to

Germany, Holland, Sweden and the US. Suddenly I could afford to give up my day job and – above and beyond my wildest dreams – become a full-time writer.

I'd been given a charmed life. But while the outside of my life had been transformed, it was taking a lot longer for my feelings to catch up with the facts. The insecurity and immaturity which had characterized my drinking were still alive and kicking and I felt confused and unworthy.

Like every other time when I'd been knocked off balance, a drink seemed deliciously attractive, but I resisted. At some very deep level I understood that my sobriety was the foundation stone for every other part of my life and if I protected it by going to meetings and sticking close to recovering alcoholics, I'd be okay.

Time passed and my third novel got published, then my fourth, all comedies about dark issues, and their reception humbled me deeply. Paradoxically, writing about feeling disconnected has connected me: I received hundreds of letters, the gist of which was, 'Your books describe exactly how I feel.' This, to the person who once felt she barely belonged to the human race.

Readers told me how well I'd captured their bleakest feelings – and how I'd made them howl with laughter. And for the first time I saw that all those horrible years, mired in alcoholism, hadn't been a complete waste.

And still I didn't drink. I had thought that my sober life would be akin to crawling through a desert for the next forty years, or however long I lived, fixated on alcohol. I thought that I would devote every day to Not Drinking, that it would be a full-time job. But, oddly, it's not an issue. I've disassociated from it entirely – knowing that I can't have *any*, not a single drop, makes it easier.

Mind you, it's very interesting being sober in a world sodden with alcohol. In my early days of recovery I went to the cinema a lot and for the first time noticed that nearly all the ads were for alcohol.

Not everyone understands why I don't drink. After I stopped, I was visiting a friend who hadn't seen me at my worst and she was baffled that I didn't drink any more. Carefully I explained that my body was so sensitized to alcohol that I couldn't take even one mouthful without triggering a blazing desire, that it made me crazy and sick and that I was much better off without it. She listened, nodding carefully, and when I finished she said, 'Of course, of course. But you'll have a glass of wine with dinner, won't you?'

There are other people who don't want to understand – people who probably suspect they might have a problem themselves; fighting off their offers of drink is the hardest.

But in so many ways, life is normal. I had thought I wouldn't be able to be around drinkers, that, green with envy, I'd be watching every mouthful of alcohol that they took and wondering how it was for them. But actually I enjoy it – at least, up until the point when people are telling me the same story for the third time or when they have me hemmed into a corner, telling me glassily that I'm their best friend and that they love me.

Because alcohol was the centre of my life for so long, I couldn't imagine ever having such freedom.

It doesn't mean that I don't crave escape. There are times

when I'm upset or angry or simply would like a night off from myself and half a bottle of wine would unwind me nicely – and it's simply not possible. I'm also sorry that there're all these new-fangled drinks for sale now that I never got to try, like Bacardi Breezers. (I'm told they're not so great, but nevertheless . . .)

And I seem to need more sleep than non-alcoholics. I think I must find full-on reality exhausting because at a certain point every evening I kind of hit a wall and think: that's enough life for one day, now, thanks.

But it's a small price to pay.

Over ten years later, I still haven't had a drink.

It's been an incredible journey. More than ten million copies of my books have been sold worldwide, they're published in thirty-two different languages, I've travelled the globe in the course of my work – but my sobriety is still the most important thing in my life. I know that if I drink again, I might never be able to stop. I got one chance and I treasure it. It's the greatest gift I've ever been given.

A version of this was first published in Marie Claire, *November 2004.*

Concerned

After I expressed interest in their work, the Irish charity Concern,
who work in the developing world, invited me to see some of the
projects they're carrying out in Ethiopia. I visited with Himself
in September 2002.

Thursday 5 September

Himself and myself visit Concern's Dublin office for final
briefing. Suddenly I realize how tough this trip is going to
be, wish I wasn't going and curse myself for ever saying I
would. Despite their assurances that we'll have a great time,
and that there's a lovely market just outside Concern's Addis
compound, I'm not convinced. Himself also has The Fear.

Monday 9 September

9.00 a.m. Leave for airport, to fly to London, then to
Alexandria, then on to Addis Ababa. Delays in London, more
delays in Egypt.

Tuesday 10 September

3.30 a.m. (two and a half hours late) we land at Addis Ababa
airport, then hang around the carousel for a very long time
until it becomes clear that our suitcase hasn't made the journey
with us. But it'll be on the next flight, the nice man tells us.

Which is on Friday. But today is Monday, I protest. Tuesday actually, he says.

All we have are the clothes we stand up in, a copy of *Vanity Fair* (read) and a selection of snacks purloined from an airport lounge. Nothing for it but to go and meet our poor driver who has been waiting outside since one-thirty.

4.45 a.m. Arrive at the Concern compound.

5.00 a.m. Head hits pillow.

5.01 a.m. Cock crows.

5.02 a.m. Another cock crows. Then four hundred of his closest friends get in on the act. A sound system kicks into life blasting Ethiopian pop. Ah yes, the market just beyond the wall.

9.30 a.m. Wake up, put on our dirty clothes and go to introduce ourselves to the Concern staff. It's a gorgeous morning, with blue, blue skies. In the distance I see lush green hills – surely some mistake? Where are the sun-bleached deserts?

Concern staff vair nice, offer to loan us clothes and suggest the market beyond the wall would be a good place to buy underwear, etc. A mixture of fear and curiosity propels Himself and myself through the gates and into downtown Addis and I swear to God, it was like going back to biblical times. A dusty red-earth road teeming with life – tall, elegant men in robes and wellingtons, women with babies tied to their backs, a man wearing a sheep around his neck like a scarf, donkeys laden with enormous bundles of firewood, mad quavery music coming from somewhere. The only non-biblical note was the mini-buses, beeping like mad as they struggled through the packed street, trying to disperse the herds of goats which were loitering in their path. Blankets spread on the roadside were offering all kinds of things for sale: onions, tomatoes, batteries, lengths of twine, chickens (live and unplucked), firewood and – oh great! – socks and knickers. The socks were fine, the knickers less so – baggy and funny-looking. But what the hell! When in Rome. The price for two pairs of socks and two pairs of funny pink knickers? Twenty birr – about two euro. Excellent value. We'd been told to haggle but how could you? On to the next stall where we purchased two pairs of underpants for Himself, a T-shirt for fifty birr and a pair of plastic sandals for me for eighty birr.

12.30 p.m. Decked out in our new and borrowed finery, we set off to see some of the Concern projects. Addis is a city at first sight constructed almost entirely of corrugated iron; miles and miles of shanty town, holes in the rotting iron patched pitifully with rush matting and polythene bags. Almost all roads are untarmacked: just bare lumpy earth like boreens, which I've never before seen in a city. And everywhere there are people – it's incredibly densely populated. An estimated five million people live in Addis.

Our first stop was at a community-based urban development programme, where Concern are working with the poorest of the poor – women-headed households and households with more than ten members – to construct houses, communal kitchens, water points, latrines and roadways. Concern provide most of the funding but the community provide the labour and become responsible for maintaining the common areas.

One of the many people I met was a beautiful woman called Darma – by and large the Ethiopians are extremely good-looking. Darma has nine children, her husband is 'gone' and she's younger than me. With great pride she ushered us into her new house, a ten-by-ten room with a packed-earth floor, no electricity and no running water. With a smile she indicated the roof – 'no holes so no rain gets in'. Which would turn the mud floor into a quagmire. I was beginning to understand. The sturdy walls provoked another smile – 'secure against rats'. Gotcha.

Darma's day begins at six when she prepares breakfast for herself and her children. This is harder than it sounds. The staple diet is injera: a bread that's made from a grass called teff, which has to be pounded into a paste – which takes up to two hours – and then cooked. Before Concern funded the communal kitchens – one between three households – Darma had to light a fire in her chimney-less home, filling it with choking smoke and upsetting her children.

After breakfast, Darma sets off on the half-hour walk to the wholesale market, buys potatoes and onions, then returns and sells them in her own neighbourhood. At six she comes home and once again pounds teff until her hands blister. She goes to bed at about midnight.

But life is so much better, she says. She has the kitchen, the communal water point – which saves an hour a day walking to buy water – and most of all, her house. I was humbled by her positivity and I hoped I'd think twice the next time I wanted to say, 'I've had a hard day.'

Before I left I was invited to admire the latrines, which I did as best I could – I mean, what do you *say*? – and then it was on to a clinic which feeds and treats thirty-six malnourished children. By the time we arrived, they'd left, which I was shamefully glad about. I didn't think I was able for the sight of three dozen malnourished babas.

Back in the Concern house I suddenly remembered that today was my birthday. Himself's present for me was in the awol suitcase. However, he gave me a celebratory Club Milk that he'd nicked from the Aer Lingus lounge in Dublin. I was very happy.

Wednesday 11 September

New Year's Day. And 1995, no less. Something to do with a dispute over the date of the birth of Christ. Great hilarity (at least on my part) as Himself dons his Ethiopian knickers – very little and snug, Bruce Lee circa 1977. Great hilarity (at least on his part) as I don mine – baggy and mad, like a granny's.

11.00 a.m. Visit a Concern-funded project which aims to educate and train girls. This is a very macho society and I'd been told that Ethiopian women would have a better life if they'd been born a donkey. They have much less chance of receiving an education than a man yet often end up being the main breadwinner as well as doing the 'invisible' work like childcare, taking care of sick relatives, cooking, carrying water and tending the animals.

This project nails its colours firmly to the mast with the sign on the office wall: 'God created man before woman. The reason why? Every artist does a rough draft before creating a masterpiece.' Right on, sisters!

We visit a girls' school they're building; it will provide education for 200 pupils when it opens in late September. Dozens of amber-eyed children appear from nowhere, to shake hands (even the toddlers do it) and have their photo taken.

3.30 p.m. On to a vocational skills training project for street children. There are an estimated 60,000 children and young mothers living permanently on Addis Ababa's streets, where they're at the mercy of anyone and everyone, including the police. This project aims to train them in all kinds of disciplines – from driving to metalwork to office skills – and make them employable.

I was introduced to a twenty-year-old girl, a graduate of the programme. She looked like Lauryn Hill – like, *exquisite* – and asked me not to use her name. Her story is that both her parents died when she was sixteen and she had to take care of her three sisters and two brothers by washing clothes and gathering and selling firewood. Her income was so low that prostitution was the next step, either for herself or for her younger sisters. But instead she managed to get a place on a training course. Now she earns 340 birr a month as a cook (good money, honestly), is able to rent a house for herself and her siblings and is going for lessons in computers and paying for herself.

When I asked her what her parents had died of, she bowed

her head, began to cry and didn't answer. Later the director of the programme told me that she has never said, but he suspects they died of Aids. Despite at least one in ten and maybe as many as one in six adult Ethiopians being infected with HIV, there's such a stigma that few will admit to being affected by it.

Among the many other success stories of the project is that two ex-street children are working for Ethiopia's previous president as a cook and a housekeeper.

It was an uplifting and energizing day. Back at the ranch, we watched *The Young and the Restless*, a spectacularly awful American daytime soap, and spent a happy hour trying to figure out which ones were the young and which ones were the restless. It was strangely compelling.

Thursday 12 September

5.30 a.m. Several of us left in a packed four-wheel drive for Damot Weyde, a six-hour drive to the south. This area was the scene of a famine in 2000 and this year the rains didn't come so the maize harvest has failed and once again the people are facing a famine.

On the drive down we passed field after field of burnt dead maize. But other than that, the countryside was spectacularly beautiful: ranges of huge mountains layered against the blue sky and, apart from the dead maize, it was surprisingly green; lots of trees. When I asked why they didn't cut the trees down to use the land for food, I was told that the trees were necessary to prevent soil erosion, already a huge problem which further exacerbates drought.

Also contributing to the look of lush vegetation is a plant

called insett or 'false banana'. It's a slow-growing but drought-resistant plant which has the huge wax leaves of the banana plant but only the roots are edible. (After being pounded for three hours.) So although the area is facing a famine, it's called a 'green famine'.

Always the roadsides were swarming with people; even though it's rural it's extremely densely populated – 250 people per square kilometre. Twice we passed people carrying a stretcher, making their way with a sick friend or relative to the nearest clinic.

9.30 a.m. Stopped for breakfast in Shashemene, a town which has a large Rastafarian community. I had to restrain Himself. He's always nursed a desire to run away and become a Rasta.

midday Arrive at Concern's compound. It's twenty kilometres off a tarmacked road and has no phone line. But there is electricity and as everyone kept telling me – their faces aglow – there's a shower, a *hot* shower. And a toilet, I asked anxiously. Yes, I was told. Well, an outside latrine, which is the same thing really. I'm not really an outside-latrine kind of girl. Well, I was about to become one.

1.30 p.m. After a quick lunch we head off to visit a spring that Concern had built. However, it had been raining and the four-wheel drive got stuck in the mud. We all had to get out and as I clambered down I landed on a donkey, who gave me a patient, I-won't-hold-it-against-you look and carried on up the hill.

We turned back and instead went to visit an Animatrice (I think that's how it's spelt) – a local woman who'd been trained by Concern to teach her community about nutrition and hygiene but most importantly to take care of malnourished children. Previously, if a child was malnourished, the mother would go to a Concern feeding centre where she and the child would stay until they were both healthy. This could take up to three weeks. Meanwhile, no one was at home to take care of the woman's other children and, moreover, the mother had no opportunity of earning money during that time. This scheme is a way of avoiding that and of handing control and responsibility to the community. All of Concern's work is about 'sustainability'; they are enabling the community to do things for themselves, so that when they leave (all non-governmental organizations have to move on after three years) the locals will be well able to look after themselves.

But the Animatrice was nowhere in sight. They'd all gone to 'the weeping' – a lyrical way of describing a funeral. Right so, we said, girding our loins. We'll visit the Kerchech health clinic.

Back into the four-by-four and after another bumpy hour on muddy roads we arrived at the three-roomed clinic. At the same time a young woman called Erberke showed with her husband, Bassa, and their sick baby girl, Jelsalem. They'd walked for forty minutes in their bare feet to reach us because Jelsalem was passing blood; she was fifteen months old, but she was so stick-like and shrunken that she looked a good year younger. Bassa was wearing what might have been Farrah slacks once upon a time but was now a collection of rags held together with yellow twine. I'd seen so many sad things but for whatever reason this was the one that did it for me. I couldn't stop crying.

Dr Degu Tinna, who runs the clinic and visits patients on the motorbike that Concern purchased, examined Jelsalem and found she was 75 per cent of the weight she should be, but she wasn't showing signs of oedema (protein deficiency). He gave antibiotics; the local method for dealing with a baby with diarrhoea is to burn the baby's stomach. (Likewise eye infections are 'treated' by branding the temples.) I went into the horrors at the thought that if the clinic hadn't been there, Jelsalem would have died.

8.00 p.m. Dinner that night was the famous injera bread. It was grey and looked like a rolled-up sponge but tasted nice. Had to get up twice in the night to use the outside latrine. Didn't get eaten by leopards.

Friday 13 September

7.00 a.m. Set off to visit another spring but once again got bogged down in the mire. This time we pressed on and arrived at 9 a.m. Yay!

The spring was a godsend – clean water for washing, cooking and most importantly drinking. Before the spring was built the only option was the dirty water from the nearby river – so filthy that a glass of it looked like drinking chocolate.

It was all go at the spring. Ofusi, a thirteen-year-old stunner, was washing her family's clothes – scrubbing like billy-o with a bar of soap. Salem, a ten-year-old girl, was filling a five-litre container of water for her home an hour's walk away.

But what I noticed most was that a lot of the children clustering around me looked sick. Their teeth were brown and most of them seemed to have an eye infection. Flies were landing in babies' mouths and some of the children's skin was patchy and piebald-looking. I thought I remembered reading that this was an indication of severe lack of protein. I was looking first hand at the effects of chronic food deprivation. They pressed closer and closer to me, but remained silent, and for the first time since I'd arrived in Ethiopia I felt slightly freaked out.

On the way back we passed several women working in the fields, including one called Tefari who was seven months pregnant. Then we got to meet Itanish the Animatrice; the work she was doing with the women in her area would make sure that the malnourished children would get better. This cheered me up.

11.00 a.m. Drive back to Addis.

5.00 p.m. Our suitcase had arrived! Because I'd had a week living with just the basics I'd suspected that I'd have no interest in it, but I'm sorry to say how wrong I was. I fell on it like it was a long-lost friend and marvelled at my lovely things. My face cream! My sunglasses! My anti-malaria tablets!

6.30 p.m. An open-air concert to raise awareness of HIV/ Aids among the young and homeless in the Merkato area (a huge market that has a lot of prostitution). I thought it would be a bit worthy and crap but I swear to God I've never seen anything so gorgeous. On stage three slender elegant boys and three lush colleens were in traditional dress and dancing like Irish people wouldn't be able to dance if they practised for a million years. Imagine people receiving electric shocks but *gracefully* and you get some idea of how wonderful they were. And they were having such fun, it was a delight to behold. The concert (a monthly event) is the brainchild of a very energetic, intelligent man called Anania Admassu who runs a Concern-funded project which helps Aids orphans. There are a huge number in Addis – 1,000 in the Merkato area alone.

Saturday 14 September

9.30 a.m. Visited Concern's Street Vendors Programme, which gives basic business skills and low-interest, collateral-free loans to the poorest street traders (nearly always women). Hundreds of women have had their lives changed by this programme and most of them have even managed to start saving.

Part of the programme has involved the construction of several latrines and I was invited to visit a couple. Well, I don't know about you, but one latrine is much the same as the other as far as I'm concerned and though they tried to talk me out of it I stood my ground. They were disappointed, but I think they got over it.

2.00 p.m. Last gig. A visit to Mekdim, an association run and staffed by HIV-positive people, who provide education, medical help, counselling, home nursing and funeral expenses for those with the virus.

HIV/Aids is a huge, huge problem in Ethiopia. Because of extreme poverty many women have no choice but to become prostitutes – it's either that or let themselves and their children starve. Nor is the situation helped by the attitude of the government who, until recently, were in denial. Now, rather late in the day, they've admitted that the problem has reached epidemic proportions.

Mekdim is run by Tenagne Alemu, a charismatic man who has lived with the virus for thirteen years – 'drug free' everyone kept telling me before I met him. Like an eejit I thought he was drug-free to make some kind of point. But not at all. He is drug-free because he can't afford the drugs. The miracle anti-retroviral drugs that are saving the lives of the thousands and thousands of HIV-positive people in the developed world are way beyond the reach of Ethiopians.

I met one of the home-care givers. She was a beautiful and articulate twenty-nine-year-old who discovered she was HIV positive when her three-year-old daughter became sick and died. No one could tell her what her daughter had died from, but she'd heard about 'the sickness' and suspected the worst. Her husband had been her first sexual partner, so she'd caught it from him. As you can imagine, her life fell apart. She divorced him and was going to kill herself but then she heard that Mekdim were looking for people to train as home-care givers.

She is constantly coming down with infections. She's ostracized by her peers. (She wouldn't let me take her photo because she got harassed enough, she said.) There are anti-retroviral drugs which can cure her but aren't available in Ethiopia because they're so expensive. And the number of those infected with the virus – particularly women – continues to escalate.

'I'm angry,' she said with vehemence. 'I'm always so angry. Will you tell the people in Ireland we need their help?' she asked. I said I would.

See www.concern.ie *for more information.*

First published in the Sunday Independent, *November 2002.*

Rebuilding Children

In the summer of 2003, I became patron of To Russia With Love. *This is the story of how the charity started and a trip I made to Russia in January 2004. All royalties from the Irish sales of the hardback of* Further Under the Duvet *are going to this charity.*

When we first arrived there were no mirrors, so none of the children knew what they looked like. Before we left we hung up a group photo of them, but the next time we came, the photo was full of holes: all the children had cut out their own face. It was the only image they had of themselves and we kept finding them under their pillows, in their pockets, all over the place . . .

These are the words of Debbie Deegan, an ordinary Dublin housewife, who, on a whim seven years ago, decided to take two Russian orphans into her home for a short Irish holiday, with no idea that it would change her life. But within days she'd fallen in love: no way could she send these little girls back. As 'luck' would have it, one of the seven-year-olds, Zina, caught meningitis, was too sick to travel home and had to stay in Ireland. But the other girl wasn't so 'lucky', no meningitis for her; when the two weeks were up she had to return to the orphanage. And that, Debbie thought, would be that. Fat chance. She was tormented that she'd sent the girl back and eventually, over a year later, she buckled and decided she had to go to Russia to track her down.

Not knowing a word of Russian, she flew to Minsk, and managed to make her way to Bryansk, a city eight hours south-west of Moscow, and finally she found the orphanage, Hortolova. As she admits herself, she was clueless, in no way prepared for what awaited her. 'It was crumbling, filthy, the stench was indescribable, the toilets were broken and the bathrooms were just one big toilet.' Almost worse than the physical privations was that the children had no sense of self or identity: they literally didn't know what they looked like. She was carried out of there, 'a basket case'.

Which was no use to anyone, she admitted. She arrived back in Ireland determined to rebuild the orphanage. Her friends and family – like most sensible people – tried to talk her out of it and waited for the rush of blood to the head to pass. She'd no connections, they pointed out to her, no money, no understanding of the Russian system. But sometimes ordinary people pull off extraordinary things. She started with a coffee morning and raised an astronomical nine grand. (Mind you, you'd want to meet Debbie – her energy, her compassion and her vision would persuade anyone of anything. She's a force of nature.)

Two months later she returned to Hortolova with a team of surveyors and builders to see how best they could rebuild the orphanage. There were 150 children, aged six to eighteen and Debbie was determined to make everything shiny and new for them. However, she'd planned on a quick in and out, and once everything was fixed, to withdraw and return to her old life.

But it was already too late because she'd become involved with the children and her focus had shifted: it was no longer about rebuilding the crumbling bedrooms, it had become, much more importantly, about rebuilding the children.

And God knows they needed rebuilding. Their backgrounds are often so horrific it's hard to believe we're talking about real people – like Lena, whose mother tried to sell her in the marketplace, as if she was an animal. And Vika, who witnessed her father killing her mother's lover. Or Sergei, who is almost blind, has TB and was a heavy smoker from the age of five. Many of these children hadn't had any affection in years, if ever, and Debbie's instinct as a mammy was that often what they needed more urgently than anything else was a hug.

That was the start of To Russia With Love. Six years on, they've rebuilt the boys' block, the kitchen, the laundry, they've added a little medical block and a life skills centre – and completely transformed the lives of all the children.

Last summer Debbie invited me to visit Hortolova, along with thirty other people – mostly fund-raisers and sponsors. The plan was to go in early January, in time for the Russian Christmas, bringing sackfuls of presents; 'Santy', the full nine yards.

I agreed to the visit so long in advance that at the time I'd never really believed it would ever happen (you know how it is). But as it drew nearer the dread kicked in. Himself was coming with me and having no children of our own I was afraid we'd start filling our suitcase with orphans to bring home. A week before the off I got the flu and I tried mind over matter to work it up into something really debilitating like pleurisy, so that I couldn't travel, but nothing doing.

We landed in Moscow just as it started to snow. (Debbie has a super-efficient Russian right-hand man called Igor. Rumour has it he can fix anything. Debbie had mentioned that the first impressions the group got of Russia would be enhanced if there was snow. Apparently Igor had a word . . .)

At the baggage carousel there was a moment of panic when it looked like Santy's red rig-out hadn't made the trip but, just before we all started sewing our red hats together, it turned up and off we went. A long journey south-west to Bryansk followed and at 4 a.m. we checked into our (surprisingly nice) hotel.

The following morning, at eleven, the orphanage bus arrived to collect us, bearing a ten-year-old emissary: Polina, our first orphan. She was a chirpy, chatty sweetheart with the look of a young, far less surly Kate Moss. She was thrilled to be the one allowed to escort us and when Santy clambered onto the bus, she nearly lost her life. Later on she told me, quite matter-of-factly, that her mother had abandoned her when she was two months old; apparently her mother has now gone on to have a new family with someone else 'far, far away' and never contacts Polina. She arrived at Hortolova when her dad was sent to prison. Many of the 'orphans' aren't orphans in the traditional sense; instead they're 'social orphans' in that one or maybe both of their parents are still alive but have been deprived of parental rights for various reasons – usually neglect due to alcoholism. However, her father has since been killed and Polina went to heartbreaking pains to let me know that her dad had been 'a good man'.

Then we arrived and, on the face of it, the orphanage didn't look grim. It wasn't one big gloomy Dickensian-looking institution, but a collection of single-storey cottage-type buildings, set in a fir forest sprinkled with snow. Even the dogs – silver-haired, blue-eyed wolf-lookalikes – added to the whole fairy-tale-with-an-edge effect.

Lots of the children were waiting, in Santy hats, as excited as if . . . well, as if it was Christmas morning . . .

When we got off the bus I was shocked to see that there was also a Russian Santy – in orange velvet, a faceful of make-up and with a much more impressive beard than our fella. I feared a Santy-off; the two Santys circled each other warily, eyeing each other's sacks, then made peace and we all went inside for the present-giving.

Debbie had told me that the children were very affectionate and would keep hugging me; but hearing that kind of creeped me out. I thought it sounded really sad – that they were so starved of affection that they'd fling themselves at any passing stranger like a sackful of needy puppies. But, as it happened, it was nothing like that. In the gift-giving melee, I bumped into Polina, the chipper little girl I'd met on the bus, and we had a moment when we grinned at each other and had a spontaneous squeeze. And as the days passed, I clicked better with some of the children than others (which is exactly as it should be) and when we met we hugged like old friends. Meanwhile Himself had 'his' children.

What really depressed me was how alcoholism featured in so many children's stories. I met Tatiana; beautiful, blue-eyed, fair-haired. She's only fourteen, but looks much older, at least eighteen, and has an unusual serenity about her, probably a consequence of surviving so much so young. She has an eleven-year-old sister, Luba, a bit of a handful, whom she evidently frets about. Their mother had died 'from drink-ing' but their father is still alive, living in a flat in the town, and Tatiana visits him once a month. She told me she worries a lot about him. He has sold all his furniture to buy alcohol and there is never any food in the flat. 'He needs to eat,' she told me. 'I worry because he doesn't eat.' I sat there, looked at her mutely and thought: you're *fourteen*. I thought I'd choke from grief.

Oddly enough, the children who moved me the most weren't children at all, but the teenage boys. And that's kind of strange because I'm vaguely terrified of teenagers. I remember myself at that age – confused, angry, scornful of adults – and I so live in dread of saying something inane or stupid to make them roll their eyes and whisper, '*Christ!*' that I tend to give them a wide berth. But the lads here were very pally – and astute. They noticed that Himself was wearing a Watford hat (his football team) and by a really strange coincidence, while we were actually at the orphanage, Wat-ford were playing Chelsea on the telly. Since they've been managed by Abramovich, Chelski seems to have become Russia's second national team. A battalion of lads came to ferry Himself off to watch the match with them, but I insisted he remain on photo-taking duty (I'm so mean). They exchanged a mano-a-mano 'Women!' look with Himself and every time someone scored, a scout was dispatched to keep him informed. It was all so *normal* and that's what made it so sad.

Maybe it's wrong to have favourites, but anyway I did. He was Andrei, aged seventeen and, like Tatiana, another 'caretaker' child. He too has a younger sibling, a brother called Dima, who's fifteen and has had a series of breakdowns. Their mother was deprived of parental rights because of her drinking and their dad was beaten to death after being released from prison. For a long time Andrei was afraid to break the news to Dima and, although he took it badly, he now knows. Andrei is a natural peace-maker and his ambition is to work as a car mechanic because he loves cars. His favourite car is a BMW and Debbie had to take me aside and warn me sternly that I was NOT to buy one for him. I mean, as *if* . . . okay, the thought *had* crossed my mind, but I wouldn't *really* have . . .

The thing is, though, you'd give these children anything, you'd cut your heart out for them. I'd expected they might be difficult, bratty, withdrawn – who could blame them considering what they've already endured in their short lives? But they were variously charming, polite, mischievous, earnest, sweet, thoughtful, affectionate and above all – and most moving – dignified. I couldn't get over it. And it's entirely down to Debbie and her team; even though there are 150 children in Hortolova, they're all treated like individuals, just as they would be in a family. I was very moved by the myriad humane little touches, the thoughtfulness, the treats – like taking a load of the lads to Moscow for the Russia v Ireland match. Or like giving children choices. Most orphans have no say in what they eat, what they wear, where they sleep: they get what they get and they can like it or lump it. But Hortolova children are brought to the market and allowed to pick out their own clothes. Mind you, when this first started, the children were completely unable to do it, they were so paralysed by lack of practice that the market visits took *for ever*.

Unlike other orphanages, the Hortolova children get to visit their siblings. Russian orphanages are – er, *why?* – run by the Department of Education, so children are 'sorted' according to their academic ability. The brighter ones are sent to one orphanage, the middling ones to another, etc., and it makes no difference if two children are from the same family. If one is smarter than another, they're sent to different places and that's that. A staggering 60 per cent of children in orphanages have siblings in other orphanages and to ameliorate the brutality, Debbie introduced the Sibling Programme: every Sunday the bus goes off, bringing Hortolova children to see their brothers and sisters.

And every child has an Irish sponsor family, who give 150 euro a year to cover things like new clothes, glasses, any emergency extras. More importantly, they exchange letters, birthday cards and photos to give them a sense of belonging, of mattering to someone, somewhere.

A hairdresser comes regularly, so does a dentist and a psychologist, and in the life skills centre the children are taught everything from how to put petrol in a car (they practise on half a Lada that someone found somewhere) to how to cook. On our final day, all the eight-year-olds cooked and served us our tea with heartbreaking earnestness.

Paradoxically the more that gets done at Hortolova, the more that needs to get done; the bar is constantly being raised. Some Hortolova children are very, very bright – three girls and one boy are being given extra tuition in an attempt to get them into university. If it happens it will be the first time any of the orphans has gone to university. Some of the older boys are preparing to leave (they're legally obliged to when they're eighteen) so the Challenger Programme has been introduced to build their self-esteem, to de-institutionalize them (until recently no such concept existed in Russia, it was literally impossible to translate) and to prepare them for the outside world.

Meanwhile TRWL is also spreading its nets in other directions. They're matching up children in other orphanages with Irish sponsor families. And Debbie has just taken on the mammoth task of Bryansk orphanage, a Dickensian place housing 350 children, where many of the teenagers are already showing problems with alcohol. Lots done, more to do, as someone once said . . .

My visit to Hortolova was life-changing, a trip I feel profoundly privileged to have made. The funny thing is, I'm not a crier, not even when I'm very sad – Himself (a man) usually cries much more than me. But I shed more tears in five days in Russia than I have in the rest of my life put together. It got to the point where it was actually embarrassing, I was making such a show of myself. It wasn't just the children's stories, heartbreaking and all as they were. What moved me most was their innate dignity. Despite all that had happened to them, they were such sweet, hopeful little human beings. Like a cluster of clean, bright flowers in a burnt-out land.

See www.torussiawithlove.ie for more information.

First published in the Sunday Independent, *March 2004.*

SHORT STORIES

Mammy Walsh's Problem Page

Those of you who have read any books featuring the Walsh family will be familiar with Mammy Walsh. I hope others will enjoy this too.

Introducing Mammy Walsh, mother, wife, home-maker, troubleshooter. She won't dress it up, she won't tone it down. Mammy Walsh tells it like it is.

Hello everyone, my name is Mammy Walsh. Send me in your problems and I'll do my best to help. Now, just so as you know, I haven't had any official training. Instead I have learnt at 'the university of life' – in other words I have five daughters who, at various times, have been a heartscald to me. My eldest, Claire, she was always a bit wild, but she got married and got pregnant and I thought she was all set up until that scut of a husband of hers ran off on her the day she had her first child. I mean, it all worked out in the end but at the time it was no fun, let me tell you.* Then the middle daughter, Rachel, decides she has a drug problem and has to go to this rehab place that cost a bloody fortune.† Myself and Mr Walsh could have gone on the Orient Express to Venice and stayed in that Chipper-iani place for a month for the same money. Then, and this

---

* You can read about it in *Watermelon*.
† You can get the gory details in *Rachel's Holiday*.

was the biggest shock of all, Margaret, the only good daughter, does a runner on her – admittedly, dull as ditchwater – husband and hightails it to Los Angeles where her pal Emily lives.* Anna, the second youngest, was always a bit away in the head. To be perfectly honest I thought she had a bit of a lack. But it just goes to show because, after years of being useless, isn't she after getting a great job in New York, working for a cosmetic house. You've probably heard of them, they're a 'hot' brand called Candy Grrrl and me and the rest of the girls get a rake of free stuff, often before they're even on sale in the shops. We're all very proud of her, even though it's still a bit hard to believe. And Helen, the youngest, she was another one that was worse than bloody useless but now she's after getting a great job too. She's a private investigator, 'a private eye' we sometimes call her, or 'a PI'. (Or 'a pain in the backside' Mr Walsh is telling me to put in, although that's just his little joke.) Sometimes, when she's very busy, she begs me to go 'on stake-out' with her and if it's not my bridge day, of course I do, because I don't like to let her down. Twice I've helped her break into people's apartments and look for documents and yokes, and I'm telling you something, you wouldn't *believe* the dirt of other people's houses when they're not expecting visitors. Of all my daughters, Helen probably has the best job – apart from the night that someone threw a brick through our sitting-room window during *EastEnders* to 'put the frighteners' on her.

Q. *Dear Mammy Walsh, I am writing to you because I have no one else to turn to. I think my wife is having an affair. We've been married only seventeen months, but five times in the last*

* You can get the fully story in *Angels*.

month there have been tyre marks in our drive that aren't from my car. They might be from a Saab. (I drive a Ford Mondeo.) Then I found a small piece of foil wrapper under my pillow which looks like it belongs to a condom packet, but not a brand I use. Also my next-door neighbour has taken to looking at me very sympathetically, like someone has died, and he has never been that pleasant before now – he didn't invite my wife and me to his homebrew evening. I really love my wife and this suspicion is doing my head in. I've asked her straight out if anything is going on, but she has denied it. What should I do?

David, Dublin

A. Dear David from Dublin, you're in luck. I can indeed help you. My youngest daughter, Helen, is a private investigator and she specializes in just this kind of work. I believe her rates are quite high, but this is because she is amoral and has no fear of breaking the law. However, I can ask her as a favour to me if she'll knock a couple of euro off. She gets great results; she sets up cameras in bedrooms and catches people up to all kinds of shenanigans. Also she hides in garden hedges and photographs people going in and out of houses. I wish she wouldn't do this, she's always catching throat infections and I'm the one who has to listen to her whingeing. She also happens to be very 'good-looking' and men are forever falling in love with her; there's a chance that you might too and the situation with your wife would no longer matter. It's only fair to tell you, however, that in such an eventuality, Helen will still charge you.

PS I spoke to Mr Walsh and he tells me that Saabs are very good cars, much better than Ford Mondeos. Actually he said Saabs were 'sexy', which I find highly annoying. Everything has to be 'sexy' these days. Tell me, how is a car 'sexy'? Bottoms are 'sexy' (or can be). Eyes are 'sexy'. Not white couches or risotto or indeed cars . . . Sorry, I lost my train of thought there, where was I? Oh right, Mr Walsh says – and I can only apologize if this sounds harsh but I'm just passing on what he said – he said if he was a woman he'd sleep with the man with the Saab.

Q. *Dear Mammy Walsh, I wonder if you could advise me. I have a boyfriend whom I love very much. We've been seeing each other for over two years and recently we moved in together. Last night he told me that his parents, who live in Nottingham, are coming to spend the weekend with us. This is not really a problem, the problem is that he says his mother will expect me to cook a large roast on Sunday, and I am a vegetarian. I find meat disgusting, and the thought of even touching it makes my skin crawl. However, my boyfriend is quite insistent that I must do this; his mother won't approve of me if I don't, he says. What should I do? Should I insist that he cooks the roast lunch and pass it off as my efforts?*
Angie, London

A. Are you off your skull? Do you want your flat burnt to the ground? Men are hopeless in the kitchen, everyone knows that. No, you need to cop on to yourself and knock off that vegetarian nonsense. My middle daughter, Rachel, was a vegetarian for a while, but she was only looking for notice. Then she became a drug addict and tried to kill herself and was able to stop being a vegetarian because she got all the attention she needed. The thing is, Angie, that meat is delicious, there is no point in a dinner without it and you need it to get iron and other essential nutrients. Otherwise, you'll get ear infections and dropsy, and who'll end up running up and down the stairs minding you? That's right, your mammy. Start with some chicken – Marks and Spencer do some very tasty all-in-one dinners – and before you know it you'll be on the fillet steak! Good luck!

A Moment of Grace

Monday

I am an angel. Go on, have a good laugh, but, really, I am. An angel. A proper, fully paid-up heavenly one with wings, halo, the whole lot.

And I'm in Los Angeles on a mission. A mission from God, since you ask.

Which all sounds very important but, to be honest, the reason I'm here isn't such a great one. Some angels just have a natural aptitude for the job. I, unfortunately, am not one of them so I've been sent to earth on a training course. In order that I can help humans I need to understand them. So while I'm here I have to commit – but not too enthusiastically, of course – each of the seven deadly sins. I've got seven days to do it in.

'Envy, Sloth, Greed,' Ibrox, my superior, listed off, 'Gluttony, Anger, Envy – no, I said Envy already, didn't I? I can never remember the seven. It's the same with the seven dwarves, I can usually do five, then I just draw a blank. You try.'

'Grumpy, Dopey, Snee –'

'No! The seven deadlies.'

'Sorry. Okay, Greed, Envy, Sloth, Anger, Gluttony . . .' I looked at him helplessly.

'Pride,' he supplied. 'And you'll remember the seventh.'

So off I went. And here I am in Silverlake, Los Angeles, standing outside the apartment which is going to be home for the next week. Apparently I've been recommended by a friend of a friend of a friend and I will have two flatmates – Nick, an actor who plays a lot of psychopaths, and Tandy, an actress who gets offered slutty-girl roles a lot.

I rang the bell. No one came. I rang again and heard some muffled shouting from inside. Then a man wrenched open the door. 'What?' He was a *mess* – wild hair, wild eyes, horrible smell. Looks like this Nick is a method actor.

I stuck out my hand and stapled on a smile. 'I'm Grace and you must be Nick!'

'And you must be out of your mind,' he growled. 'Nick lives next door.'

'Ah . . . right . . . sorry.' See what I mean about me being crap at my job? Imagine if I was the Archangel Gabriel? I'd probably call at the wrong house and tell the wrong woman that she was the mother of God. I'll never make the big time, not if I carry on like this.

I moved one apartment along and a woman I assumed must be Tandy answered the door. She gave me a speedy but thorough once-over and when she saw that she was thinner than me, she visibly relaxed, then smiled. 'Come on in.'

She was really, really pretty, but I could see why she kept getting the hooker-type roles. Her lips were so pneumatic they looked as if they were about to burst and she was X-ray skinny, apart from a very large pair of breasts which clearly belonged on a different body.

'Nick, come and say hey to your new roommate,' she called.

In came Nick. I took one look at him and remembered the elusive seventh sin. Lust!

'Hey,' he said vaguely.

Hey, indeed!

Dark-haired, gangly, loose-limbed, and his eyes had a not-known-at-this-address distance to them. Just out of curiosity, I wondered if I was his type. I look a bit like those Renaissance paintings of angels, except without the halo, the wings and the nakedness – no need to freak people out, I always say. But I've all the other stuff – blonde curly hair, a round, rosy-cheeked face and I'm a little plumper than they generally seem to like them in Los Angeles.

Just then a girl emerged into the room after Nick. She was weeping.

'Nick –' she beseeched, trying to grab on to him. She was sloe-eyed, silky-haired and tiny; with a sudden, fierce passion I wanted to be her.

'Take care, baby.' He steered her, very firmly, to the door. 'Missing you already.'

'But –' she tried again. Nick kissed her tenderly on her forehead, while managing to deposit her in the hallway.

From the way Tandy rolled her eyes at me, this clearly happened a *lot*.

Nick clicked the door shut, waited, tensed against a storm of crying and yelling from outside, then relaxed when nothing happened. She'd obviously decided to limp away and lick her wounds quietly.

'Why do I always hurt those I love?' he enquired of no one in particular, then absent-mindedly left the room.

Suddenly I was very glad I *wasn't* that dainty, exquisite girl.

'Granola,' Tandy called. 'Come and meet Grace.'

For the first time I noticed a little white terrier, sitting alert in a basket. He was staring, as though mesmerized by me. Yikes! You can fool people into believing you're a human being, but animals work on a different level. Granola knew there was something very weird about me.

'What's wrong, doggie?' Tandy coaxed.

'Okay,' she shrugged. '*Be* rude. So, Grace, you want to go out tonight and get trashed on strawberry cheesecake martinis?'

'That would be delightful!' I'd just been shot through with that lonesome, away-from-home feeling. Getting trashed on strawberry cheesecake martinis sounded exactly what I needed.

Later, as we left to go out, I told Tandy about calling first to the wrong apartment.

'You did what? You called into crazy Karl's?' She was horrified. 'He is, like, a totally insane alcoholic. He's always yelling and howling at the moon, like a crazy dawg. Although,' she said, as we passed his door, 'he's quiet right now.' She sounded almost disappointed.

As we drove along, palm trees were silhouetted against the skyline. The sun was setting and the sky was layered with colours: pale blue low down, rising and darkening overhead to a deep luminous blue, in which the first twinkling stars were set like diamonds.

We went to a bar on Sunset. It was a cool, vibey place, packed with good-looking people. If I hadn't been with Tandy I'd have never gone in – way too intimidated.

Almost as soon as we sat down, a bottle of champagne

was sent over by a handsome dude who liked the look of Tandy. 'Take it back,' she told the waiter. Then to me, 'I don't want to hook up with him so it wouldn't be fair.'

'Oh. Okay.'

Over flavoured martinis I got Tandy's life story. She came from a rich, academic family back East. Her elder sister had a PhD in something scarily impressive *and* managed to run a home *and* was very good at tennis. Her younger sister made her first four million by setting up an internet site selling lovely handbags *and* she was so good at horseriding she could have made the Olympic team if she'd wanted. Tandy's entire family were aghast at her decision to become an actress and even more aghast that she was working as a temp while waiting to hit the big time.

'It's hard when you come from a place where everyone else is perfect,' she said wearily.

Tell me about it!

'So how about you?' Tandy asked. 'You're an actress too?'

They've given me a whole new identity, a bit like the Witness Protection Programme. Apparently I'm an actress, but on account of there being a little too much of me, my résumé shows only wallpaper parts – the fat best friend, the jolly fat work colleague, the weird fat roommate. *Fat* being the common thread.

'So what age are you?' Tandy asked.

I froze. What age was I? In real time I was several hundred millennia, but in LA years . . . ? What had they told me?

'It's okay,' she whispered. 'Same for me. My résumé says twenty-two years old, but I'm actually in my mid-twenties.'

'Looking good.'

'Well, twenty-seven,' she admitted with a sigh.

'And I'm twenty-nine.' I'd just remembered.

'So am I.'

We gazed at each other fondly and decided to order another lot of martinis. I was having a Really Good Time, but I mustn't forget that I was here to WORK.

I got my first break when we went to the ladies' room to fix our make-up.

Tandy held a little bottle up to me. 'You want some Envy?'

Envy! One of my seven deadlies. 'You mean . . . in that container . . . is Envy?'

She twisted the label-side towards her and studied it quizzically. ''S what it says.'

I couldn't believe my luck. I'd been here only a few hours and already I was making progress. They had told me I would experience the sins in the most unexpected ways. Now I knew what they meant.

Tandy squirted me and I beamed at her from my cloud of fragrant mist. One down, six to go.

Tuesday

Sleep is a wonderful thing. We don't have it where I come from. But I'm a human now – so I will sleep, I will eat, I will work and, in the process, I will commit the seven deadly sins. Then I can go home, a better, wiser angel and no one will ever refer to me again as 'Not the sharpest knife in the drawer'.

Already I was ahead of the game. On earth less than twenty-four hours I'd been sprayed with Envy. Would it be possible to just proceed to the local mall and buy Pride,

Gluttony, Anger, Sloth and . . . and . . . the others (I'll remember in a minute what they are), experience the lot in half an hour and spend the rest of the week working on my tan? Unfortunately a discreet enquiry revealed that none of the other deadly sins were available in perfume form.

I awoke to a citrus-bright morning and I was hungry. Nick was in the kitchen, hunched over a bowl of marshmallow Cheerios.

'Sleep well?' he murmured darkly. Nick was good at murmuring things darkly. He didn't seem to communicate in any other way.

'Yes! It was great, I kind of saw all these movies in my head.'

He looked at me like I was insane. 'Dreams,' he said faintly.

'Um . . . of course.' Yikes!

Luckily the phone rang and Nick, giving me another odd look, threw himself at it. I heard a high-pitched gibbering, like the noise a broken cassette makes. A woman. She sounded upset.

'Sure, baby,' Nick crooned, 'I know, baby, I'm sorry, baby, I never meant to hurt you, baby. Take care, baby. Bye.'

He slammed down the phone, sighed with enough force to almost knock the chairs over, then slumped into moody silence.

The noise of a key scratching at the door heralded the arrival of Tandy, back from walking her dog. Granola raced into the room, stopped dead when he saw me and took a couple of careful steps backwards. Tandy's gorgeous face was flushed and angry. 'Why do I go to the dog park? Like, WHY?'

'So your liddil doggie can play with the other liddil doggies,' Nick said, his head in his hands, staring into his bowl.

'I go to meet men!' She addressed her rant to me. 'Instead I get all these women coming up to me. How old is Granola? How long have I had him? What is the *point*?'

'Calm down,' Nick said. 'Eat something. Oh no, I forgot, you don't do that, do you?'

'So, Grace,' Tandy ignored him, 'what are you going to do today?'

Actually, today I was hoping to commit Sloth. Just as soon as I found out what it was. But I had to play my part as a wannabe actress from Smallsville looking for a foot in Hollywood's door. 'I'm meeting an agent. There's a chance she might take me on.'

On account of Nick and Tandy also being actors this provoked a storm of enthusiastic enquiry. Who was she? Who did she represent?

In the middle of their interrogation the phone rang again. Another woman for Nick. 'I hear you, baby,' he murmured. 'But I never said I wanted a relationship.'

'Why do I always hurt those I love?' Tandy said, in a brooding voice that was uncannily like Nick's.

Nick glared at Tandy. Tandy glared back.

I went to get ready for my meeting. I'd been sent to earth with *beautiful* clothes, everything a girl would need.

'Oh my God, I love your purse,' Tandy breathed

reverentially. Then I felt her tense up. 'But . . . but isn't this from the new collection? I thought you couldn't buy it for another six months!'

Of course Tandy would know! What with her high-achieving sister – well, one of her high-achieving sisters – selling lovely handbags. I had to mumble something about having a contact in the design room and getting a sample copy. Honestly, sometimes they can be so inefficient Up There. And they have the nerve to complain about me . . .

As I was leaving I hesitated and said, 'This may sound a little weird, but does either of you know what Sloth is?'

'You're right,' Tandy said. 'It sounds a little weird.'

'It's an animal,' Nick said. 'A small British animal. I'm pretty sure.'

I wasn't so certain. Like, how could I *commit* a small British animal?

To be fair to my superiors they'd pulled out all the stops to equip me for life in Los Angeles. I had a hire car and – even better – the ability to drive it, a fake résumé and a glossy collection of eight by twelve headshots.

As I drove under clear blue skies and along palm-fringed highways to Beverly Hills, I passed skanky-looking motels, dentists, adobe-style houses, nail-salons, gun shops, pet care outlets, tanning salons, more dentists . . . and I wondered about the personality I'd been given. Generally, I didn't seem to be too neurotic, I hadn't had one urge to self-mutilate. I also seemed to be punctual. And a non-smoker. All a little dull, however.

*

The agent, Robyn Dude, was a power-suited power-house. She spoke extremely quickly, out of one side of her mouth. She was the kind of woman who'd look magnificent pulling the pin out of a grenade with her teeth.

'Yeah, I think we could get you some parts. But,' she said, 'I'm going to give it to you straight. Your face is great, that cherubic look is kinda now, but if you don't drop to ninety pounds, soaking wet, you're gonna be playing character parts for, like, for ever.'

'The fat best friend, the fat roommate,' I said, almost sulkily.

'Right!'

I felt a strange resentment. Okay, this wasn't my body, I'd only got it on loan and only for a week, at that, but couldn't they have given me something a little more appropriate for an actress?

There seemed to be nothing further to say. Just before I left something occurred to me. 'Do you know the meaning of the word Sloth?' I asked.

Her face filled with dark colour and she looked like she might pop. She opened her mouth and yelled, 'Some nerve! No one works as hard as me. *No one.* Okay, we'll try and get you some non-fat parts, if that's how you feel, but you'd better get to a spinning class *right now* and don't leave until you've dropped three dress sizes!'

I had no clue what she was talking about. None. Nervously, I thanked her for her time and closed the door on her. In the waiting room was a brainy-looking young woman. Or at least she was wearing those rectangular, tortoiseshell-framed spectacles that people wear if they want to look brainy.

On impulse I said, 'Sorry to bother you, but do you know what Sloth is?'

She shrank back against the wall like I was a crazy person.

'Sorry,' I mumbled, making for the sunshine and my car.

'It means lazy,' she called after me.

'It's not a small British animal?' I called back.

'No, that's a *stoat*. A sloth is a lazy South American animal.'

'Thank you.'

So sloth meant being lazy. *Lazy*. No wonder Robyn Dude had been so offended!

I drove home, depleted of any energy. All this being human was exhausting. For the rest of the day I lay on the sofa, watched talk shows and energetically committed sloth. I also ate many, many small, round, wonderful things. Pringles, I believe they were called.

Wednesday

The following day, Los Angeles behaved totally out of character – it was *raining*. As I watched the drops scoot down the window, I composed a letter of complaint in my head. 'I was *distinctly* promised blue skies and endless sunshine, yadda, yadda. *Imagine* my disappointment . . . I'd like a *full* refund . . .'

Tandy and Nick went to work and I hung around the mall, but eventually I had to return to the apartment – lured by savoury snacks.

Late afternoon, Nick came home and did a bit of that moody-prowling-around-the-room stuff that he was so good at, then came to a halt in front of me.

'You've eaten that whole tube of Pringles. You glutton!'

'I'm a glutton?' I asked faintly, hardly able to believe my luck. 'Do you mean that I'm committing . . .' I could hardly say the word with excitement, '. . . Gluttony?'

'Hey, I'm kidding. It's just nice to see someone eating around here now and again.' He looked meaningfully at Tandy's bedroom door as he said this.

'It's not a problem.' I was very excited. 'I just need to know if being a glutton is the same as committing Gluttony.'

'Yeah, I guess,' he admitted reluctantly.

There went Gluttony off my list. And it had been great! Almost as comforting as Sloth. And Envy had smelt very nice. I could see why people enjoyed the seven deadly sins so much – my empathy and understanding were simply *exploding*. Next on my list was, let me see, Lust, perhaps. Or Greed.

'You can be –' Nick studied me, '– a little strange, sometimes.'

I swallowed, suddenly nervous. The expression in those eyes of his unsettled something in me.

'Well, I'm a woman,' I said heartily. 'Think of a man, then subtract all reason and intellect!'

This got a half-hearted laugh out of him.

'How was your day?' he asked cautiously. 'Did your agent call?'

'No, seeing as how I haven't dropped twenty pounds since yesterday. How was your day? In fact, what do you do?'

'Carpenter. Just until I get my big Hollywood break,' he said drily.

'I thought all resting actors worked as bellhops.'

'Not me. I haven't got the right look for a bellhop.'

I knew what he meant. He did have a touch of the psychopath about him. No wonder he'd got typecast as a man who can hold his hand in a flame while remaining impassive.

'Well, you know my closet door? It's the worst piece of carpentry I've ever seen. Could you fix it for me?' I asked.

'Fix it? I made it.'

'Whoops,' I said, my face, rosy at the best of times, igniting into an inferno of shame. 'Sorry, I . . . er, sorry.'

Come home, Tandy. Oh please, come home.

And then Tandy walked through the door. I am not a very accomplished angel, but sometimes, if I try really, really hard, I can make things happen.

'You're early,' Nick accused.

'Yeah, I am.' Tandy looked in confusion at her watch. 'What's going on? It's five after six now but I didn't leave work until six-thirty. I must've read five-thirty as six-thirty. Or something . . . That is so spooky . . .'

Yes, I felt ashamed, since you ask. Freaking her out like that.

Only the fantastic news she'd had earlier in the day was enough to distract her from my dirty low-down manipulations in the space–time continuum. She'd been sent a script by her agent and she was going for an audition in the morning.

'Isn't that the best news? I'll be in my room learning my lines.'

I have to admit I was disappointed. I'd been hoping we could get dressed up, go out to a bar, flirt with men and see if I could get a Lust thing going on with one of them.

'I just hope,' she sighed, 'that Crazy Karl doesn't do anything too crazy tonight. I could use a good night's sleep.'

'What's with Crazy Karl?' Nick suddenly sat to attention and looked at the wall that divided the two apartments. 'It's very quiet out there.'

'Too quiet,' the three of us chorused.

'But seriously, we haven't had to call the cops in days. There hasn't been one drunken tantrum from him since . . . since *Sunday*.'

'Not since Grace called on him.'

'Grace called on him?' Nick sounded slightly *too* interested.

'When I first arrived I got the wrong apartment,' I hastily explained. 'He told me I was out of my mind.'

'Sounds like Karl.'

Tandy went to her room with Granola and I spent the evening watching TV, while a succession of heartbroken women kept Nick on the phone murmuring, 'I know, baby, I'm sorry, baby, you'll meet someone else, baby, no, your life is *not* over, baby . . .'

Then I went to bed where I had another great night, with all those movies showing in my head. The plots were a little far-fetched and inconclusive at times, but who cares? And I awoke to another dazzling Los Angeles morning.

Nick wasn't much of a talker first thing. In silence he hunched over his cereal (apple and cinnamon Fruit Loops this morning) while I sipped coffee.

When Tandy marched into the kitchen, I actually thought she'd just got home after a night of hard partying. She wore a barely-there pink dress, which revealed her long, lean, gold-leaf legs. Pink marabou-feathered, spindly heeled sandals were on her sparkly toed feet. Her car-tyre lips were defiantly sexy, her honey-blonde hair a heavy swishy sheet and her hip bones were sharp enough to fillet plaice.

'Guys,' she commanded, 'I want to know if you want to sleep with me?'

'Suuuurrrre.' Nick's eyes were half-closed as he looked her up and down appreciatively.

'Grace?'

'Sure. If I was gay.' Except I didn't think I was.

'Excellent.' She smacked those lips with satisfaction. 'That part is so mine.' She handed me the script. 'Will you do a read-through with me?'

I began, but two lines in I had to stop. 'But, Tandy . . .'

'What?'

'Your part. You're supposed to be a nun dying of cancer.'

'So?' Her stance got even more defiant.

'So you look like a hooker,' Nick interrupted.

'It doesn't matter,' Tandy said in exasperation. 'This is Hollywood. Doesn't matter if I'm playing a crack addict dying of Aids, a nine-month pregnant woman, or a suicidal depressive, I'll never get the part unless every man in that casting room wants to sleep with me!'

Her words fell into shocked silence.

Nick was the first to break it. 'Fair enough,' he conceded.

'Read,' she ordered me.

'Okay. "But, Sister Martha, you must rest!"'

'"How can I rest? Those poor, motherless children need me . . ."'

Thursday

Nick and I waved Tandy off by yelling affirmations at her. 'You will get the part, you will get the part. Good luck, break a leg!'

As I closed the door I was sorry I'd said the 'break a leg' bit. Tandy's endless legs looked thin enough to snap all by themselves.

All I'd meant was I wanted her to get the part because I really liked her. Well, I would I suppose. Being an angel I tend to like everyone, even the bad ones. I don't get much choice in the matter. But there was something sweet and vulnerable about Tandy that touched me, something totally at odds with her sassy, sexy appearance.

Nick hung around for a little longer, somehow managing to look dark and mysterious as he ate another bowl of cereal. (Lucky Charms, this time.)

'I gotta take off.' He clattered his bowl into the dishwasher. 'Work calls. Have a great day.' With the fluid, careless grace that had half the women in the greater Los Angeles area beating down his door, he swung out of the apartment.

Then – apart from Granola, who still wouldn't come near me – I was alone. So what was I to do? So far I'd managed to commit three of the seven deadlies, leaving less than four days to do Greed, Anger, Pride and . . . and . . . what was the other one? Oh yeah, Lust, how could I forget?

A dangerous little thought wriggled in. The apartment complex had a pool. How about if I lay beside it and scoped for men? Surely that way there was a very good chance of taking care of Lust?

And when I rummaged among the clothes I'd been given

for my mission, I found a sleek jade bikini, with a matching sarong. This convinced me that catching some rays was the Right Thing To Do.

There was only one other person by the pool. A man – as luck would have it. But the wrong kind of man. He was astonishingly thin and pale. You don't get too many pale people in Los Angeles. On the other hand you get plenty who are thin, in fact it's very hard to find people who *aren't*. But this man looked thin in the way someone who's been sick for a very long time looks thin. He lay inert on a sunbed, asleep behind his shades.

I tried a couple of exploratory swings past him, but no dice. So I stretched myself out on a bed and Thought About Things.

Perhaps it was actually A Good Thing that I hadn't been a high-achiever. If I'd been a perfect superbeing, with an innate grasp of humanity, I'd never have been sent here. Dreamily I let the sun beat down on me while I wrestled with a philosophical conundrum: can angels get sunburnt?

After a while the worry became compelling so I jumped in my car, drove to the nearest drugstore and bought a bottle of factor 25.

But when I came out of the store, disaster struck. Suddenly I heard myself calling, 'Hey! That's my car.'

The two front wheels were off the ground, attached to a hook, attached to a truck. *I was being towed!* A man in a uniform said, 'You shouldn'ta parked there.'

A feeling stirred in me. A strange, outward-spiralling rush where I had an irresistible impulse to physically assault this man.

'I was only in there for five minutes!' I yelled.

'Hey, lady, no need to get so angry.'

'I'm angry?' I squeaked.

'Too right you're angry.'

I took a moment – and he was right. *I do believe I'm experiencing . . . ANGER!*

I lunged towards the man and he put his hand up to deflect the blow. But there was no blow. Instead I hugged him. 'Thank you so much.'

He was transfixed.

'Aw, hey.' He gestured to another man who was in the truck. 'What the hell? She was only five minutes. Give her her car.'

'No, no, no,' I insisted. 'You're just doing your job.'

A small crowd had gathered. As my car was lowered back to the ground, a smattering of applause broke out.

'This kinda thing,' I heard one of the onlookers say, as I drove away, 'restores your faith in human nature.'

Back by the pool, slathered in suntan lotion, I noticed that my pale, bony man was still immobile. Anxiety about his tender skin getting burnt began to gnaw at me. Gently, taking care not to wake him, I gave him a speedy once-over with my factor 25. But as I rubbed lotion into his arm I saw that he'd lifted his shades and was staring at me quizzically out of pale blue eyes.

'You angel,' he said hoarsely.

'Sssshhh,' I hissed – angrily, as it happens, now that I knew how to feel it.

The last thing we wanted was him figuring out what I was. Either he'd get locked up or I would.

*

That evening, back at the ranch, things weren't so good. Not only had Tandy not got the part but they'd told her she'd never make it because her look 'is so over'.

'What can I do?' she moaned. 'This is how I look. What am I supposed to do?'

'Plastic surgery?' Nick suggested.

'I've had it,' she said.

'Really?' I asked curiously. 'What, exactly?'

'Nose, lips, eyelids, cheekbones.'

'Boobs,' Nick chipped in. 'You forgot your boobs.'

She lifted her face from her hands just long enough to scorch him with a look.

'But you have so much talent,' I told her.

'Talent, shmalent.' She gave a scornful wave of her hand. 'This is Hollywood. What use to me is talent?'

She turned her tear-stained face to mine. 'We must go out and drink white chocolate martinis.'

'That's the closest you get to a square meal, right?' Nick said.

'Gimme a break! I eat. Often.'

'Oh yeah, I forgot. You had an aspirin last Tuesday.'

'I'm an actress! Eating isn't an option.'

'I'm giving you a hard time because I care about you.'

'You don't care about anyone but yourself.'

'Not true.'

'Is true.'

'Guys, guys,' I said hastily. 'Break it up.'

'I'm going to the store.' Nick swung from the room.

Fifteen minutes later he was back, looking out of his mind with worry.

'You are not going to believe this. I've just met crazy Karl, our unfriendly neighbourhood alcoholic –'

'– He pulled a knife on you?' Tandy asked, in alarm.

'No, far worse. He said hey and asked me how I was.'

'Then he asked you for a dollar?'

'No, he said he was real sorry for all the crazy stuff, the yelling and the howling like a dawg. Says it won't happen again. He's cleaned up his act.'

'Really?'

'Really.'

'I'm going to miss him howling like a dawg,' Tandy admitted. 'So what's happened to him?'

'Dunno,' Nick shrugged. 'Far as I can see he hasn't been the same since Grace called in on him.'

'I met the man for two seconds,' I defended myself.

'What is it about you?' Nick considered me with his bleak dark eyes.

Later, in some white-tiled, glass-fronted bar, after three different men asked for and didn't get Tandy's number, she got maudlin about her audition.

'They way they treat people is the way I used to treat shoes. I used to stroll through the store, ignoring some, picking others up, then saying the most *hurtful* stuff.'

'Like?'

'Like . . . too high, weird heel, wrong colour, too low. It's so CRUEL.'

I nodded sympathetically. People at the other tables were beginning to look.

'And now when I'm at the market buying, like, apples, I pick the shiniest, reddest ones, RIGHT? But I try to send out vibes to the apples I left behind, to let them know that just because I didn't choose them doesn't mean that they're all not WORTHWHILE and UNIQUE. In case any of them feel BAD, you know? Oh no!'

Two martinis had just arrived courtesy of a man who was winking energetically from across the room.

'Take them back,' Tandy beseeched the waiter. 'Please.'

'He's really cute,' I tried to persuade her.

'Thank you,' the waiter said, warmly. 'So are you.'

'I ... um ... actually meant the man who'd sent the drinks,' I explained. 'But thank you.'

Friday

The next day Tandy had already left for her job before Nick surfaced, wafting into the kitchen in a morning-fresh, citrus cloud. He had a strangely alluring unkempt look about him, and he always seemed as if he could do with a good scrub. Even when he'd just had one. Even when he was actually *having* one, according to Tandy, who'd admitted last night that she'd had sex in the shower with him one 'horrible' (her word) evening when they'd both had about ten vodkatinis too many.

'Won't you be late for work?' I asked him.

'No work today, Grace.'

'Why not?'

'Audition.'

'That's great! Why didn't you say?'

He shrugged. 'Tandy was so bummed over her lousy audition yesterday I thought telling her about mine might bring her down.'

'So what's the part?'

'Mild-mannered, happily married father of three who blows the whistle on a chemical company that's poisoning the water system.'

'*Real*ly? That's excellent.' And what a change from the stalker/slasher/wacko parts he was usually up for!

'Nah, just kidding.' He slung himself into a chair. 'Psychopath. Neo-Nazi tendencies. Impressive collection of knives.'

As he ate his Captain Crunch, he looked kind of depressed.

Then the phone rang. Another heartbroken woman for Nick. Except it wasn't. The call was for me! And there was only one person in Los Angeles who had my number: Robyn Dude, theatrical agent and ass-kicker extraordinaire. This could only mean one thing – an audition!

I know I'm not a human being. I know I'm an angel whose mind is on higher things. Or at least it should be. But when Robyn growled at me to show up at some suite in Wilshire with my résumé and headshots, I suddenly wanted that part. Fiercely. Violently.

So desperately that for a while I forgot why I was actually on earth. Seven Deadly Sins, I reminded myself sternly. Perhaps today I'd see if I could tick off, ooh, let's see, how about . . . Pride!

'Tell me what you know about Pride,' I said to Nick.

'It comes before a fall.'

'That's all you can tell me?'

'Pride is a big ole march they have in San Francisco every year.'

'Ohhh-kaaaay.' Why did I expect him to make sense? After all, this was the man who'd told me that Sloth was a small British animal.

Nick loped off to his audition and I dressed for mine. The part was for the fat, supportive sister of the kooky, beautiful heroine. Another fat girl part to add to my fat girl résumé . . .

In the suite in Wilshire there were dozens of us, all doing our best to exude fat, supportive, sisterly energy. But in a strange, smug way I suspected I was the best. At one hundred and twelve pounds I was certainly the fattest, and humming in a warm place inside me was the conviction that the part was *mine*. So sure of myself was I that I was able to chatter brightly to the sweet girl next to me. Who confided that nothing had gone right in her life for so long that she was beginning to suspect her ex-boyfriend had put a curse on her. Her car had been stolen, her highlights had turned a funny colour and she hadn't worked in six months. When I heard my name being called, I touched her on the shoulder and said, 'I hope you get the part.'

'I hope you do too,' she replied. Which was a kind of stupid conversation because there was only one part and there were two of us, but I suppose we were bonding.

I'd never been to an audition before but having done a run-through with Tandy for *her* audition I knew exactly what to do. A girl called Lana fed me my lines and Wayne, the director, watched from the back of the room.

'I am so kurrr-ay-zee,' Lana said, acting the part of the kooky heroine.

'Hahaha,' I laughed, in what I hoped was a fat, supportive, sisterly way.

'Thank you!' Wayne shouted.

'You're welcome,' I said, then turned back to Lana, waiting to be fed my next line. She remained oddly silent.

'Go ahead,' I encouraged.

'Thank you,' Wayne called again. 'You can go now.'

'But I'm not finished.' I held up my page of dialogue.

'We would like you to leave now.'

Then I understood. When they shout, 'Thank you,' they're not actually thanking you, they're telling you you're crap. As I slunk towards the door, Wayne yelled, 'Next!' I was barely aware of the nice girl I'd been talking to in the waiting room being ushered in past me.

I was crushed. *Crushed.* Tandy had warned me about auditions: meat racks, cattle markets, where they treat you as if you're not human. (Well, obviously I'm not, but how were they to know?)

As I trudged towards my car I wanted to go home. Not home to Silverlake, but *home* home.

I'd been so sure I'd get the part. I burnt as I remembered how I'd thought it was in the bag when it wasn't. What's that Nick had said? 'Pride comes before a fall.' And he'd been right. I'd certainly taken a tumble . . .

Then the sense of that began to dawn on me. If I'd had the fall, I must've had *pride*. Pride.

And all at once it was as if the sun had come out from behind the clouds. I'd done five now. Only Greed and . . . and . . . what was the other one? Oh right, Lust. Only Greed and Lust to go.

There was the sound of running feet behind me. It was the sweet girl I'd spoken to in the waiting room.

'I got the part,' she gasped. 'They just took one look at

me, before I'd even read, and they said, "You're our Mary Ann." It's totally weird,' she added. 'They don't usually do it this way. Like, never. They've sent everyone else away.'

And sure enough, flooding out into the car park came a stream of supportive, sisterly women, now looking peeved and disappointed. A disgruntled mutter reached me.

'It's like you were my good-luck charm or something . . .' She looked at me in a kind of confused wonder, a little like the way Granola did.

'I'm really happy for you,' I said, because, actually, I was.

To celebrate my ritual humiliation at the audition I went to a bar with Tandy for apple martinis. It was wall-to-wall beautiful people.

'Why was it horrible?' I asked.

'What?'

'You said when you slept with Nick that it was horrible.'

'The sleeping bit wasn't horrible,' she said awkwardly. 'It was afterwards . . . He never mentioned it again. And there were – are – all these other girls.'

I nodded. There *were* a lot of girls around Nick.

'No, thank you, she doesn't want it.' Irritably I shooed away a waiter who'd showed up with a bottle of champagne and a phone number.

'No, wait. Which guy?' Tandy asked.

'The gentleman raising his glass like a character in a low-rent James Bond movie,' the waiter said politely. 'May he join you?'

'Sure,' Tandy sighed. 'If it's okay with you, Grace?'

'Er, sure.'

By the time we left two hours later, Tandy had agreed to go on a date with James – I'm sure that wasn't his real name – the following evening.

Back home Nick had celebrated getting the part of the neo-Nazi psycho by going to the movies. With Karl.

'Crazy alcoholic Karl?' Tandy was aghast.

'Who hasn't had a drink since Sunday,' Nick replied.

'He was talking about you.' He addressed this to me. 'He decided to stop drinking, he says, when he had a moment of Grace.'

'Just because my name is Grace doesn't mean it's anything to do with me.'

'What is it about you?' Nick stared at me, lost in consideration.

'Nothing. There's nothing about me.'

Saturday

Tandy and I stood in the Rodeo Drive store, struck dumb by the beauty of the leather goods before us – the sturdy, curvy shapes, the way the light caught the devilishly pliant hide, the slender long handles just begging to be slung over our shoulders.

I wanted to possess them so *badly*.

'Other people go to art galleries,' Tandy admitted. 'I come here and look at the purses. They're so beautiful that sometimes I cry. I used to be like that about shoes, but –'

'– handbags are the new shoes,' I finished for her. I may have been on earth for only six days, but I'd taken care to learn the most important stuff. That kind of knowledge would take me anywhere.

'When I do my first not-straight-to-video movie,' she promised, 'I'm going to come in here and buy every purse they have.'

'Me too. When I play my first non-fat girl part,' I said. 'Tandy, can I ask you something?' And yes, I admit it was a trick question. 'Is it greedy to want to steal one of these bags?'

Tandy was appalled. 'Greedy? It's totally normal.'

I tried again. 'Would it be greedy to want to steal *more* than one?'

'Depends. What were you planning on doing with the both of them?'

'*Both?* Well, I was thinking of more than two.'

This seemed to impress her.

'Okay, what would you do with them all? You can't really wear more than two at the one time.'

'I'd have some next to my bed so they'd be the first thing I'd see when I woke up. I might frame some and hang them on my wall and I'd keep the rest in my closet, and when I was depressed I'd take them out and kiss them.'

After an awkward pause she asked, 'Are you going to give one to me?'

And, shamefaced, I had to admit, 'No, Tandy, I want to keep them all for me.'

'*That*'s greedy,' she said huffily. 'That's, like, not nice. I thought you were my friend.'

'Sorry,' I whispered, suddenly restored to normality. Of course I'd give Tandy one of the bags I wanted to steal from Prada. All of them, if she wanted. (But hopefully she wouldn't.)

'Hey.' Her smile was sweet. 'This is crazy. No one's going to steal anything.'

'Good,' said the male assistant who'd materialized behind us. 'I have a horror of scenes.'

I perked up. I'd just committed my sixth deadly sin. So that was how greed operated – blinding you to friendship and generosity. All for the sake of some nicely stitched leather. *Very* nicely stitched leather, I thought, in lovely colours, with zips and locks and ... I could feel myself getting sucked in again.

Of my seven deadly sins I only had Lust to go. As if on cue, a woman hurtled into the store and flung herself on a purple ostrich-skin evening bag.

'Ohmigod,' she shrieked. 'I totally *lust* after this. One of these is better than sex!'

Naturally enough this gave me pause for thought. In my great yearning for a bag had I also done Lust? It would be very useful if I had, of course, because I could spend my last day on earth lying by the pool. Maybe I'd even get to talk to that pale and interesting man who'd been there two days ago. But I'd always expected that I'd feel Lust about a man, not about a handbag. I wasn't ready to give up on that yet.

All week men had been coming on to Tandy. Every time we'd gone out she'd spent her time wearily dismissing bottles of champagne and phone numbers and cheap pick-up lines. So why was she going on a date with this James guy? What was so special about him?

'I'm going to give it my best shot,' she said. 'It's stupid to keep hoping and –' She stopped abruptly and put another layer of shine on her cheekbones.

By the time she was ready she was so dazzlingly gorgeous she would take the sight out of your eyes.

Dark and downbeat at the best of times, Nick had gone into overdrive. He slouched on the couch like a human black hole.

'How do I look?' Tandy danced into the room and pirouetted in her date finery.

'You're blocking my view of the TV.' Nick rubbernecked as he tried to see around her.

'Doesn't she look great!' I said heartily.

Nick pressed the remote and raised the sound.

'Nick?' Tandy asked, above the raucous canned laughter.

'What can I say, Tandy?' His voice was flat. 'You look beautiful. You always look beautiful.'

This seemed to confuse her and some of her dancing, lit-up quality dimmed.

'You'd be even more beautiful if you ate occasionally,' he added. She marched from the room and slammed the door. Yikes!

After she'd left, Nick and I watched a movie and ate popcorn in companionable silence. Well, companionable*ish*. Nick was so broodingly self-contained, I couldn't help sneaking glances at him. Suddenly he turned and caught me looking. After more silence, he spoke: 'How come you're not on a date tonight, Grace?'

'No one asked me. Tandy's so beautiful,' I shrugged, 'it's hard not to disappear beside her.'

Alright, so I was milking it.

'Aw, but you're so cute,' he said softly, swinging his legs off the table and moving closer along the couch. 'You've got these curls,' he wound a hand into my bouncy hair, 'and beautiful skin,' with his other hand he touched my face, 'and a perfect mouth . . .' With his thumb he pulled gently at my lower lip and moved his face so that it was level with mine.

He was going to kiss me. And I wanted him to. My heart was knocking echoes into my ears, and I was wound tight with longing. I leant into the heat of him, feeling the grip of his hand on the back of my head and then, and then . . . Something changed and it was all trickling away.

'I'm sorry,' he said, pulling back with a heavy sigh. His eyes were weary but the touch of his hand on my face was kind. 'I'm so sorry, Grace. It's not you.'

'Whatever.' But my voice was helium high and didn't convince.

I burnt with humiliation. What made things worse was that I'd been enjoying the movie and now I had no choice but to slink away to my room.

I'll level with you. Of all the seven sins, Lust was the one I'd been most looking forward to. And see what had happened – over before it had begun.

The phone rang and I heard Nick saying to some heart-broken girl, 'I'm sorry, baby.' The line he'd been saying all week since I arrived: he was like a broken record. And some kind of understanding began to stir in me, something to do with Tandy saying that things would never work with her and Nick because there were all these women around him . . . But before my realization was fully formed the doorbell rang and I lost my train of thought. I've always had a very short attention span.

I strained to hear who it was. *Please don't let it be a girl*, I begged. But thank God, it was only crazy, alcoholic Karl. Who, if Nick was to be believed, was no longer so crazy or so alcoholic. They left to shoot some pool.

Sunday

My last day on earth. That sounds really dramatic, right?

I'd successfully completed my mission, done all seven of my deadly sins in six days and I was shipping back to Up There this evening, a more confident, experienced, *humane* angel. Yet I was left with the feeling that there was still something very important to do. THE most important thing, actually.

It was another beautiful morning. Granola was scampering around chasing dust motes but as soon as I came into the room he bolted to his basket and crouched in it, trembling. Looks like winning the dog over isn't going to be one of my success stories.

Tandy was swinging around the apartment taunting Nick.

'I had the best time last night. James is really cute and smart and funny.' She was watching Nick very carefully as she said all this, but he was utterly engrossed in the sports pages.

'He is the funniest guy,' Tandy said dreamily. 'Let me tell you what he –'

With a sharp rustle of paper, Nick sat up. 'So, you gonna go out with him again?'

'What do you care?'

'You're right, I don't.'

They stared each other down, looking like they hated each other.

Clearly, they were in love with each other. How had I not noticed until now? Well, last night, really. At least I got it in time.

I needed to speak to Tandy; there wasn't much time before I left for home.

'Nick . . .' I began.

'That jerk!'

'Yeah. So let's see if I've got this straight. You slept with him –'

'I was loaded,' she furiously defended herself.

'Then afterwards nothing happened and you were cross because he always had a bunch of girls around him.'

'Yeah.' She sounded uncertain, as if she wasn't really sure where this was going.

'But,' I said dramatically, 'since I've been here I admit there have been a lot of girls around but Nick keeps telling them to go away. Seems to me he's clearing the decks.'

'For what?'

'Dduuuuhhh! For you! Who do you think?' Well, it certainly wasn't for me. Not that I was sore. Angels don't really do sore. But if I wasn't an angel I think I might have been very sore indeed. Anyhow . . .

'For me? You think?' Tandy couldn't keep the hope out of her voice, then she changed tack. 'He thinks I'm anorexic.'

'You are very thin,' I said carefully. 'And you don't seem to eat very often.'

'I'm not anorexic,' she yelled. 'I'm –'

'Yes, I know; you're an actress.'

'No. I'm in love with him! I was a hundred and twenty pounds before I moved into this apartment.'

'When exactly was that?' I was very keen to know how long it took her to lose thirty pounds.

'A year ago. Back then I used to play a lot of fat best friend parts.'

'Like me!'

'Just like you. I preferred them to the hooker roles I get now.'

We were getting diverted from our main purpose.

'So what about James?'

'Oh he's an asshole,' she said dismissively.

Next stop, Nick. We hadn't spoken since he'd acted as though he was about to kiss me, then changed his mind with those immortal words, 'It's not you.'

Anyone who's ever been told, 'It's not you,' knows immediately that it *is* them. But this particular case is the one exception. It wasn't me – it was Tandy! Nick loved Tandy, but old habits die hard and a ghostly flicker of his former behaviour meant he'd probably felt it would be *impolite* not to try to jump me.

He was on the deck, staring at nothing.

'Can we talk?'

The poor guy looked horrified. He thought I was going to be a girl and insist on doing a big analysis of how we nearly, but not quite, got it together the night before.

'Sure,' he croaked, doing a wild retreat behind his eyes.

I sat down and smiled reassuringly at him. Okay, so he hadn't found me attractive. But I'm bigger than all that. Well, I'm working on it.

'About Tandy . . .' I began.

'Yeeaaahhh?'

'Since I've been here, you've been on the phone a lot saying goodbye to girls. Is it because of her?'

He tried to stare me down. But I can stare longer and harder. Sometimes it's *great* being a supernatural being.

With a sigh he caved in. 'Okay. I wanted her to know that I wasn't going to be fooling around with anyone else. But what happens? She goes on a date with cute, smart, funny James.'

'He's an asshole.' I was thinking how *lucky* it was that I was here. They'd never sort this mess out if I wasn't.

'Says who he's an asshole?'

'Tandy.'

'Yeah? For real?' A rare smile played on the corners of his mouth. He really *was* devastatingly attractive.

If you like that sort of thing.

'You two need to talk. But you're kind of hard to approach, you know?'

'I wasn't always like this,' he bristled. 'I was a really happy guy until she moved in. But I see her, so beautiful, and I, you know, I get, like, depressed. I usedta do a lot of comedy roles once, now I only seem to get offered psychos.'

'Talk to her now,' I commanded, very excited about the way things were going.

But before we got any further, we had a guest.

'Karl!' Nick exclaimed. 'So have you met Grace?'

It was the pale, ill-looking man who'd been lying by the pool. He was also – though I hadn't recognized him – the shouty smelly bloke I'd accidentally called on when I'd first arrived in Los Angeles nearly a week before. He certainly scrubbed up well.

'It's you!' he sort of gasped.

Yes, it was indeed me. No point denying it.

He ran his eyes over me with the same sort of awed wonder that Granola looked at me with.

'What did you do?' he asked. 'You called into my apartment and when you left I didn't want to drink any more. Then you stop me from burning in the sun.'

'How'd she do *that*?' Nick demanded.

'I put suntan lotion on him.'

'Who are you?' Karl wondered. 'Some sort of angel?'

Nick followed the exchange with interest. I knew Nick had had his suspicions about me, so I was surprised when he said matter-of-factly, 'She's Grace from Hicksville and you were long overdue to quit drinking, buddy. It's no biggie.'

Karl was adamant. 'I know you've had something to do with it. Thank you.'

'You're welcome,' I said shyly.

'I knew it!' Karl said.

'Karl, buddy,' Nick cut in. 'Can I catch up with you later, I got something really important to do.'

'Sure.'

Tandy was in her room and, after a push from me, Nick knocked and went in. I was going mad wanting to know what was happening, but I wasn't able to see through the wall — I really needed to do some work on my X-ray vision. Luckily, though, Nick didn't fully close the door behind him, so through the narrow gap I could see Tandy.

First she looked a little suspicious, then she was listening, then she smiled and said something. Another bit of listening, then suddenly Nick was also in the frame, taking her in his arms and holding her like he was never going to let her go.

The situation was just begging for a soundtrack. I simply couldn't resist it — the air trembled and swelled with the sublime sound of heavenly violins. In his basket in the kitchen Granola began to howl happily along with it.

Previously unpublished.

Q. *Dear Mammy Walsh, I'm writing to you with quite an embarrassing problem. It's my boyfriend. When he 'wees', he sprays it everywhere. The bathroom is spattered with drops and smells disgusting. I've asked him to be more careful but he hasn't. What should I do?*
Fiona, Edinburgh

A. In the early days of our marriage, Mr Walsh was guilty of the same carry-on. My advice to you is, rub his nose in it.

Q. *Dear Mammy Walsh, I have a daughter who says she's a lesbian and she walks up and down our road holding hands with her 'partner' in broad daylight. I am mortified. What should I do?*
Anon, address withheld

A. Dear Marguerite (I recognized your writing), I won't plaw-maws you because I've seen them myself with my own two eyes, and everyone in the cul-de-sac gawking out from behind the curtains at them. They don't care who sees them and they even stopped beside my leylandii for a 'snog'. But the thing is that Angela is a lovely girl and she's only looking for notice. They all do it, daughters, and I have often wondered if a son would have been any easier. If daughters are not being lesbians, they're insisting they're vegetarians or drug addicts or hiding in wet hedges with a long-range lens, catching throat infections, then spending a week in bed belly-aching for Lemsip and KitKat Chunkies. It's the cross we mothers have to bear. Offer it up, Marguerite. Think of our Lord on the cross, with six-inch nails through his hands and feet, dying for our sins and several people not even grateful.

PS Maybe your husband, Mr Kilfeather, for once in his lazy, gombeen life, could help out by having a little word with her. Small wonder she thinks she's a 'lezzer' with him as her only male 'role model'.

Q. *Dear Mammy Walsh, can you help with a dilemma? I love to read 'chick-lit' books, they cheer me up, especially the happy endings where the heroine always gets her man. However, I recently read an article where a leading feminist criticized these books as being 'anti-feminist' and deleterious to the cause of female equality. I was terribly shocked because I've always thought of myself as a committed feminist but one who believes in love between men and women. Please help.*
Camilla, Gothenburg

A. I am sick to my craw of feminists. They're nothing but shouty, bad-tempered termagants who try to make women feel guilty about everything. They're worse than men. Telling me that I'm letting myself be exploited by wearing a bra and cooking Mr Walsh his dinner! As it happens, I *don't* cook Mr Walsh his dinner and haven't since the early eighties. It wasn't that he was exploiting me, it was because those five brats of daughters never ate anything except bowls of Frosties. I'd cook myself blue in the face and they'd laugh and pretend they didn't know whether the end result was animal, vegetable or mineral. So, I thought, I'm not going to make a gom of myself, slaving over a hob when I could be watching *Neighbours* and playing bridge. But it's not because I'm a feminist, it's just because I no longer fecking felt like it. And nor do I do much housework, but that isn't because I'm afraid of being exploited there either, it's because I have a bad back and can't do much bending (hoovering is out). Show what an independent, free-thinking woman you are by reading what you like and telling the feminists to stick it.

PS Is that your real name?
PPS Have you already written to me? Are you 'stalking' me?

Q. *Dear Mammy Walsh, can you give me advice on applying fake tan? Mine always goes streaky or too orange and I've been the subject of a whispering campaign at work.*
Dawn, Cardiff

A. Did they laugh at you, pet? I'd know all about that. Patience is the key. Also, and this might sound like I'm promoting my own daughter, but Candy Grrrl does a lovely fake tan – and that's another thing, Dawn – we don't call it fake tan any more, love. It's self-tan now. Just a little tip. Yes, Candy Grrrl's is very nice. You put it on with latex gloves, like something out of *ER*, and the shade comes up nicely after three goes. Not streaky and not too orange. Quite smelly, though, but then again, they all are. Mr Walsh goes mad. He says I stink the bedroom up. But I tell him to shut up, that it's a small price to pay for me looking lovely. Another thing that might help is if you 'exfoliate', that means to give yourself a good scrub with granuley stuff, before you put on your self-tan. If you don't want the extra expense of buying the exfoliator, just rub harder with your face-cloth. Although, and again it might sound like I'm promoting Anna, but Candy Grrrl do a lovely exfoliator, it smells like pineapples. Mind you, it's easy for me to say because I get mine free.

Mammy Walsh regrets she cannot enter into private correspondence, as she has a home to run, a husband who is next to useless and five daughters who are always getting themselves into terrible mix-ups.

First written for Penguin Books' website, 2004

A Woman's Right to Shoes

*T*hin morning light, grey pavement, counting forty-eight seconds from the front door to the end of my road. Turn onto bigger road and start again, counting seventy-eight seconds before the traffic lights. Across the road in thirteen, then counting twenty-nine to the shops.

I've only started this counting lark lately – just in the last few weeks. But now I do it all the time, I count everything. It's very handy, it stops me from going mad.

As I got nearer to the pub, I wondered if my silver sandal would still be outside. Probably. Because who would want it? Mind you, there was no accounting for pissed people. They took big orange traffic cones home, why not a single, silver sandal?

Nearer I got and nearer; there was something there alright and it was the right size for a shoe. But already I knew it wasn't mine. Alerted by some instinct, already I knew something strange was happening. And sure enough, once I was close enough, I saw that my sandal was gone – and, as if by alchemy, shimmering in its place was a different shoe, a man's shoe. It was astonishingly beautiful: a classic brogue shape, but in an intense purple leather. It sat on the grey pavement, looking almost as though it was floating and it seemed to throb, as if it was the only thing of colour in a black and white world. Slightly mesmerized, I picked it up and turned it over. There were no scuffs on the sole, like it had never been worn. Butter-soft, biscuit-coloured leather lined the insides and it made my aching eyes feel better just to look at it.

Should I bring it to the police station? It looked important enough. But it was a shoe, a single shoe. Lost by a man who'd had one alcopop too many last night. I'd be cautioned for wasting police time.

Perhaps I should put up a sign saying it had been found – if it was a puppy or a kitten people would, and shoes were beloved also. Next door to the pub was the newsagent with its noticeboard of ads. I could post something there: 'Found: One magical shoe.' Then I remembered the last time I'd placed an ad there about shoes. Look at where that had landed me.

But this shoe was too beautiful to abandon. Quickly I gathered it up, wrapped it in my scarf, put it in my bag and hurried to work.

The previous night

Yes, perhaps wearing a single, high, silver sandal mid-November smacked a little of histrionics. But it was necessary for people to know I was making a statement, a protest, even.

As I had walked to the pub I'd plumped for practicality and worn an old pair of trainers – pre-Hayley trainers that for some reason I had kept, even though I had thought those days were long gone – but just before I entered into the bright, convivial warmth, I took them off and replaced them with a single spindly sandal on my right foot. On my left foot – the shoe-free one – my tights had a hole in the toe. I regarded it steadily. So be it. I couldn't falter now.

Listing to one side, I stood just inside the door. Were they here? Not yet. This was good, I could settle myself for maximum impact. There were many sofas – this was a lady-friendly pub – but I required elevation and visibility. I hop-alonged to the bar and climbed up onto a stool, then I rotated so that I was facing into the room. You couldn't have missed me or – more importantly – my uneven feet, one shod, one bare.

My eyes were doing that constantly-scudding-swimming-fish thing that very dislocated people do and I counted between events (people coming in, people lighting cigarettes, people gently moving a strand of their girlfriend's hair out of her eyes, etc.; I started back at zero each new time). In between the counting, I drank steadily. The plan had been to stick to mineral water, but somehow, between the ongoing shock and my proximity to strong drink, that fell apart. All evening, I sat, my back rigid with righteousness, waiting for them to appear, but they didn't. This was very annoying. How else could I shame them?

Nick, the barman, though clearly a little bit alarmed by my behaviour, was kind. Unlike Naomi, a mutual friend of mine and Steven's who said, 'Alice, please put some proper shoes on; this whole thing, it's just so undignified.'

Undignified? Me? I was dignity personified, as much as anyone can be in one sandal and one betighted foot in mid-November. In an attempt to defuse me, Naomi tried subsuming me into her group of sofa-based friends, but I refused to abandon my post.

Around eleven o'clock, I gave up; they weren't coming. I hadn't known for sure they would, the real world isn't like *Coronation Street*. But they had been sighted there together. Which was very tactless, considering Steven and I used to go there. Not every night, maybe only once or twice a week and as much for food as for drink. (Salmon fishcakes, Pacific-rim salads, mocha bread-and-butter pudding, etc. Like I said, a lady-friendly pub.)

As I left, I see-sawed across the pub – now quite crowded, which was unfortunate because my great shoe imbalance was not as instantly visible as I would have wished. Indeed, I feared that several people simply dismissed my side-to-side swaying as the result of inebriation. I was aware of general nudgage as I limped past. I even heard someone say, 'So she's pissed, so what? After what's happened, who'd blame her?'

Only when I got through the doors and out into the street did I retrieve my trainers from my bag and take the sandal off. I was going to put the sandal back into the bag, and then I thought: but why bother? What use is it to me now?

So I left it. Exactly mid-way across the two doors (well, as mid-way as I could manage after an evening of grim, heavy drinking).

I nursed a vague plan that I might do the same the next night with a different shoe. And every night thereafter, until all thirty-one of my shoes were gone. Just over a month, it would take.

How I met Hayley

Most people are unbalanced. Or asymmetrical, as it's more commonly called. My problem area is my feet: my right foot is a size four and my left a size five. I used to get round the problem by buying shoes in a size five and employing insoles, but it wasn't always a great solution, especially if the objects of my desire were sling-backs or open-toed, minxy stuff.

However, one day I was visited with a brilliant, life-changing idea: if I had a size-four right foot and a size-five left foot, could there be someone in the metropolis I lived in who had a size-five *right* foot and a size-four *left* foot? My pedi mirror image. If we could only find each other, we could buy two identical pairs, one in size four, one in size five – and divvy them up according to our needs.

I considered advertising in *Time Out* or a national newspaper, but in the end I placed an ad on the noticeboard in the local newsagent – and got a reply! A local girl, she lived less than ten minutes' walk from me and Steven.

I was wild with excitement before I met her, charmed by the idea of symbiosis, and the thought that this woman would complete me.

I am quite freakishly short and therefore fond of high heelage. (Sometimes when I step out of my four-inch heels, people look around in confusion and ask, 'Where's she gone?' and I am obliged to call out, 'I'm down here.') Hayley, by contrast, was tall and slender. I feared she would spurn high-heelage and embrace flattage, and unfortunately, most of the time, she did. Right from the start it was a battle of wills and our shared asymmetry didn't kick-start a friendship. From time to time we bumped into each other locally, but we only ever arranged to meet on a 'Need to Buy' basis. Which we did for over two years: in March, when the fresh sandals crop hit the shops and September, when the new boots arrived. There were also occasional unscheduled events – the need for glittery Christmas party shoes or just a random spotting of a beautiful pair, which it would have been criminal to pass up.

Sometimes Hayley was game and agreed to the purchase of sky-scraper heels, which made me happy. Even at the best of times, though, it was never as much fun as I'd expected. In fact, it was slightly uneasy. But I pretended it wasn't. We were girls! We were shopping for shoes! We had a special bond! The bottom line was that Hayley was horrible. An important life lesson for me, and one I'd learnt too late – just because someone loves shoes doesn't necessarily mean she's a good person.

When Steven told me he was leaving me for her, the shock plunged me into a grey-tinged nightmare. It was then that I began counting. I even found myself doing it in my dreams, because as soon as I stopped, the panic rose steadily until it threatened to choke me.

There was worse to come. Two days later I came home from work to find that all my size-five shoes had been stolen. Hayley had taken them. I was left with thirty-one single right-foot shoes. The only complete pairs I had left were the boots I stood up in and a manky pair of ancient trainers.

Popular psychology has it that when a person undergoes a trauma – a mugging or perhaps an abandonment – they often respond by thinking they're worthless. As it happened,

I hadn't got around to it yet. But Hayley had – even though the trauma was mine. In her eyes, I had become utterly insignificant; after helping herself to my husband, she felt she could take anything else she wanted. Apparently, she had decided that, actually, her feet were suddenly the same size. After a lifetime of one size four and one size five, both her feet were now a size five. An unbelievable turnabout? Well, why not? Was it any more incredible than Steven's defection, after he'd once promised that he'd always love me, so much so that he'd married me? (I'd had the shoes – white satin pumps – made specially; for once both my feet were perfectly shod.)

I rang them to ask for my shoes back. Hayley told me to stop harassing them. I said I just wanted the return of my shoes. Hayley said they'd get a barring order.

Deflated as I was, I knew I was in the right. But all that remained to me was the moral high-ground. I decided I would wear a succession of single shoes to the local pub in the hope of shaming them publicly.

The search

That evening, after work, when I emerged from the underground, I was expecting to see photocopied flyers stuck to the lamp posts. Big bold type asking, 'Have You Seen This Shoe?' Then a blurry photo – or an artist's impression, even – of the magical purple shoe. 'Last seen on my foot on 17 November. Reward offered.'

But there was nothing. Didn't anyone care?

I would have cooked dinner, except I didn't bother eating any more. I counted my way through three soaps until it was time to go to the pub. Tonight I chose a brown suede boot. Then I wrapped the magic shoe in a soft old pashmina – I was glad to get some use from it, it had cost a fortune and four seconds after I'd bought it, it had plummeted out of fashion.

Nick's face fell as I repeated my hop-along through the pub to the same stool I'd sat on the previous night. I was an embarrassment. Well, tough. I unwrapped the purple shoe, as though I was revealing a valuable artefact, and asked if he had any idea who it might belong to. No, he said, but he agreed that it was a magnificent-looking shoe and he was very taken with the Cinderella overtones. 'You're like Prince Charming. When you find the bloke who owns the shoe, maybe you'll fall in love.'

I looked at him scornfully. 'This is no fairy story. And why,' I wanted to know, 'do men always think that a new man is the solution to women's problems?'

'Sorry,' he said quietly, taking the shoe and placing it in a position of high visibility behind the bar. There it remained for the entire evening, but no one claimed it.

I counted my way through every man who came in, my eyes going straight to their feet, as I sought that special man in one shimmering purple shoe and one besocked foot. But nothing.

Nor was there any sign of Steven and Hayley. When I was leaving, I left my brown boot in the street. Then I went home and slept with the purple shoe on my pillow. It wasn't the first time I'd slept with a shoe, but it had never been someone else's before. It seemed to glow in the dark, filling the room with a benign violet light.

The next morning, on my way to work, I wondered if my abandoned boot had been replaced by another purple shoe. I'd half-expected it to be like the elves and the shoemaker – a new shoe every day. But this time there was nothing except an empty cigarette box and that didn't count.

Days passed and I brought the purple shoe everywhere. I felt edgy (okay, edg*ier*) without it and sometimes, when even the counting wasn't working, I took it out of my bag and touched it to my face and, amazingly, it calmed me down. One night I had a dreadful scare when I couldn't find it in my bag to put on my pillow. I was deeply unsettled without it. But when I woke in the morning, it was on my bedroom carpet, twinkling at me as it always did, like a puppy happy to see me. Now, how had that happened? Magic? Or simple muddlement brought about by a surfeit of alcohol? I didn't care, I was massively relieved and hugged the shoe to me.

Mind you, now and then I caught a glimpse of my behaviour, as seen from the outside, and wondered about it. But I'd had my husband stolen and all my left-foot shoes stolen. If I was a little unhinged, who could blame me?

Every night I went to the pub, sat on a stool and watched for one-shoed men. Every night I wore one shoe and left it behind when I went home. Although I had left nine shoes on nine different nights there had been no sightings of Hayley and Steven.

One night I arrived at the pub to find Nick bubbling over with excitement. 'I have your Cinderella,' he hissed. 'He was here the night before you found the shoe. And he's the kind of bloke who'd have a cool shoe like that.' He jerked his head discreetly. 'It's him over there.'

I looked and immediately I knew this wasn't our man. This one was too good-looking. Wasn't it traditional to make approaches to the ugly sisters first?

However, we went through the motions and, actually, he wasn't even nice about it. He seemed baffled when I withdrew the purple shoe from my bag, then he looked at my feet, at the shiny black stiletto on one foot and the big toe poking through the hole in the tights on the other. (Yes, all my tights had developed holes.) Fear scooted across his face; he suspected he was being set up, that he was the subject of a big, shoe-based leg-pull and that the whole pub was in on it. 'That's not my shoe.' He dropped eye-contact, then moved away as fast as anyone can in Oliver Sweeney Chelsea boots. Seconds later, he left.

Nick and I exchanged a look. 'It was worth a try,' I said, then Nick went back to polishing glasses and I resumed counting and drinking.

'Give me another look at it,' Nick asked later. 'Remind me of the brand name again.'

I unfolded the pashmina and purpleness blazed around the bar counter. Nick and I shared another meaningful look. I knew what he was thinking: normal non-magical shoes don't behave that way. The brand name was picked out in gold leaf on the leather insole. Merlotti.

'I'll look it up on the internet,' Nick said.

'No point,' I said. I'd already googled the brand and got nothing . . .

Suddenly a voice behind me cut into our conversation. 'Excuse me,' it said, 'but that's my shoe!'

I froze. I knew that voice. And from Nick's expression, he knew that face. I stayed as I was, facing towards Nick and all those nice shiny bottles behind the bar. Still and defiant, I refused to turn around because once I did, I knew that every single sprinkle of magic would disperse, the magic I had come to depend on.

Stupid bastard. He had to ruin bloody well everything.

I started counting. From the outside it might have looked as though the three of us and the shoe were in the grip of a hideously embarrassing silence, but I was far away inside my head. I'd got as far as twenty-four before he said, 'Alice, won't you look at me?'

'Nope.' Now I had to start again. One, two, three, four, five, six . . .

'It's my shoe,' he repeated.

'What do you want, a medal?' I asked.

'Yeah, but how do we know it's yours?' Nick challenged, a little sneery about the lip.

Silently, a plastic bag was placed on the bar top from which a shoe-sized flannel sleeping bag appeared. A second of hesitation, as if to build anticipation, then the sleeping bag's drawstring was loosed and a purple shoe was slid out. From the violet light that burst forth, there was no mistaking it. It was the matching shoe, the other one in the pair.

He placed it next to mine and, almost hypnotized, I watched both shoes as they sat on the wooden counter. Side by side they hummed with a transcendent wholeness, such astonishing completeness. Two things had never belonged more together and created a greater-than-the-sum-of-their-parts perfect oneness.

I sighed and swivelled around. There he was, doing his concerned face – furrowed brow, 'kindly' eyes – the face he'd presented the day he'd left me for Hayley, as he asked if I'd be okay. At the time I was meant to play ball and promise that yes, of course I'd be okay. But I hadn't. I had assured him I would never be right in the head again. 'Good,' he'd said absently. 'Good.' And then he'd taken his leave – a guilt-free one because he'd behaved with honour by acting concerned.

'Steven, what's going on?'

'These are my shoes. Hayley had them handmade for me in Paris. My feet were measured specially, they cost a fortune.'

I set my face in an expression of polite but condescending and-exactly-what-the-fuck-does-this-have-to-do-with-me?-ness. (Note to self: handmade shoes take a very long time. I'd never been able to establish just how long this Steven and Hayley thing had been up and running. Quite a while, it seemed.)

And what was Hayley doing giving purple, handmade, French shoes to Steven? Steven cared as much about shoes as I cared about the mating habits of crisp packets. But I understood that Hayley was such an unempathetic, self-obsessed type that the presents she gave would have to be something she wanted herself. (Like those stupid men who buy their wife a car global positioning system for her birthday and are baffled when she shrieks the house down.)

'I'm very sorry about your shoes,' Steven said. 'About you

being left with all those single ones. I heard about you showing up here in only one shoe. Naomi rang me. I came over, I saw you leave the silver shoe behind. I thought if I left my expensive handmade one in its place, you'd know I was sorry.'

Behind my polite face, I processed this ridiculousness. The appearance of the magical purple shoe in place of my silver sandal was a coded apology from Steven for letting his girlfriend into my flat to steal my shoes. How lovely!

It would have been a million times better had he got my own shoes back for me, instead of leaving me one of his own. Dickhead. But what had I expected? I was reminded of the time I'd had an excruciating toothache and instead of Steven ringing a dentist and sorting me out with extreme painkillers, he'd lain down on my bed and cried with me.

'But you kept coming here every night, doing that one-shoe thing. I realized you didn't know I'd apologized. I thought I'd better tell you.'

'Take your shoe back.' I slid it over to him. I no longer wanted it, it had been leached of all magic. I'd miss it tonight on my pillow but I was going to have to get used to sleeping on my own at some stage.

Twenty-seven months later

I was on the tube when I saw a man I recognized. For a moment I couldn't remember where I knew him from. Oh yes, I used to be married to him, didn't I?

I couldn't say it was nice to see him, it would never be nice to be reminded of my stupidity, but I was certainly able to be civil.

I enquired after Hayley. Unfortunately she was well. She and Steven were still together.

'And you?' Steven said. 'You'll meet someone else too.'

'I already have.'

'Oh?' He looked a little shaken. 'Is it . . . um . . . serious?'

'Yes. I'm very happy. Here's my stop, I have to go now.'

I jumped off the train, thrust back briefly into those terrible, terrible days when I was as mad as a cut snake, fixated only on single shoes. When getting through a whole day was out of the question, when even an hour was unmanageable, when I'd had to break the process of endurance down to each individual second. Hard to believe how hopeless I'd felt then, convinced utterly that I'd never meet someone else.

But I did. This time through an ad in *Time Out*. Her name is Jenny. Like me, she's short and, like me, she loves high heels. Won't wear anything else. It's only been a couple of months but already it's been a great success (two pairs of boots, one knee, one ankle, dull but worthy navy work shoes and some whimsical little pumps) and I certainly don't anticipate having the same trouble with her as I did with Hayley.

Written for the BBC's End of Story, *2004.*

Q. *Dear Mammy Walsh, I've been with my boyfriend for almost three years and last night we were sitting at home watching* EastEnders *and suddenly he blurted out, 'Have you put on weight? You have, haven't you?' And yes, I must admit I have. I was a size twelve when I met him and now I'm a size sixteen, so I said, 'Yeah, a bit, I s'pose. But you still love me, don't you?' And he said, 'Course I love you.' But he was looking at me strangely, as if he hadn't really seen me for months. His eyes lingered far too long on my belly, which wasn't fair because I was wearing my slobbing-around clothes, as you do, in the evenings after work, and obviously no one looks their best in them. So I sucked in my stomach and said, 'Well if you love me, then there's no problem.' Then he said, 'But I liked it better when you were thin.' I was absolutely gutted. If people love each other, how they look should have nothing to do with things. What should I do?*

Holly, London

A. Dear Holly from London, have you tried Weight Watchers? Deirdre McMahon from four doors up got great results from it. She was quite stout before she started, but now she is down to her 'target weight' and is pure skin and bone. Mind you, we've heard about nothing else for the past year, except points and plateaus.

Sometimes when it was 'Weigh-in day' and I'd see her coming, I used to pretend to have cystitis, just so I wouldn't have to invite her in. And since she reached that bloody 'target weight' she has got her hair cut and coloured, bought an entire new wardrobe and talks about nothing but sex. And this is a woman, like me, in her sixties. She was over only yesterday, wearing a tight top that said 'Bad Angel', a pair of 'hipsters' and a pink 'thong' sticking up for all to see, even though I happen to know that that 'thong on display' look is 'so' 'over'. She never sits down any more, because she can display her weight loss better standing up. We were talking about ordering turkeys for Christmas and I said, 'I need a nice big one,' and she said, 'Wehay, missus!' and did that vulgar action where you thrust your hips forward and pull your arms back. Then she wasn't able to open the biscuit tin (she always insists on having biscuits present just so she can show how great she is not to be having any). And I said, 'Give it a good yank,' and she said, 'As Des said to me last night!' Des is her husband, a huge big heavy man, who could do with a bit of Weight Watching himself. Helen, my daughter, sometimes calls him Dessy McFive-Bellies (to his face) and says that she bets he hasn't seen 'Little Dessy' for over a decade. (Also to his face and he sort of broke down and admitted it was true and Helen was horrified because then she had to try to be nice to him until she could find an excuse to run away.)

So, as I say, I can personally endorse Weight Watchers. If you stick with it for a few tough months, it'll be worth it, because at the end your boyfriend will love you again. (I know he's saying he still does, but let's face it, you know it and I know it: you're on thin ice.)

However, if you are one of these people who is 'addicted' to chocolate and has to have it no matter what, Weight Watchers mightn't be enough; you might have to be hypnotized. There was a programme about it. There was this woman and in her own words she 'just had to have it'. As Deirdre McMahon might say – Fnnarr! Anyway, this woman, if she hadn't had chocolate for a day or so, used to start fights with people and crying in the street and whatnot, so this man hypnotized her by telling her to associate chocolate with terrible things – the Stalinist purges of the thirties, little calves in abattoirs, Westlife singing 'Mandy', especially how they keep reaching out their hands and clutching at the air, always out of sync with each other. It was marvellous television, really interesting. And the hypnotherapy worked. They started shoving bars of chocolate at her – Flakes, Crunchies, Snickers (or is it Snickers*es*? I'm never sure), Bounties, Yorkies – like they were baiting a bear with a stick, and she begged them to take them away. (To be honest, though, I thought I detected a little flicker of interest when they produced the Bounty, but maybe I was only imagining it.)

Anyway, she was going great guns, eschewing chocolate left, right and centre, but after three days she cracked and started milling into the Fruit and Nut, then lying about it and saying that chocolate still repulsed her. But because of the hidden cameras in her flat, we knew all about it and the producers did a surprise raid on her and she was brought into a viewing room and made to sit down and watch reruns of her guzzling. Obviously she was shamed to the core but three months later they did a follow-up show and she was still on the chocolate.

If you are lucky enough to be 'mortally obese' you could qualify to have your stomach stapled. This is an operation where they cut away several miles of your large intestine and staple up your stomach until it is the size of a pea (marrowfat, rather than petit pois). This means that if you have more than two spoonfuls of mashed potato at your dinner, your stitches will burst open and you will die a slow, horrible, lingering death. Something to focus the mind when you're looking at that slice of Black Forest Gateau!

Anyway, Holly, good luck with it all, whichever route you choose, but for God's sake, don't go for the cabbage soup diet. You will suffer from severe flatulence and if your boyfriend doesn't leave you for being stout, he will leave you because of the smell.

Happy to be of help!

Q. *Dear Mammy Walsh, thank you for your detailed diet advice. But that wasn't the advice I wanted. I was thinking that if my boyfriend loves me, surely he should love me, no matter what I look like?*

Holly, London

A. Well, Holly, I'm sorry I misunderstood, so I am. But the thing is, in my day it was all different. Once you had the ring on your finger, you could go to hell altogether and guzzle scones and brown bread and jam all day long. You could put on four stone in four months and there wasn't a damn thing your husband could do about it, because there was no divorce in Ireland. Mind you, all these eating disorders and whatnot weren't invented in my day and although we certainly got stout, it was more to do with having a clatter of children than 'compulsive overeating'.

But, Holly, my point is, *there is no ring on your finger*. And even if there was, he could divorce you in the twinkling of an eye. There isn't the same security for women these days. To use a term I heard in an economics programme on telly (God knows why I was watching it) you are 'a seller in a buyer's market'.

Helen has just told me that I'm 'a fossilized old dinosaur for whom feminism might never have happened'. Well, maybe I am, but I'm not ashamed of it; I'm simply saying what everyone else is too 'politically correct' to say. However, Holly, maybe you would be better off going to a different 'agony' aunt, one of those feathery-stroker ones who will tell you that you are perfect as a size sixteen, that you are a whole and beautiful person, that you don't need to change an iota and that if your boyfriend doesn't agree, you should both go for couple counselling to 'resolve your issues', where you will be charged seventy euro a week for twenty-six weeks. (Payment up front.)

Holly, I'm sorry you and I didn't see 'eye to eye'. I haven't had a failure yet so you're my first and, I must admit, it smarts. But I wish you and your boyfriend well with this feathery-stroker approach. Just please remember that it could all be avoided if you cut out desserts and did a bums 'n' tums video three times a week.

Wishing Carefully

*B*e careful what you wish for, they say. So when Siobhan came back from Australia with an Aboriginal dreaming bowl and invited us all to place a wish in it, I'm ashamed to say I wished for a fairy-tale romance. It wasn't the kind of thing I would normally do but I was a bit wounded at the time. Even while I was folding up the note to put in the bowl, I hated Mark for turning me into the sort of person who made such pathetic wishes.

Naturally enough, I told everyone that I'd wished for peace in the Middle East. The only person I told the truth to was Siobhan, who confessed that she already knew because after everyone had left she'd unfolded the notes and read them all. She was quick to reassure me that I wasn't alone; the person who'd claimed he'd wished for his mother's arthritis to improve had in fact wished for a silver SL320 Merc with many optional extras, including heated leather seats and a CD player.

'It's just a bit of fun,' Siobhan said, but I was keen to have faith in the future, and hoped it would come true. And, in a way, it did . . .

Because, would you believe it, less than a week later I met a man. Not just any man, but a fireman. The job alone was sexy, and he was gorgeous – arms the size of my thighs, hugh barrel chest all the better to crush me against. He was slightly shorter than I expected firemen to be and this suited me fine; I was right off tall men. *And* he was a kind and caring person; only a kind and caring person would put their life at risk entering burning buildings to rescue sleeping children and climbing up trees to bring home beloved cats.

We hit it off, he asked me out, Siobhan smiled proudly from the sidelines as if it was all her doing and suddenly I was in great form. I embarked on the round of shopping and ablutions that a first date calls for and Saturday night couldn't come fast enough.

But on Saturday afternoon my phone rang. It was my hero and he was yawning so hard his jaw cracked. 'I'm sorry, Kate, out on a job last night, just got back, need some sleep, on a shift again tomorrow.' Another huge big yawn.

What could I say? Huffiness simply wasn't an option – no sniping about freshly done nails, new sandals, having turned down four other invitations and now what was I supposed to do, spend my Saturday night cleaning the bathroom? (Like I'd done every previous Saturday for the past month.) This man was a *hero*. So I sympathized, praised and rearranged for Thursday night. 'I'll be wide awake and full of beans,' he promised.

So on Thursday I came to work in my going-out clothes. I caught Mark watching me as I click-clacked in my high sandals to the photocopier, but he said nothing. Briefly the pain of our separation knocked the breath from my body, then – with gratitude – I thought of my hunky fireman and I started to breathe again.

But that afternoon, minutes after I'd got back from spending my lunch hour getting my hair blow-dried, my fireman rang. He'd just got home after a fifteen-hour stint dousing a huge conflagration in a rubber-goods warehouse.

'I'm sorry, Kate.' A five-second yodelly yawn followed. 'I really need some zeds, I'm so sleepy.'

The disappointment was intense and as I thought of my good hair and my inappropriate clothes, I swallowed, braced myself, then went for it. Brazenly, I said, 'I could come over and keep you company.'

'I'm sorry,' he said gently. 'All I'm capable of is sleep. How about we try again on Saturday night?'

But even though I took the precaution of not doing my hair, Saturday night didn't happen either: he'd been rescuing people from a house fire and he was exhausted. It was then I made my decision. The rest of the world needed him more than I did. It would be selfish to try to get a go of him, so I turned him free.

But there was no time to be miserable because within days I'd met Charlie – at a party where he walked straight over to me, pointed a finger and said, 'You, babe, are the woman I'm going to marry.'

'What a fool,' Siobhan murmured and even while one part of my brain was agreeing with her, another part found his confidence strangely alluring.

'The name's Charlie,' he said. 'Remember it because you'll be screaming it later.'

'I don't think so,' I replied, and he just laughed and said he wouldn't take no for an answer.

Over the next two weeks he pursued me rapaciously and he seemed so sure he'd win me over that in the end he managed to convince me of it too. When I finally agreed to go out with him he promised he'd show me the best night of my life and I must admit I was intrigued.

First he took me to a party, but he made us leave after fifteen minutes because he was bored, then he took me to a bar, which I'd read about but hadn't been to, but we were barely there half an hour before he wanted to be off again. Two more parties and a club followed. He had the shortest attention span of anyone I'd ever met and in a way all that variety was exciting.

There were three or four more nights like that and at the time I thought of myself as glamorous, but now what I remember most is the number of times I had to gulp back the drink which had just arrived, while Charlie eyed the exit and tapped his foot impatiently.

So convincing was Charlie's wide-boy swagger that it took me some time to notice that he was shorter than me. A *lot* shorter when I wore my boots. And when he couldn't sit through a film – and we're not talking *Dances With Wolves* or *Heaven's Gate* here, only a normal ninety-minute one – his attention deficit disorder began to annoy me.

Worse still, he always seemed to have a cold and his constant sniffing was driving me mad. *Mad.* As soon as one sniff was over, I was tensing my shoulders in irritation against the next one. Occasionally he sneezed and he baffled me by treating it like a major disaster.

Then I discovered the cause of the constant sniffing – and the short attention span – when I accidentally walked into his bathroom and found him crouched over the edge of the sink, a rolled-up fiver at his nostril.

It wasn't the cocaine itself that shocked me. It was that he was taking it for a Saturday afternoon's shopping. And that he'd been snorting it all this time and he'd never once offered me any. Marching orders were swiftly dispatched and not even him prostrating himself and swearing that we'd get a video and a Chinese takeaway and stay in for an entire evening made any difference.

The disappointment of Charlie set me back, and I was missing Mark a little too much for my liking, so to take my mind off things I decided to throw a party, which is where I met Owen.

The moment we made eye-contact he began to blush and I'd never seen anything like it. It roared up his neck and face like red-hot lava, rushing to the furthest reaches of his head, then kind of 'pinged' on the outer edges of his ears. For some reason I thought of an advertising slogan: Come home to a real fire.

Flustered, he turned around and bumped into a bottle of red wine with such violence it splashed Siobhan's dress and my pale-gold curtains and the only reason I didn't start shrieking like a termagant was because I felt attracted to him.

Owen was, quite simply, the shyest man I'd ever met but after the cocaine-fuelled arrogance of Charlie, I liked his self-effacing charm. And though he was short, he was very good-looking – a neat handsome little package.

He asked if he could take me for a drink some time and when I said yes, he was so pleased that he knocked over and smashed my good flower vase into smithereens.

Our first date wasn't much better. He came to pick me up, said, 'You've lovely eyes. Even though they're quite close together,' then swept the phone off the wall with such force that it never worked properly again.

I urged myself to give it time, that he would eventually relax with me. But each outing was as bad as the first time: the blush that could be seen from outer space, the stammering compliment that managed to be an insult, then the ceremonial knocking over and breaking of something.

I had to end it with him before he'd destroyed all that I owned.

And into the breach stepped Shane, a friend of Siobhan's youngest brother. He was too young for me but I didn't care. He was cute-looking – another dinky one, actually; I was having quite a run of short men asking me out – and he was sweet.

He took me to Brittas Bay to fly kites which might have been fun had he not told me that we were going to an art exhibition and had I not dressed accordingly. Shane claimed to have no memory, no memory *at all* of telling me about the exhibition. Then he raced off down the beach with his big, yellow kite and I almost ended up flat on my back as I chased after him and my four-inch heels sank into the sand.

Eventually the kite-flying torment ended and we went to the pub and the real date began. But within minutes Shane disclosed that he thought:

a) Jack Nicholson and Jack Nicklaus were related,
b) that flour was made from flowers,
c) that the Mona Lisa's real name was Muriel.

At the Muriel bit I sighed heavily; this was awful. And thick and all as he was Shane said, 'You're not really into this, are you, Kate? Some guy wrecked your head, yeah? Siobhan said.'

I sighed again; Siobhan was so indiscreet. But all of a sudden the idea of spilling the beans about Mark to this dim, sympathetic boy was enticing.

'It was great for ages and I don't really know what happened but in the end he just rode roughshod over me.'

'He rode *who?*' Shane was all indignation.

That was it! But Shane was mad keen to see me again. 'We could go to this exhibition you keep talking about,' he beamed.

Gently I turned him down. I couldn't see him again. He was simply much, much, *much* too stupid.

Then I was depressed. I'd gone out with so many men and I was still thinking about Mark. I saw him at work but we never spoke. He'd been smiling a bit at me lately, probably because he thought enough time had elapsed for us to start behaving like civilized people again. Well, he could think again.

I squared my shoulders and told myself it would all be fine eventually.

I thought the good times had finally arrived when I met a short, clever doctor who kept trying to get me into bed by tugging at my clothes and saying, 'Let me through, I'm a doctor.' It was funny the first time he said it, though not funny enough for me to sleep with him. Quite funny the second time too. By the fifth time I was worried. Was this what counted as a sense of humour with him?

Unfortunately it was and I stopped letting him through.

It was Siobhan who twigged what was happening.

'Hiho,' she greeted me. 'How are you enjoying your fairy-tale romance?'

'Still waiting for it,' I said glumly.

'What are you talking about? You're slap-bang in the middle of it. You're Snow White and you're working your way through the seven dwarves.'

I told her she was off her rocker and that I wasn't going to play, but she insisted. 'They've all been very short, haven't they? *Haven't* they? And their personalities fit. The poor fireman who couldn't get out of bed? Sleepy, obviously. Charlie the coke-fiend is Sneezy, of course.'

'There wasn't much sneezing, mostly sniffing,' I said, but Siobhan was undeterred.

'Poor shy Owen is an open-and-shut Bashful. Shane is Dopey – the funny thing is that's what his friends call him anyway. And the doctor? Well, Doc, obviously.'

'So which ones haven't I done?' It's impossible to remember the names of all seven of them.

'Grumpy and Happy.'

Mark asked if I'd meet him for a drink after work. With a heavy heart I agreed. It had been seven months now; I supposed he was entitled to his stuff back.

But we'd barely sat down when he blurted out, 'I'm sorry, Kate. I was such a grumpy bastard to you.'

As soon as I heard the word 'grumpy' my heart almost stopped in my chest. But Mark couldn't be Grumpy! He was too tall!

'You were right not to put up with me. I've had plenty of time to think and, Kate, I feel small. I feel so very, very small.'

'Small?' I repeated.

'Small. Tiny.' He held up his thumb and first finger, barely leaving a gap. 'This small.' Then he told me he loved me, that he was miserable without me and asked if there was any chance that I'd take him back.

'I know I don't deserve it.' He hung his head. 'But if you'd give me just one chance I'd make it up to you and I'd do everything I can to make you happy. If you come back to me, Kate, I'll be happy. I'll be so *happy*.'

First published in Woman's Weekly, *February 2002.*

Q. *Dear Mammy Walsh, I am a young man (aged twenty-seven) and I have developed a slight crush on you. I dig your no-nonsense approach. Tell me, if they made a film of your life, who would you like to play you?*
Darren, Cork

A. Dear Darren from Cork, me, of course! However, I know that often the Hollywood studios insist on a 'star', in which case I think Halle Berry would be perfect. She and I have very similar ears, Mr Walsh has remarked on it more than once. Thank you for your interest, also your gracious comments. I recently had my first failure, due to the no-nonsense approach you mentioned and it's nice to be reminded that you can't please all of the people all of the time.

Q. *Dear Mammy Walsh, me again. I was just wondering if you could do any job in the world, what would it be?*
Darren, Cork

A. Dear Darren from Cork, I would like to present *Top Gear*.

Q. *Dear Mammy Walsh, why?*
Darren, Cork

A. Dear Darren from Cork, I would like to drive fast cars. I've had a lifetime of sensible stuff like Nissan bloody Sunnys and Toyota fecky Corollas and I'd love a go of a Maserati or a Merc SL55. I like the thought of motorbikes too but the helmet would have my hair destroyed.

Precious

*H*e was the most beautiful man I'd ever seen.

Granted, I was only twenty, and not much of a judge, but all the same.

I was three weeks into my first 'proper' job and I'd just come back from the bar after a frustrating attempt to buy a post-work round of drinks. Not only had it taken for ever to get served but then the barman had seemed disinclined to believe I was over eighteen. That's how young I was – desperate to look older.

I banged a glass in front of Teresa and another one in front of my chair and I blazed indignantly, 'If they went any slower, they'd be taking drinks back from people and refunding them their money!' He laughed and I fell silent. Where had he come from? This creature with his dark wavy hair and skin so pale it almost had a bluish hue.

My colleague and, as it happens, new best friend – you bond quickly at that age – Teresa introduced us. 'Orla, this is my friend Bryan.'

Suddenly Bryan, second only to Nigel in the pantheon of dorky boy names, blossomed into something violently romantic.

He was small and slight, but not boyish. More like a fully grown man who'd been reduced by, say, 20 per cent. And the thin wrists that stuck out beneath his white cuffs were covered with fine black hair.

I was convinced he was foreign, perhaps of Russian ancestry. No Irish man could be so elegant and delicate. But when I mumblingly asked him what nationality he was, he sounded surprised and said, 'Irish.'

Was he sure, I pressed.

Quite sure, he said. His mother was from Limerick, one of the Limerick McNamaras and his father's family had lived in Meath since time immemorial.

The next day at work, Teresa delivered the news that almost caused me to levitate. 'Bryan likes you.' To my dumb, idiotic face she expanded, 'He was asking all about you.'

Eventually I released the question which tormented me. 'Have you ever, you know . . . with him?'

'Bryan?' She laughed a laugh I didn't understand. 'Nah, he's a bit too –' another laugh '– *mysterious* for me.'

I wasn't inclined to believe her. How could she not want him? How could anyone not want him?

That night we all went out again. This was when I discovered I was taller than him.

His movements mesmerized me. He did everything – lit cigarettes, fiddled with his glass – with a hard, easy grace. Next to him I was a lumpish peasant and my coarse unworthiness rendered me mute.

'Are you alright?' Teresa's voice was innocently surprised. 'It's just that normally you're so . . . lively.'

'Fine,' I insisted, a sickly smile nailed to my face.

He looked as if he'd spent his childhood as a pale face at a bedroom window, watching sadly while the other cruder, more robust children rough-housed with each other on the grass. But it turned out that he'd been very good at football.

When he wasn't answering questions he was a man of few words. He didn't bother with small talk, which impressed me no end and served to silence me further. 'I wonder . . .' he said at one stage. 'I wonder what it's like to be a loofah.'

'Yeah, I wonder . . .' I tried to make my voice sound musing, although until that very moment I hadn't entertained an atom of curiosity about the inner workings of a loofah. 'Scratchy, I suppose.'

'Scratchy!' He acted as if I'd said something profound and I nearly burst with pride – and relief.

Being kissed by him was like being pelted with marshmallows and I was so grateful that he wanted to sleep with me.

But my inadequacy burgeoned. He was just too beautiful, too perfect, too refined, too self-contained. Then I discovered I was six months older than him. It made me worse. I somehow felt like a horny-handed, meaty pervert who was taking advantage of him.

Waiting for him to discover that I wouldn't do became unbearable, so I hastened it myself. I watched his exasperation grow with my awkward, giggly silences. It was like seeing an out-of-control truck speed down a hill, directly towards me. I was powerless to stop it and powerless to get out of the way.

Every night when he dropped me home I swore to myself that next time – if I was lucky enough to get a next time – it would be different. I'd talk, I'd laugh, I'd make *him* laugh. But when the next time came, my words would disappear on me and we'd end up going to bed more out of needing something to do.

From the beginning I'd known he was moving to New York and that the most I would ever get with him was a couple of months. Even while I fantasized about him staying for me, I knew he wouldn't.

So he went, just as expected. The only jarring note was that he was going to work for a bank.

And I never got over him. Sometimes I used to say it. I liked the sound of it. 'There was this bloke when I was twenty and I suppose I . . .' brave smile, deep breath, '. . . never got over him.'

It was actually a relief when he was gone. I was sick and crazy, but it was easier to deal with when he wasn't around.

Teresa wouldn't let me be heartbroken. 'I like him,' she said, 'he's my friend, but isn't he a bit precious?'

For a long, long time I thought calling someone 'precious' was a compliment.

Perhaps six months after he'd left news filtered back from New York that he was going out with a painter. When I'd recovered from the initial kick-in-the-stomach shock, I thought: oh but of course. A painter, a tormented artist. What else? I could see her. Neurotic and sexy, with an elusive, quicksilver quality which held Bryan in her thrall. She was tiny – she'd have to be, to be worthy of him. Skinny with childlike buttocks, but nothing childlike about her sexuality. She never ate, but subsisted on cigarettes and black coffee. She dressed entirely in black, her black polo-neck covered with paint stains which she never noticed. Sometimes she deliberately cut herself with the scalpel she used on her canvasses. While the rest of the world slept she prowled around her loft, flinging paint at canvas and exclaiming with insomniac despair. I scorned my own regular seven-hour slumbers – how stolid, how embarrassingly stable.

Time passed and I went out with other men, and did my very best to let them break my heart. Some of them made quite a good stab at it too, but not enough to wipe out his memory.

'I'm sorry,' I said more than once. 'You see there was this bloke when I was twenty and I . . .' brave smile, deep breath, '. . . never got over him.'

Most of them bought it. Some were quite sympathetic, some were hurt, some angry and one of them told me I had an over-active imagination and that I'd want to cop on to myself.

The day I heard he was marrying the neurotic, insomniac painter, I thought I took the news quite well. Until I was on the bus on the way home and, with a sweaty rush of hot and cold, realized that if I didn't get off at the next stop, there was a good chance I'd vomit.

And somehow it was ten years since he'd left Ireland, Teresa was getting married, and Bryan was coming home from New York for the wedding, bringing Danielle his wife with him.

From the moment I heard they were coming, I became clenched and oxygen-deprived with waiting. And I wound ever tighter as the big day hurtled towards me. You'd swear it was *me* who was getting married.

The morning of the wedding I spent a long, long time on my appearance, prepared to embrace any small setback – a chip in my nail varnish, a missing earring – as a major disaster.

I didn't see them in the church, but when we got to the hotel and saw the seating plan I couldn't decide if I was glad or appalled to find I was at the same table as them. But my friend Jennifer was also at the same table, she'd provide a buffer.

I was twisted up, tight as a walnut, my eyes working the reception room. Then I saw him. Patiently I waited to see if I'd fall in a faint or break out into a sweat or rush to vomit. Nothing happened. .

At the same time he saw me and came towards me, as my heart knocked ever louder echoes into my ears. We smiled and our greeting was the height of polite, apart from the fact that he had forgotten my name. Still 'not quite of this world', I thought. Then I focused on the woman next to him. I'd seen her already: she was impossible to miss. She didn't look the way I expected Bryan's wife to look. For a start she was tall, taller than him. About my height, actually. And her hair was bright yellow. Not exactly blonde, more like the Day-Glo dazzle of yellow Opal Fruits. Glorious. Her dress was also yellow, but not quite the same shade. How brave, I thought, suddenly angry with my own tweely coordinated look. She wore lots of red lipgloss, as if she'd fallen into a patch of raspberry jam. And I was surprised that she didn't look as if she subsisted on just cigarettes and coffee. One or two square meals got past those raspberry-jam lips. I could see no obvious scalpel scars on her bare arms, either.

'How's New York?' I asked him.

'Fine,' he said.

'Good,' I said, 'I was worried about it.'

No, I didn't actually say it, but I thought it. To be fair, I didn't exactly set the conversation alight either. Even ten years on he could deprive me of the power of speech.

During the meal she was very loud and drank a lot. Of course she drank a lot. Most creative people had a drinking problem. Tossing back the yellow hair that didn't quite go with her yellow dress, she seemed to like Jennifer. During one break in conversation she confided loudly into Jennifer's face that her cellulite was so bad she could see Calista Flockhart's profile in it.

As I discreetly checked beneath the table for scars on her legs I couldn't help but notice that her legs were quite hairy. For a second this didn't fit with my picture of her, then it all made sense. She was a free spirit, thumbing her nose at convention. My respect for her went through the roof and I felt ashamed of my own smooth, waxed legs. I was nothing but an unimaginative slave.

After the speeches all the smokers stampeded out to the lawn. En route, Jennifer got me in a headlock. 'Christ in the marketplace, that Bryan is so boring! Getting conversation out of him is like trying to get blood out of a turnip. Where's Al? I need a light.'

Al was my escort, my 'plus one'. Actually he was the man who'd told me that I had an overactive imagination and that I'd want to cop on to myself. I'd grown quite attached to him. I liked his plain-spokenness. The fact that he spoke *at all* was very attractive, I suddenly acknowledged, as I eyed Bryan across the table and realized conversation would be non-existent until one of the smokers returned.

Time dragged, then next thing Jennifer catapulted at high speed across the room. A liver-coloured patch crawled up her neck and her eyes were bright with indignation.

She pulled me away from the table. 'You know that

Danielle?' Her voice had a tremble. 'She's just tried to start a fight with me in the ladies'. Lairy piece of work.'

'Well, she's an artist,' I shrugged. 'They're temperamental.'

'What are you talking about?' Jennifer asked. 'She's a painter.'

'Yeah, an artist.'

'No,' she corrected impatiently. 'She's a house painter, a lairy painter and decorator. She's drunk and lairy and awful.'

A house painter. Not a picture painter, a *house* painter. Of course it was a shock. Until I began to process it. How cool was that? A woman in a man's world, confounding expectations, bucking the trend . . .

Abruptly, I stopped. That was *enough*. As if on cue, across the room came Al, homing straight at me, looking so happy to see me, even though he'd only been gone ten minutes. I began walking towards him.

Lairy, I said to myself. I liked that word. Lairy, I repeated. Lairy.

First written for BBC Radio, broadcast on 29 December 2000.

Q. *Dear Mammy Walsh, you rock! Do you believe in monogamy?*
Darren, Cork

A. Dear Darren from Cork, of course I do, you cheeky imp! I'm a devout Catholic.

Q. *Dear Mammy Walsh, hey, you can't blame a guy for trying! Tell me two things, Mammy Walsh. One, if you could be any animal, what would it be? And two, what's your real name? I can't keep calling you Mammy Walsh, can I?*
Darren, Cork

A. Dear Darren from Cork, why can't you? Mammy Walsh is my professional name. I can't be revealing my real name to every Tom, Dick and Darren who wants to know it. Darren from Cork, I am beginning to think you are a bit of a 'weirdo' and I know what you're trying to do with that animal question – that sort of thing is as old as the hills. If I say my favourite animal is a tiger (which it isn't) you will say that it means I'd be like a tiger in bed. As it happens, I don't like any animals, they are dirty, stupid creatures. I have enjoyed our correspondence, but I now consider it to be at an end. For the love of God, make friends with people your own age, instead of badgering the likes of me.

Q. *Dear Mammy Walsh, wooh! Tough babe! Love it! But I hear ya!*
Darren, Cork

Soulmates

'So was it a disaster?' Peter begged Tim. 'Did they try to kill each other?'

Watched by seven avid pairs of eyes, Tim shook his head sorrowfully. 'They got on like a house on fire. They're going to do it again in July.'

A murmur of *Isn't that marvellous?* started up.

But Vicky couldn't take any more. In despair, she put her face in her hands. 'How do they do it?' she whispered, echoing everyone's sentiments. 'How do they bloody well do it!'

Georgia and Joel were born on the same day in the same year in the same city – though they didn't meet until they were twenty-six-and-a-half, whilst moving and shaking their way around a launch party for a Japanese beer. When Joel discovered the momentous connection, he declared, above the clamour, 'We're twins! Soulmates.'

Georgia was called the golden girl, an inadequate attempt to convey how fantastically energetic, gorgeous and *nice* she was. In every group of human beings there's a natural leader and she was one. Only a very special man could keep up with her: Joel was the perfect candidate. The kindest and best-looking of his good-looking group of prototype New Lad friends, how could he not help gravitating to Georgia, the deluxe version of her coterie of glossy, shiny girlfriends?

And now she had a soulmate. She *would*, her best friend Vicky thought, with shameful envy. Georgia was always the first. With the first ankle-bracelet, the first wedge sandals, she had an unerring instinct for what was good and new and right. Some years back Vicky had tried to trump her with a pair of boots she'd joyously ferried back from New York. *This time I'm the winner*, Vicky had thought, breathlessly ushering her new boots ahead of her. But Georgia had beaten her to it. Again. By wearing a similar pair of boots – similar, *but better*. The heel was nicer, the leather softer, the whole élan simply much more convincing. And she'd only bought them in Ravel.

Soulmates. It was the start of the nineties and New Age stuff had just started being fashionable. Katie had recently bought four crystals and dotted them about her flat, but four crystals couldn't hold a candle to a real live soulmate. It was about the best thing you could have – better than a tattoo or henna-patterned nails or a cappuccino maker. Quickly others followed their example by claiming that they too had found their SM. But it was only a spurious intimacy based on chemical connection, which dissolved just as soon as the cocaine or Ecstasy or Absolut had worn off.

'We're twins,' Georgia and Joel declared to the world, and paraded their similarities. A crooked front tooth that she'd had capped and that he'd had knocked out in a motorbike accident and replaced. Both had blond hair, although hers was highlighted. Indeed rumours circulated that perhaps his was too.

Within weeks they'd moved in together and filled their flat

with a succession of peculiar things, all of which assumed a stylish lustre the minute they became theirs. But no matter how much others tried to emulate their panache it was never quite the same. The liver-purple paint which Georgia and Joel used to such stylish effect on one room in their south-facing flat, never survived the transition to anyone else's wall. Especially not Tim and Alice's north-east-facing living room. 'I can't bear it,' Tim eventually admitted. 'I feel as though I'm watching telly inside an internal organ.'

Georgia and Joel spent money fast. 'Hey, we're skint,' they often laughed – then immediately went to the River Café. On receiving a particularly onerous credit card bill they tightened their belts by buying champagne. Attached to them, debt seemed desirable, stylish, alive. 'Money is there to be spent,' they claimed and their friends cautiously followed suit, then tried to stop themselves waking in the night in overdrawn terror.

After four years together Georgia and Joel surprised every-one by getting married. Not just any old wedding – but you could have guessed that. Instead they went to Las Vegas; hopped on a plane on Friday night after work, were married on Saturday by an Elvis lookalike, were back for work on Monday. The following weekend they rented a baroque room in Charterhouse Square, draped it in white muslin and had the mother of all parties. Proving they were ahead of their time they served old-fashioned martinis which made a comeback amongst the Liggerati a couple of years later.

Close friends, Melissa and Tom, who were having a beach-front wedding ceremony in Bali a month later, went into a trough of depression and wanted to call the whole thing off.

Two years later Georgia once more reinvented the right lifestyle choices by announcing her pregnancy. Stretch marks and sleepless nights acquired an immediate cachet. They called their little girl Queenie – a dusty, musty old ladies' name, but on their child it was quirky and charming. In the following months, various acquaintances named their newborn girls Flossie, Vera and Beryl. Georgia regained her figure within weeks of having the baby. Even worse, she claimed not to have worked out.

Then one day, pension brochures appeared on their circular walnut coffee table.

'Pensions?' asked Neil, hardly believing his luck. Joel had finally cocked up and done something deserving of scorn.

'Got to look to the future,' Joel agreed. 'You know it makes sense.'

'Pensions,' Neil repeated, throwing his head back in an elaborate gesture of amusement. 'You sad bastard.'

'You want to be old and skint?' Joel said with a smile that was very obviously not a cruel one. 'Up to you, mate.'

And Neil wanted to hang himself. They were always moving the bloody goalposts.

But most of all, it was Georgia and Joel's relationship that no one could ever top. They'd been born on the same day, in the same year, within four miles of each other; they were so obviously meant to be together that everyone else's felt like a making-do, a shoddy compromise. Georgia and Joel fitted together, like two halves of a heart; symbiosis was the name of the game and their devotion was lavish and public. Every year one or other of them had a 'surprise' birthday party, 'for my twin'.

Their friends were tightly bound to them by a snarl of admiration, hidden envy and the hope of some of their good fortune rubbing off.

But as they moved forward into the late nineties, perhaps Georgia and Joel's mutual regard wasn't as frantically fervent as once it had been. Perhaps tempers were slightly shorter than previously. Maybe Joel got on Georgia's nerves once in a while. Perhaps Joel wondered if Georgia wasn't quite as golden as she'd once been. Not that they'd ever consider splitting up. Oh no. Splitting up was for other people, those unfortunate types who hadn't found their soulmate.

And other people *did* split up. Tom left Melissa for Melissa's brother in a scandal that had everyone on the phone to each other in gleeful horror for some weeks, vying to be the biggest bearer of bad news, outdoing each other in the horrific details. 'I hear they were shagging each other on Tom and Melissa's honeymoon. On the *honeymoon*. Can you believe it!'

Vicky's husband left her. She'd had a baby, couldn't shift the weight, became dowdy and different. Unrecognizable. She'd once been a contender. Of course, never exactly as lambent or lustrous as Georgia, but now she'd slipped and slipped behind, well out of the race, limping and abandoned.

Georgia was a loyal and ever-present friend in their times of woe. Tirelessly she visited, urged trips to hairdressers, took care of children, consoled, cajoled. She even let Vicky and Melissa say things like, 'You think that your relationship is the one that won't hit the wall, but it can happen to anyone.' Georgia always let them away with it, bestowing a kindly smile and resisting the urge to say, 'Joel and I are different.'

People gave up watching and waiting for Georgia and Joel to unravel. The times people said, 'Don't you think Georgia and Joel are just *too* devoted? Methinks they do protest too much,' became fewer and fewer. People ran out of energy and patience waiting for the roof to fall in on the soulmates and their 'special relationship'.

But the thing about a soulmate is that it can be a burden as well as a blessing, Joel found himself thinking one day. You're stuck with them. Other people can ditch their partner and forage with impunity in the outside world, looking for a fresh partner, where *everyone* is a possibility. Having a spiritual twin fairly narrows your choice.

And Georgia found herself emotionally itchy. What would have happened if she hadn't met Joel? Who would she be with now? And she experienced an odd yearning; she *missed* the men she hadn't loved, the boyfriends she'd never met.

So acute was this unexpected sadness that she tried to speak to Katie about it.

'Sounds like you're bored with Joel,' Katie offered. 'Do you still love him?'

'Love him?' Georgia exclaimed, with knee-jerk alacrity. 'He's my *soulmate*!'

Then one night Joel got very, very drunk and admitted to Chris, 'I fancy other women. I want to sleep with every girl I see. The curiosity is too much.'

'That's normal,' Chris said in surprise. 'Have an affair.'

'It's not normal. This is me and Georgia.'

'Sounds like you're in trouble, mate.'

'Not me and Georgia.'

They believed their own publicity and, in time-honoured

tradition, attempted to paper over the cracks by having another baby. A boy this time. They called him Clement.

'That's an old man's name!'

'We're being ironic!' But their laughs lacked conviction; and when they painted Clement's room silver no one copied them.

On they laboured, shoulder to shoulder. While all around them people danced the dance of love: merging and splitting, blending anew with fresh partners, sundering, twirling and cleaving joyously to the next one. And shackled to their soulmate, Georgia and Joel watched with naked envy.

It was only when Georgia began questioning her mother on the circumstances of her birth that she realized how ridiculous the situation had become. 'What time of the day was I born, Mum?' she asked, as Clement bellowed on her lap.

'Eleven.'

'Could it have been a little bit later?' Georgia heard herself ask. 'Like gone midnight?' *So that it was actually the following day*, she thought but didn't articulate.

'It was eleven in the *morning*, nowhere near midnight.'

Three weeks later when Joel and Georgia split up it caused a furore. Everyone declared themselves horrified, that if the golden couple couldn't hack it, what hope was there for the rest of them? But there wasn't one among them who couldn't help a frisson of long-awaited glee. Now Mr and Mrs Perfect would see what it was like for the rest of them.

The 'press release' insisted that they were still friends, that it was all very adult and civilized, that they were in complete agreement over finances and custody of the children. Sure, everyone scorned. *Sure.*

But, disconcertingly, Georgia wouldn't join in an 'all men are bastards' conversation with Vicky, Katie and Melissa. Not even when Joel began going out with a short, plump dental nurse called Helen.

'Tim has met her,' Alice consoled. 'He says she's not a patch on you.'

'Oh don't,' Georgia objected. 'I think she's really sweet.'

'You've met her?'

And when Georgia began seeing a graphic designer called Conor, Tim assured Joel that Alice said he was a prat.

'Nah,' Joel protested. 'He's a good bloke. We're all going on holiday with the kids at Easter.'

'Who are?' Tim wanted to pass out.

'Me and Helen, Georgia and Conor.'

Everyone declared that it was wonderful they were being so mature about the split and only the certain knowledge that the holiday would be a bloodbath consoled them. Itching to find out just how bad it was, Tim rang Joel the day he got back. Then Tim, Alice, Katie, Vicky, Melissa, Chris, Neil and Peter gathered in the pub, ostensibly for a casual drink. Conversation glanced off the usual subjects – house prices, hair-straighteners, Pamela Anderson's breasts – until no one could bear any more. Peter was the first to crack, the words were out of his mouth before he could stop them.

'So was it a disaster?' he begged Tim. 'Did they try to kill each other?'

Watched by seven avid pairs of eyes, Tim shook his head sorrowfully. 'They got on like a house on fire. They're going to do it again in July.'

A murmur of *Isn't that marvellous?* started up.

But Vicky couldn't take any more. In despair, she put her face in her hands. 'How do they do it?' she whispered, echoing everyone's sentiments. 'How do they bloody well do it!'

First published in You *magazine, May 2000.*

Q. *Dear Mammy Walsh, I am in a dilemma. My boyfriend has bought me a nurse's outfit and wants me to wear it while we're having sex. I love him but don't feel very happy about it, especially because it isn't even a short sexy nylon nurse's uniform, the type you buy from Ann Summers or somewhere like that, but a real nurse's uniform which he bought from Oxfam. What should I do?*

Aileen, Cambridge

A. Don't write to me again, young lady, that's what you should do! This column is not some kind of 'sexpert' thing. I dispense solid common sense about matters of the heart. I have no interest whatsoever in anyone's 'sex' life and I consider our correspondence to be closed. And what is it with men and nurses? Clearly your 'boyfriend' has never been in hospital because if he had he wouldn't consider nurses to be in any way sexy. Nurses are hard-hearted types who dress you in humiliating blue paper nighties that are wide open at the back for the whole world to see your bottom. And nurses say things like 'How are "we" today?' when there's only one of you in the bed and they make you do your wees into a shallow metal bowl when you're perfectly capable of walking to the bathroom. Mind you, men wanting to have sex with nurses isn't the half of it. I believe there are some men who find it a 'turn on' to dress

347

in babies' nappies and waddle around the place, knocking things over and being fed puréed carrots and behaving exactly like babies – no shallow metal bowls needed for them, if you get my drift.

And other people (in the US, of course, where they're stone mad for the 'kinkiness') dress up in – wait till you hear – bunny rabbit outfits and furry bear outfits and the sort of chicken outfits that sometimes a grown man will be wearing as he stands in the street handing out leaflets about a new fast-food chicken restaurant. There are 'clubs' for these people and they meet up in their furry rig-outs and, for reasons that baffle me, they find it a ferocious 'turn on'.

The latest thing, I hear, is something called 'dogging'. Have you heard of it? I thought it meant doing it 'doggy style', which of course I have heard of, because I am a woman of the world, even if I have never tried it. Then I thought it must mean having 'sex' with dogs, which is an unholy thought. But it transpires to be something entirely different. What it is, is lots of people going to a park or forest in the dark of night and 'having sex' with strangers. Some people 'have sex' in their car, leaving their lights on and other people stand around watching and 'pleasuring' themselves, although I cannot see the connection to 'dogs' in all this. I first found out about it when my daughter Helen told me she was going out for an evening's 'dogging' and although it was a quarter past twelve, I thought she meant she was going to the greyhound track to try to win some money, as she was 'skint'. But she soon put me right on what 'dogging' means and at first I thought she was making it up, because that's the sort of thing she does. Having a little laugh at her gullible mother. But then she showed me an article about 'dogging' in Mr Walsh's *Marie Claire* and there it was in black and white and not even Helen could pull that much of a 'hoax' on me. It beggars belief. Wouldn't you get cold standing around in the raw night air, 'pleasuring' yourself? Or what if you bumped into your dentist? Or someone from bridge?

However, as I said, I have no interest whatsoever in discussing 'kinky' sex. Also your boyfriend sounds very stingy – how much did the second-hand nurse's uniform from Oxfam cost, as opposed to a lovely new nylon one from Ann Summers? That's what you'd want to be considering, young lady. No one likes a man who won't put his hand in his pocket. (Unless he's the kind of man who puts his hand in his pocket to 'interfere' with himself.)

Please do not contact me again.

PS Unless you find out the origin of the word 'dogging'. I am keen to know.

The Truth is Out There

*L*os Angeles International Airport: teeming with passengers, filmstars, illegal immigrants, a dazed English girl called Ros and, of course, the odd alien or two freshly landed from another planet. Well, only one alien, actually. A small, yellow, transparent creature who liked to be called Bib. His name was really Ozymandmandyprandialsink, but Bib was just much more *him*, he felt. Bib was in Los Angeles by accident – he'd stolen a craft and gone on a little joyride, planning to go only as far as planet Zephir. Or planet Kyton, at the most. But they'd been repairing the super-galaxy freeway and diverting everyone and somehow he'd lost his way and ended up in this place.

Ros Little hadn't landed from another planet, she just felt like she had. The twelve-hour flight from Heathrow, the eight-hour time difference and the terrible row she'd had the night before she'd left all conspired to make her feel like she was having a psychotic episode. Her body was telling her it should be the middle of the night, her heart was telling her her life was over, but the brazen mid-afternoon Californian sun dazzled and scorched regardless.

As Ros dragged her suitcase through the crowds and the drenching humidity towards the taxi rank, she was stopped in her tracks by a woman's shriek.

'It's an alien!' the helmet-haired, leisure-suited matron yelled, jabbing a finger at something only she could see. 'Oh my Lord, look, just right there, it's a little yellow alien.'

How very Californian, Ros thought wearily. He first mad person and she wasn't even out of the airport yet. In other circumstances she'd have been thrilled.

Hastily Bib assumed invisibility. That was close! But he had to get out of here because he knew bits and pieces about planet Earth – he'd been forced to study it in Primitive Cultures class. On the rare occasions he'd bothered to go to school. Apparently, Los Angeles was alien-spotting central and the place would be overrun with X-filers in a matter of minutes.

Looking around anxiously, he saw a small girl-type creature clambering into a taxi. Excellent. His getaway car. Just before Ros slammed the door he managed to slip in beside her unnoticed, and the taxi pulled away from the crowd of people gathered around the hysterical matron.

'But, Myrna, aliens ain't yellow, they're green, everyone knows that,' was the last thing that Ros heard, as they skidded away from the kerb.

With heartfelt relief, Ros collapsed onto the air-conditioned seat – then froze. She'd just got a proper look at her cabbie. She'd been too distracted by Myrna and her antics to notice that he was a six-foot-six, three-hundred-pound, shaven-headed man with an eight-inch scar down the back of his scalp.

It got worse. He spoke.

'I'm Tyrone,' he volunteered.

You're scary, Ros thought, then nervously told him her name.

'This your first visit to LA?' Tyrone asked.

'Yes,' Ros and Bib answered simultaneously, and Tyrone looked nervously over his shoulder. He could have sworn he'd heard a second voice, an unearthly cracked rasp. Clenching his hands on the wheel, he hoped to hell that he wasn't having an acid flashback. It had been so long since he'd had one, he thought he'd finally grown out of them.

When the cab finally negotiated its way out of LAX, Los Angeles looked so like, well, *itself* that Ros could hardly believe it was real – blue skies, palm trees, buildings undulating in the ninety-degree haze, blonde women with unfeasibly large breasts. But as they passed by gun shops, twenty-four-hour hardware stores, adobe-style motels offering waterbeds and adult movies, and enough orthodontists to service the whole of England, Ros just couldn't get excited. 'It's raining in London,' she tried to cheer herself up, but nothing doing.

To show willing she pressed her nose against the glass. Bib didn't, but only because he didn't have a nose. He was enjoying himself immensely and thoroughly liked the look of this place. Especially those girl-type creatures with the yellow hair and the excess of frontage. Hubba *hubba*.

Tyrone whistled when he drew up outside Ros's hotel. 'Class act,' he said in admiration. 'You loaded, right?'

'Wrong,' Ros corrected, hastily. She'd been warned that Americans expected lots of tips. If Tyrone thought she was flush she'd have to tip accordingly. 'My job's paying for this. If it was me, I'd probably be staying in one of those dreadful motels with the waterbeds.'

'So, you cheap, huh?'

'Not cheap,' Ros said huffily. 'But I'm saving up. Or at least I was, until last night . . .'

For a moment terrible sadness hung in the air and both Bib and Tyrone looked at Ros with compassionate interest laced with a hungry curiosity. But she wasn't telling. She just bit her lip and hid her small pale face behind her curly brown hair.

Cute, Bib and Tyrone both realized in a flash of synchronicity. She's cute. Not enough happy vibes from her, though, Tyrone felt. And she's not quite yellow-looking enough for my liking, Bib added. But she's *cute*, they nodded in unconscious but undeniable male bonding.

So cute, in fact, that Tyrone hefted her suitcase as far as the front desk and – unheard of, this – waved away a tip.

'Maaan,' Tyrone muttered to himself, as he lumbered back to the car. 'What is *wrong* with you?'

After the glaring mid-afternoon heat, it took a moment in the cool shade of the lobby for Bib's vision to adjust enough to see that the hotel clerk who was checking Ros in was that Brad Pitt actor person. What had gone wrong? Surely Brad Pitt had a very successful career in the earth movies. Why had he downgraded himself to working in a hotel, nice as it seemed? And why wasn't Ros collapsed in a heap on the floor? Bib knew for a fact that Brad Pitt had that effect on girl-types. But just then Brad shoved his hair back off his face and Bib realized that the man wasn't quite Brad Pitt. He was *almost* Brad Pitt, but something was slightly wrong. Maybe his eyes were too close together or his cheekbones weren't quite high enough, but other than his skin having the correct degree of orangeness, something was off.

Before Bib had time to adjust to this, he saw another earth movie star march up and disappear with Ros's suitcase. Tom Cruise, that was his name. And he really *was* Tom Cruise, Bib was certain of it. Short enough to be, Bib chortled to himself smugly. (Bib prided himself on his height, he went down very well with the females on his own planet, all two foot eight of him.)

The would-be Brad Pitt handed over keys to Ros and said, 'We've toadally given you an ocean-front room, it's rilly, like, awesome.' Invisible, but earnest, Bib smiled and nodded at Ros hopefully. This was bound to cheer her up. An ocean-front room that was rilly, like, awesome? What could be nicer?

But Ros could only nod miserably. And just as she turned away from the desk Bib watched her dig her nails into her palms and add casually, 'Um, were there any messages for me?' While Brad Pitt scanned the computer screen, Bib realized that if he had breath he would have been holding it. Brad eventually looked up and with a blinding smile said, 'No, *ma'am!*'

Bib wasn't too hot on reading people's minds – he'd been 'borrowing' spacecraft and taking them out for a bit of exercise during Psychic lessons – but the emotion coming off Ros was so acute that even he was able to tune in to it. The lack of phone call was bad, he realized. It was very bad.

Deeply subdued, Bib trotted after Ros to the lift, where someone who looked like Ben Affleck's older, uglier brother pressed the lift button for them.

Bib was very keen to get a look at their room and he was half impressed, half disappointed. It was very . . . *tasteful*, he supposed the word was. He'd have quite liked a waterbed and adult movies himself, but he had to say he was impressed with the enormous blond and white room. And the bathroom was good – blue and white and chrome. With interest he watched Ros do a furtive over-her-shoulder glance and quickly gather up the free shower cap, body lotion, shampoo, sewing kit, emery board, cotton buds and soap and shove them in her handbag. Somehow he got the impression that she wasn't what you might call a seasoned traveller.

A gentle knock on the door had her zipping her bag in a panic. 'Come in,' she called and Tom Cruise, all smiles and cutesy charm was there with her case. He was so courteous and took such a long time to leave that Bib began to bristle possessively. *Back off, she's not interested,* he wanted to tell Tom. Who'd turned out not to be Tom at all. He only looked like Tom when he was doing the smile, which faded the longer he fussed and fiddled in the room. At the exact moment that Bib realized why Tom was lingering, so did Ros. A frantic rummage in her bag and she found a dollar (and spilt the sewing kit onto the floor in the process). Tom looked at the note in his hand, then looked back at Ros. Funny, he didn't seem pleased and Bib cursed his own perpetual skintness. 'Two?' Ros said nervously to Tom. 'Three?' They eventually settled on five and instantly Tom's cheesy, mile-wide smile was back on track.

No sooner had Tom sloped off to extort money from someone else than the silence in the room was shattered. The phone! It was ringing! Ros closed her eyes and Bib knew she was thanking that thing they called God. As for himself he found he was levitating with relief. Ros flung herself forward and surfed the bed until she reached the phone. 'Hello,' she croaked, and Bib watched with a benign smile. He almost felt tearful. But anxiety manifested itself as he watched Ros's face. She didn't look pleased. In fact she looked bitterly disappointed.

'Oh Lenny,' she said. 'It's you.'

'Don't sound so happy!' Bib heard Lenny complain. 'I set my clock for two in the morning to make sure my favourite employee has arrived safely on her first trip in her new position, and what do I get? "Oh Lenny, it's you"!'

'Sorry, Lenny,' Ros said abjectly. 'I was kind of hoping it might be Michael.'

'Had another row, did you?' Lenny didn't sound very sympathetic. 'Take my advice, Ros, and lose him. You're on the fast track to success here and he's holding you back and sapping your confidence. This is your first opportunity to really prove yourself, it could be the start of something great!'

'Could be the *end* of something great, you mean,' Ros said, quietly.

'He's not the only bloke in the world,' Lenny said cheerfully.

'He is to me.'

'Please yourself, but remember, you're a professional now,' Lenny warned. 'You've three days in LA so put a smile on your face and knock 'em dead, kiddo.'

Ros hung up and remained slumped on the bed. Bib watched in alarm as all the life – and there hadn't been much to begin with – drained out of her. For a full half an hour she lay unmoving, while Bib hopped from pad to pad – all six of them – as he tried to think of something that would make her happy. Eventually she moved. He watched her pawing the bed with her hand, then she did a few half-hearted, lying-down bounces. With great effort of will, Bib summoned his mind-reading skills. *Jumping on the bed.* Apparently she liked jumping on beds when she went to new places. She and Michael always did it. Well, in the absence of Michael, she'd just have to make do with a good-looking – even if he did say so himself – two-foot-eight, six-legged, custard-yellow life-form from planet Duch. *Come on*, he willed. *Up we get.* And he took her hands, though she couldn't feel them. To Ros's astonishment, she found herself clambering to her feet. Then doing a few gentle knee-bends, then bouncing up and down a little, then flicking her feet behind her, then propelling herself ceiling-wards. All the while Bib nodded unseen encouragement. *Attagirl*, he thought, when she laughed. *Cute laugh. Giggly, but not daft-sounding.* Ros wondered what she was doing. Her life was over, yet she was jumping on a bed. She was even enjoying herself, how weird was that?

Now you must eat something, Bib planted in her head. *I know how you humans need your regular fuel. Strikes me as a very inefficient way of surviving, but I don't make the rules.*

'I couldn't,' Ros sighed.

You must.

'Okay, then,' she grumbled, and took a Snickers from the mini-bar.

I meant something a bit more nutritious than that, actually.

But Ros didn't answer. She was climbing, fully dressed, into bed and in a matter of seconds fell asleep, the half-eaten Snickers beside her on the pillow.

While Ros slept, Bib watched telly with the sound turned

off and kept guard over her. He couldn't figure himself out: his time here was limited because they could find the space-craft at any time, so he should be out there cruising, checking out the females, having a good time at somewhere called the Viper Room (owned by one Johnny Depp, who modelled himself on Bib, no doubt about it), but instead he wanted to remain here with Ros.

She woke at 4 a.m., jolted upright with jet lag and heart-break. He hated to see her pain, but this time he was powerless to help her. He managed to tune into her wavelength slightly, picking up bits and pieces. There had been a frenzied scream-ing match with the Michael person, the night before she left. Apparently, he hadn't wanted her to come on this trip. Selfish, he'd called her, adding that she cared more about her job than she did about him. And Ros had flung back that *he* was the selfish one, trying to make her choose between him and her job. By all accounts it had been the worst row they'd ever had and it showed every sign of being their last.

Human males, Bib sighed. Cavemen, that's what they were, with their fragile egos and sense of competition. Why couldn't they rejoice in the success of their females? As for Bib, he loved a strong, successful woman. It meant he didn't have to work and – Oi! What was Ros doing, trying to lift that heavy case on her own? She'll hurt herself!

Puffing and panting, Ros and Bib manoeuvred her case onto the bed and when she opened it and started sifting through the clothes she'd brought, Bib realized just how distraught she must have been when she'd packed. Earth still had those quaint, old-fashioned things called seasons and, even though the temperature in LA was in the nineties,

Ros had brought clothes appropriate for spring, autumn and winter, as well as summer. A furry hat – why on earth had she brought that? And four pairs of pyjamas? For a three-day trip? And now what was she doing?

From a snarl of tights, Ros was tenderly retrieving a photograph. With her small hand she smoothed out the bends and wrinkles and gazed lovingly at it. Bib ambled over for a look – and recoiled in fright. He was never intimidated by other men but he had no choice but to admit that the bloke in the photo was very – and upsettingly – handsome. Not pristine perfect like the wannabe Brads and Toms but rougher and sexier-looking. He looked like the kind of bloke who owned a power screwdriver, who could put up shelves, who could stand around an open car bonnet with six other men and say with authority, 'No, mate, it's the alternator, I'm telling ya.' This, Bib deduced with a nervous swallow, must be Michael. He had dark, messy curly hair, an unshaven chin and his attractiveness was in no way marred by the small chip from one of his front teeth. The photo had obviously been taken outdoors because a hank of curls had blown across his forehead and halfway into one of his eyes. Something about the angle of his head and the reluctance of his smile indicated that Michael had been turning away when Ros had clicked the shutter. *Real men don't pose for pictures*, his attitude said. Instantly Bib was mortified by his own eagerness to say 'Cheese' at any given opportunity. But could he help it if he was astonishingly photogenic?

For a long, long time Ros stared at Michael's image. When she eventually, reluctantly, put the photo down, Bib was appalled to see a single tear glide down her cheek. He rushed to comfort her, but fell back when he realized there was no need because she was getting ready to go to work. Her heart was breaking – he could *feel* it – but her sense of duty was still intact. His admiration for her grew even more. Luckily, in amongst all the other stuff she'd brought, Ros had managed to pack a pale grey suit and by the time she was ready to leave for her 8 a.m. meeting she looked extremely convincing. Of course Bib realized she *felt* like a total fraud, certain she'd be denounced by the Los Angeles company as a charlatan the minute they clapped eyes on her, but apparently that was par for the course in people who'd recently been promoted. It would pass after a while.

Because of her lack of confidence, Bib decided he'd better go with her. So off they went in a taxi to DangerChem's headquarters at Wilshire Boulevard, where Ros was ushered into a conference room full of orange men with big, white teeth. They all squashed Ros's little hand in their huge, meaty, manicured ones and claimed to be 'trullly, trullly delighted' to meet her. Bib 'trullly, trullly' resented the time they spent pawing her and he managed to trip one of them up. And not just any of them, but their *leader*. Bib knew he was the leader because he had the orangest face.

Then Bib perked up – a couple of girls had just arrived in the meeting! Initially, he thought they were aliens too, although he couldn't quite place where they might be from. With their unnaturally elongated, skeletal limbs and eyes so wide-spaced that they were almost on the sides of their head, they had the look of the females from planet Pfeiff. But when he tried speaking to them in that language (he knew only a couple of phrases – 'Your place or mine?' and 'If I said you had a beautiful body would you hold it against me?') they remained blankly unresponsive. One of them was called Tiffany and the other was called Shannen and they both had the yellow-haired, yellow-skinned look he usually found so attractive in a girl-type. Although, perhaps not as much as he once had.

The meeting went well and the orange men and yellow girls listened to Ros as she outlined a proposal to buy products from them. When they said the price she was offering was too low she was able to stop her voice from shaking and reel off prices from many of their competitors, all of them lower. Bib was bursting with pride.

When they stopped for lunch, Bib watched with interest as Tiffany used her fork to skate a purple-red leaf of radicchio around her plate. Sometimes she picked it up on her fork and let it hover in the general vicinity of her mouth, before putting it back down. She was *miming*, he realized. And that wasn't right. He switched his attention to Shannen. She was putting the radicchio on her fork and sometimes she was putting some of it into her mouth. He decided he preferred her. So when she said, 'Gotta use the restroom,' Bib was out of his seat in a flash and going after her.

He'd really have resented being called a peeping Tom. An opportunist, he liked to think of himself. An alien who knew how to make the most of life's chances. And being invisible.

But how strange. He followed Shannen into the cubicle and she seemed to be ill. No, no, wait – she was *making* herself ill. Sticking her fingers down her throat. Now she was brushing her teeth. Now she was renewing her lipstick. And she seemed happy! He'd always regarded himself as a man of the universe, but this was one of the strangest things he'd ever seen.

I should be nominated for an Oscar, Ros thought, as she shook her last hand of the day. She'd given the performance of a lifetime around that conference table. But she tried to take pride that she *had* done it. Between jet lag and her lead-heavy unhappiness over Michael she was surprised she'd even managed to get dressed that morning, never mind discuss fixed costs and large order discounts.

However, when she got back to her hotel, she insisted on shattering her fragile good humour by asking a not-quite-right Ralph Fiennes if anyone had phoned for her. Ralph shook his head. 'Are you sure?' she asked, wearing her desperation like a neon sign. But unfortunately, Ralph was very sure.

Trying to stick herself back together, Ros stumbled towards her room, where no force in the universe – not even one from planet Duch – could have stopped her from ringing Michael.

'I'm sorry,' she said, as soon as he picked up the phone. 'Were you asleep?'

'No,' Michael said, and Ros's weary spirits rallied with hope. If he was awake at two in the morning, he couldn't be too happy, now could he?

'I miss you,' she said, so quietly she barely heard herself.

'Come home, then.'

'I'll be back on Friday.'

'No, come home now.'

'I can't,' she said gently. 'I've got meetings.'

'Meetings,' he said bitterly. 'You've changed.'

As Ros tried to find the right words to fix things, she wondered why it was always an insult to tell someone that they'd changed.

'When I first met you,' he accused, 'you were straight up. Now look at you, with your flashy promotion.'

He can't help it, Ros thought. Too much had changed too quickly. In just over eighteen months she'd worked her way up from answering phones, to being a supervisor, to assisting the production manager, to assisting the chairman, to becoming vice-production manager. None of it was her fault; she'd always thought she was as thick as two short planks. She'd been *happy* to think that. How was she to know that she had a natural grasp of figures and an innate sense of management? She had bloody Lenny to thank for 'discovering' her, and she could have done without it. Everything had been fine – better than fine – with Michael until she'd started her career ascent.

'Why is my job such a problem?' she asked, for the umpteenth time.

'"My job"!' Michael said hotly. '"My job, my job." You love saying it, don't you?'

'I don't! You have a job too.'

'Mending photocopiers isn't quite the same as being a vice-production manager.' Michael fell into tense silence.

'I can't do it,' he finally said. 'I can't be with a woman who earns more than me.'

'But it'll be our money.'

'What if we have kids? You expect me to be a stay-at-home househusband sap? I won't do it, babes,' he said, tightly. 'I'm not that kind of bloke.' She heard anger in his voice and terrible stubbornness.

But I'm good at my job, she thought, and felt a panicky desperation. She didn't want to give it up. But more than her job, she wanted Michael to accept her. Fully.

'Why can't you be proud of me?' She squeezed the words out.

'Because it's not right. And you want to come to your senses. You're no good on your own, you need me. Think about it!'

With that, he crashed the phone down. Instantly she started to ring him back, then found herself slowly replacing the receiver. There was nothing to be gained by ringing him because he wasn't going to change his mind. They'd had so many fights, and he hadn't budged an inch.

So what was the choice? She loved him. Since she met him three years ago, she'd been convinced he was The One and that her time in the wilderness was over. They'd planned to get married next year, they'd even set up a 'Meringue Frock' account. How could she say goodbye to all that? The obvious thing was to give up her job. But that felt so wrong. Oughtn't Michael to love her as she was? Shouldn't he be proud of her talents and skills, instead of being threatened by them? And if she gave in now what would the rest of their lives together be like?

But if she didn't give in . . . ? She'd be alone. All alone. How was she going to cope? Because Michael was right, she had very little confidence.

For some minutes she sat abjectly by the phone, turning a biro over and over, as she pondered the lonely existence that awaited her. All she could see ahead of her was a life where she jumped on hotel beds by herself. The bleakness almost overwhelmed her. *But just a minute*, she found herself thinking, her hand stopping its incessant rotation of the biro – *I managed to get all the way from Hounslow to Los Angeles without Michael's help*. And *I managed to get a taxi to and from work. Even held my own in a meeting.*

To her great surprise she found that she didn't feel so bad. Obviously, she felt awful. Frightened, heartbroken, sick and lonely. But she didn't feel completely suicidal, and that came as something of a shock. She was so used to hearing Michael telling her that she was a disaster area without him that she hadn't questioned it lately . . .

How about that? She remained on the bed, and her gaze was drawn to the window. In all the trauma, she'd forgotten about her 'toadally awesome' ocean view and it couldn't have been more beautiful: Santa Monica beach, the evening sun turning the sea into a silver-pink sheet, the sand rose-coloured and powdery. Along the boardwalk, gorgeous Angelenos skated and cycled. A sleek couple whizzed by on a tandem, their no-doubt perfect baby in a yellow buggy attached to the back of the bike. He looked like a little emperor. Another tall, slender couple roller-bladed by, both sun-glassed and disc-manned to the max. Hand in hand, they glided past gracefully, their movements a ballet of perfect synchronization.

'Fall,' Bib wished fiercely. 'Go on, trip. Skin your evenly tanned knees. Fall flat on your remodelled faces.' He had hoped it might cheer Ros up. But, alas, it was not to be, and on the couple glided.

Ros watched them go, gripped by a bitter-sweet melancholy. And then, to her astonishment, she found herself deciding that she was going to try roller-blading herself. Why not? It was only six-thirty and there was a place right next to the hotel that rented out roller-blades.

Hardly believing what she was doing she changed into leggings, ran from her room and in five minutes was strapping herself into a pair of blades. Tentatively, she pushed herself a short distance along the board walk. 'Gosh, I'm quite good at this,' she realized in amazement.

Bib held onto Ros's hand as she awkwardly skidded back and forth. It had been a huge struggle to convince her to get out here. And she was *hopeless*. If he hadn't been holding onto her hand, she'd be flat on her bum. Yet her ungainly vulnerability made her even more endearing to him.

Bib had followed the evening's events with avid interest. He'd been appalled by Michael's macho attitude, the cheek of the bloke! He'd longed to snatch the phone from Ros and tell Michael in no uncertain terms how fabulous Ros was, how she'd terrified a roomful of powerful orange men. Then when Michael hung up on Ros, Bib had used every ounce of will he could muster to stop Ros from ringing him back. He'd worked desperately hard at reminding Ros how wonderfully she'd coped since she'd arrived in this strange threatening city, even though it was so obvious, she should know it herself . . .

'Careful, careful!' he silently urged, squeezing his eyes shut in alarm, as Ros nearly went flying into a woman who was holding onto a small boy on a bike.

'Sorry,' Ros gasped. 'I'm just learning.'

''S okay,' the little boy said. 'Me too. My name's Tod and that's my mom, Bethany. She's teaching me to ride my bike.'

Bethany was in the unfortunate position of having to hold tightly onto the back of Tod's bike and run as fast as Tod cycled. Bib eyed Bethany with sympathetic understanding because he was in the unfortunate position of having to run as fast as Ros was roller-blading. Which got faster and faster as her confidence grew.

'Wheeeeeh!' Ros shrieked, as she sped a good four yards, before losing Bib and coming a cropper.

When she returned the skates to the hire office, her knees were bruised but her eyes were asparkle. 'I had a lovely time,' she laughingly announced. Then she sprinted joyously across the sand to the hotel, Bib puffing anxiously behind her, tangling himself in his six legs as he tried to keep up.

She woke in the middle of the night, the exhilaration and joy of the night before dissipated and gone. She felt cold, old, afraid, lonely. She wouldn't be able to cope without Michael, she didn't want a life without him.

But then she remembered the roller-blading. She wasn't normally adventurous, usually needing Michael with her before trying new things. Yet she'd done that all on her own and it was a comfort of sorts.

'I am a woman who roller-blades alone,' she repeated to herself until she managed to get back to sleep. Then she woke up, got dressed and went to work, vaguely aware that there was a new steadiness about her, a growing strength.

When she returned from her day's work, exhausted but

proud from holding her own as they inched their way tortu-
ously towards a deal, she bumped into Brad Pitt in the hotel
lobby. From the look of things he was just knocking off work.

'Did you have a good day?' he enquired.

Ros nodded politely.

'So, what kind of business are you in?' Brad asked.

Ros considered. She always found this awkward. How
exactly did you explain that you worked for a company
that made portaloos? A very successful company that made
portaloos, mind.

'We, um, take care of people,' she said. Well, why shouldn't
she be coy? Americans were the ones who called loos *rest-
rooms*, for goodness sake!

'D'ya take care of people on a movie set?' Brad never
missed an opportunity. The door to his career could open
absolutely anywhere – there was the time he'd seen the
director of *Buffy The Vampire Slayer* in his chiropodist's
waiting room, or the occasion he'd crashed into the back of
Aaron Spelling's Beemer – so he was always prepared.

'Actually, we have,' Ros said with confidence.

Quick as a flash, Brad's lightbulb smile burst onto his face
and he swooped closer. 'Hey, I'm Bryce,' he murmured.
'Would you do me the honour of having a drink with me
this evening?'

A good-looking man had invited her for a drink! What a
shame that nothing would cheer her up ever again. Because
if anything would do the trick, this would. But even as a
refusal was forming in her mouth, Ros found herself pausing.
Wouldn't it be better than sitting alone in her room waiting
for the phone to ring?

'Okay,' she said wanly.

Bryce looked surprised, women were usually delighted to spend time with him. Then he clicked his fingers. 'Oh I get it. You're English, right? You kinda got that Merchant–Ivory repressed thing going on. Love it! Meet me in the lobby at six-thirty.' And smoothing his hair, he was gone.

In her room, Ros checked the phone, picked it up, trembled with the effort of not dialling Michael's number and frog-marched herself into the shower. America, the land of oppor-tunity. She should at least try; after all Bryce really was gorgeous.

From the jumble of clothes thrown on the bed, she man-aged to make herself presentable. A short – but not too short – black dress, a pair of high – but not too high – black sandals. But as she watched herself in the mirror, it was like seeing a stranger. Who was this single girl who was going out on a date with a man who wasn't Michael?

When the lift doors parted, Bryce was loitering in the lobby, sunbleached hair gleaming on his golden forehead, white teeth exploding into a flashgun smile. Ros's spirits inched upwards. Maybe things weren't so bad. On the way to his car, she noticed Bryce patting his hair in the window as he passed by, then pretended she hadn't.

The bar was low-lit and quiet. 'So as we can really, like, *talk*,' Bryce said with a smile that promised good things, and the mercury level of Ros's mood began its upward climb again. As soon as they'd ordered their drinks, Bryce started the promised talk.

'. . . and then I got the part as the shop clerk in *Clueless*. They toadally cut it, right, but the director said I was great, really great. It was a truly great performance. I gave and gave until it hurt, but the goddamn editor was, like, toadally on my case . . .'

Ros nodded sympathetically.

'. . . of course, I should have got the Joseph Fiennes part in *Shakespeare in Love*. It was mine, they even toadally told my agent, but on-set politics, it's a toadal bitch, right?'

Ros nodded again. Despite Bryce's many tales of woe, his smile glittered and flashed. But as his litany of bad luck continued, Ros began to notice that he didn't ever make eye-contact with her. Yet the intimate smiles continued anyway. Eventually, wondering if he was coming on to some girl behind her, Ros looked over her shoulder. And saw a mirror. Ah, that explained everything. Bryce was flirting with his favourite person. Himself.

On and on he droned. Great performances he nearly gave. Evil directors, cruel editors, leading men who had it in for him because they were threatened by his talent and looks.

'Hey, I've done enough talking about me.' He finally paused for breath. 'What do *you* think of me?'

Ros could hardly speak for depression. With Bryce she felt more alone than she had on her own. 'Would you mind terribly if I left? Only I'm ever so sleepy. Must be jet lag.'

'We've hardly been here thirty minutes,' Bryce objected. 'I'm just warming up.'

To her dismay, Bryce offered to see her back to the hotel. And up to her room. At her bedroom door she realized he was about to try to kiss her. She braced herself – she didn't have the energy to resist him. He looked deep into her eyes and trailed a gentle finger along her cheek. Despite him being the world's most boring man, Ros couldn't help a leap of interest. After all, he was *so* handsome. Slowly Bryce lowered his perfect lips to hers, then paused.

'What are you doing?' Ros whispered.

'Close-up,' Bryce whispered back. 'A three-second close-up of my face before the camera cuts to the clinch.'

'Oh for goodness sake!' Ros shoved the key in the lock, twirled into her room and slammed the door.

'Hey,' Bryce was muffled but unbowed. 'You ballsy English girls, toadally like a Judi Dench thing! Y'ever met her? I just thought with you both being English . . .'

'Go away,' she said, her voice trembling from unshed tears. This was the worst that Ros had felt. Wretched. Absolutely wretched. Was this all she had to look forward to? Boring, self-obsessed narcissists?

Bib had been against the idea of a drink with Bryce from the word go. He just hated those men who thought they could fell women with one devastating smile. He'd tried to warn Ros that Bryce was nothing but a big, pink girl's blouse, but she wouldn't listen and . . . *Now* what was going on? Someone was outside their room, pounding and demanding to be let in. It was a man's voice – perhaps it was Bryce back to try his luck again?

'Open the bloody door!' a voice ordered, and as Bib watched in astonishment, Ros moved like a sleepwalker and flung the door wide. A man stood there. A man that Bib recognized. But he wasn't any of the would-be film stars, he was . . .

'Michael!'

Though it killed him to do it, Bib had to admit that Michael was looking good. With his messy curly hair, rumpled denim shirt and intense male presence he made all the wannabe Toms and Brads look prissy and preened.

'Can I come in?' Michael's voice was clipped.

'Yes.' Ros looked as though she was going to faint.

'What are you doing here?' she asked as Michael marched into the room.

'I wanted to kiss you,' he announced, and with that he pulled Ros to his broad, hard chest and kissed her with such lingering intimacy that Bib felt ill.

Finally he let Ros go and said into her upturned face, 'I've come to get this sorted, babes. You and me and this job lark.'

'You flew here?' Ros asked, dazedly.

'Yeah. Course.'

Hmmm, Bib thought. *Hasn't got much of a sense of humour, has he?* Most normal people would have said something like, 'No, I hopped on one leg, all six thousand miles of it.'

'I can't believe it.' Ros was a picture of wonder. 'We're skint but you've travelled halfway around the world to save our relationship. This is the most romantic thing that's ever happened to me.' And Bib had to admit that Michael did cut a very Heathcliffish figure as he strode about the room, looking moody and passionate.

Bad-tempered, actually, Bib concluded.

'You come home with me now,' Michael urged. 'You knock the job on the head, we get married and we live happily ever after! You and I are meant to be together. We were terrif until you got that promotion, it was only then that things went pear-shaped.'

With his words, the joyous expression on Ros's face inched away and was replaced by an agony of confusion.

'Come on,' Michael sounded impatient. 'Get packing. I've got you a seat on my flight back.'

But Ros looked paralysed with indecision. She leant against a wall and made no move, and the atmosphere built and built until the room was thick with it. Bib was bathed in sweat. And he didn't even have perspiration glands.

Don't do it, he begged, desperately. *You don't have to. If he loved you he wouldn't ask you to make this choice.*

To his horror he watched Ros fetch her pyjamas from under her pillow and slowly fold them.

'Where's your suitcase?' Michael asked. 'I'll help you.'

Ros pointed and then began scooping her toiletries off the dressing table and into a bag. Next, she opened the wardrobe and took out the couple of things that she'd hung up. It seemed to Bib that her movements were becoming faster and more sure, so in frantic panic he summoned every ounce of energy and will that he possessed and zapped her with them.

You don't need this man, he told Ros. *You don't need any man who treats you like a possession with no mind or life of your own. You're beautiful, you're clever, you're sweet. You'll meet someone else, who accepts you for all that you are. In fact, if you're prepared to be open-minded and don't mind mixed-species relationships, I myself am happy to volunteer for the position . . .* He stopped himself. Now was not the time to be sidetracked.

'I'll fetch your stuff from the bathroom,' Michael announced, already briskly en route.

Then Ros opened her mouth to speak and Bib prayed for her words to be the right ones. 'No,' she said, and Bib reeled with relief. 'No,' Ros repeated. 'Leave it. I can't come tonight. I've got a meeting tomorrow.'

'I know that, babes,' Michael said tightly, as if he was struggling to keep his temper. 'That's what I mean, I want you to come with me *now*.'

'Don't make me do this.' Misery was stamped all over Ros's face.

'It's make your mind up time.' Michael's expression was hard. 'Me or the job.'

A long nerve-shredding pause followed, until Ros once again said, 'No, Michael, I'm not leaving.'

Michael's face twisted with bitter disbelief. 'I didn't know you loved the job that much.'

'I don't,' Ros insisted. 'This isn't about the job.'

Michael looked scornful and Ros continued, 'If you love someone, you allow them to change. If marriage is for life, I'm going to be a very different person in ten, twenty, thirty years' time. How're you going to cope with that, Mikey?'

'But I love you,' he persisted.

'Not enough, you don't,' she said, sadly.

For a moment he looked stunned, then flipped to anger. 'You don't love me.'

'Yes, I do. You've no idea how much.' Her voice was quiet and firm. 'But I am who I am.'

'Since when?' Michael couldn't hide his surprise.

'I don't know.' She also sounded surprised. 'Since I came here, perhaps.'

'Is this something to do with Lenny? Are you having it off with him?'

Ros's incredulous laugh said it all.

'So have I got this right?' Michael was sulky and resentful. 'You're not coming home with me.'

'I've a job to do,' Ros said in a low voice. 'I fly home tomorrow night.'

'Don't expect me to be waiting for you, then.'

And with the same macho swagger that, despite everything, Bib admired, Michael swung from the room.

The door slammed behind him, silence hummed, and then – who could blame her, Bib thought sympathetically – Ros burst into tears.

No more Michael. The thought was almost unbearable. She lay on the bed and remembered how his hair felt, so rough, yet so surprisingly silky. She'd never feel it again. Imagine that, never, *ever* again. She could smell him now, as if he was actually in the room, the curious combination of sweetness and muskiness that was uniquely Michael's. She'd miss it so much. As she'd miss the verbal shorthand they had with each other, where they didn't have to finish sentences or even words because they knew each other so well. She'd have to find someone else to grow old with.

It was all over, she was certain of it. There would be no more rows, no further attempts to change the other's mind.

They'd had so many angry, bitter fights, but what was in the air was the stillness of grief. The calmness when everything is lost. She'd moved beyond the turbulence of rage and fury into the still static waters of no return.

What would she do with the rest of her life, she asked herself; how was she going to fill in all the time between now and the time she died?

Roller-blade, planted itself in her head. Immediately she told herself not to be so ridiculous. How could she go roller-blading?

But why not? What else was she going to do until bedtime? And despite all the events of the evening it was still only eight-thirty. She pulled on her leggings, even though they had a tear on one knee, and ran across the sand. She was surprised to find how uplifted she was by whizzing back and forth at high speed on her skates. It had something to do with pride in what a good roller-blader she was – she really was excellent, considering this was only her second time doing it. Her sense of balance was especially wonderful.

The little boy Tod who had been there the previous night was there again, with his long-suffering mother. Bethany was red-faced and breathless from having to run and hold onto Tod while he cycled up and down the same six yards of boardwalk and Ros gave her a sympathetic smile.

Then Ros went back to her room and against all expectations managed to sleep. When morning came she woke up and went to work, where, with a deftness that left the Los Angeles company reeling in shock, she negotiated a thirty per cent discount when she'd only ever planned to ask for twenty. Blowing smoke from her imaginary gun, she gave them such firm handshakes that they all winced, then she swanned back to the hotel to pack. Successful mission or what?

Bib was in agony. What was he going to do? Was he going to England with Ros, or home to his own planet? Though he'd grown very fond – too fond – of Ros, he had a feeling that somehow he just wasn't her type and that revealing himself, in all his glorious, custard-yellowness would be a very, very bad idea. It killed him not to be able to. In just over two days he'd fallen in love with her.

But would she be okay? She *thought* she was okay, but what would happen when he left her and there was no one to shore up her confidence? Would she go back to Michael? Because that wouldn't do. That wouldn't do *at all*.

He worried and fretted uncharacteristically. And the answer came to him on the evening of the last day.

Ros had a couple of hours to kill before her night flight, so instead of moping in her room, she ran to the boardwalk for one last roller-blading session. Bib didn't have anything to do with it – she decided all on her own. He'd have preferred a few quiet moments with her, actually, instead of trundling alongside her trying to keep up as she whizzed up and down, laughing with pleasure.

Bethany and Tod were there again. Time after time, Bethany ran behind the bike, holding tightly as Tod pedalled a few yards. Back and forth on the same strip of boardwalk they travelled, until, unexpectedly, Bethany let go and Tod careened away. When he realized that he was cycling alone, with no one to support him, he wobbled briefly, before righting himself. 'I'm doing it on my own,' he screamed with exhilaration. 'Look, Mom, it's just me.'

'It's all a question of confidence.' Bethany smiled at Ros.

'I suppose it is,' Ros agreed, as she freewheeled gracefully. Then crashed into a jogger.

As Bib helped her to her feet, he was undergoing a realization. *Of course*, he suddenly understood. He'd been Ros's training wheels and, without her knowing anything about it, he'd given her confidence – confidence to do her job in a strange city, confidence to break free from a bullying man. And just as Tod no longer needed his mother to hold his bike, Ros no longer needed Bib. She was doing it for real now, he could feel it. From her performance in her final meeting to deciding to go roller-blading without any prompting from Bib, there was a strength and a confidence about her that was wholly convincing.

He was happy for her. He really was. But there was no getting away from the fact that the time had come for him to leave her. Bib wondered what the strange sensation in his chest was and it took a moment or two for him to realize that it was his heart breaking for the very first time.

LA airport was aswarm with people, more than just the usual crowd of passengers.

'Alien-spotters,' the check-in girl informed Ros. 'Apparently a little yellow man was spotted here a few days ago.'

Aliens! Ros thought, looking around scornfully at the overexcited and fervent crowd who were laden with Geiger counters and metal-detectors. *Honestly! What are these people like?*

As Ros strapped herself into her airline seat, she had no idea that her plane was being watched intently by a yard-high, yellow life-form who was struggling to hold back tears. 'Big boys don't cry,' Bib admonished himself, as he watched Ros's plane taxi along the runway until it was almost out of sight. In the distance he watched it angle itself towards the sky, and suddenly become ludicrously light and airborne. He watched until it became a dot in the blueness, then traipsed back through the hordes of people keen to make his acquaintance, to where he'd hidden his own craft. Time to go home.

Ros's plane landed on a breezy English summer's day, ferrying her back to her Michael-free life. As the whining engines wound down, she tried to swallow away the sweet, hard stone of sadness in her chest. But, even as she felt the loss, she knew she was going to be fine. In the midst of the grief, at the eye of the storm, was the certainty that she was going to cope with this. She was alone and it was okay. And something else was with her – a firm conviction, an unshakeable faith in the fact that she wouldn't be alone for the rest of her life. It didn't make sense because she was now a single girl, but she had a strange warm sensation of being loved. She felt surrounded and carried by it. Empowered by it.

Gathering her bag and book, slipping on her shoes, she shuffled down the aisle towards the door. As she came down the plane's steps she inhaled the mild English day, so different from the thick hot Los Angeles air. Then she took a moment to stand on the runway and look around at the vast sky, curving over and dwarfing the airport, stretching away for ever. And this she knew to be true – that somewhere out there was a man who would love her for what she was. She didn't know how or why she was so certain. But she was.

Before getting on the bus to take her to the terminal, she paused and did one last scan of the great blue yonder. Yes, no doubt about it, she could feel it in her gut. As surely as the sun will rise in the morning, he's out there. Somewhere . . .

First published in That's Life *magazine, summer 1999.*

Q. *Dear Mammy Walsh, you seem like a devout, respectable woman, with very high standards, yet you swear like a trooper. I have often heard you use the expletive 'fecking'. I don't understand.*
Byron, Auckland

A. Byron pet, you're not Irish, are you? Let me explain. 'Fecking' is a lovely Irish word our Lord gave us when we're irate enough to want to say 'fucking' but we're in polite company. It's barely a swear word at all. 'Fecking' is a beautiful, effective catch-all phrase that you could say to a bishop. As a result I almost never employ 'fucking'. Rarely, very rarely. Like the time when Margaret arrived home to tell me she'd left her droopy-drawers husband, and even then I waited until I was in my bedroom and only said it to Mr Walsh. (I believe the exact phrase I used was, 'For fuck's fucking sake, why can't just fucking one of my fucking daughters stay fucking well married for five fucking minutes?' And Mr Walsh replied, 'Fucked if I know.' And then I said, 'No fucking need for language like that.' Then we had a little laugh because you have to under those sorts of circumstances.) I hope this clears the fecking matter up for you.

Q. *Dear Mammy Walsh, my problem is that I'm addicted to chocolate. I have to have something every afternoon at around three-thirty (usually a Hazelnut Caramel or a Biscuit Boost). I mean, I HAVE to have it. Then, coming home from work, if I'm a little later than usual and hungry, I sometimes buy something for the walk from the bus stop to my flat. (Often a Time Out or a Twirl.) But the biggest problem of all is with boxes of chocolates. Once I open a box, I can't stop. I literally can't. I keep saying, this will be the last one but it never is and the next thing you know the box is empty apart from the coffee cremes and those yukky strawberry ones that – weirdly – are my sister's favourite, but I hate them. Sometimes we are given boxes of chocs at work and they're handed around and everyone takes one and goes back to work, but I keep thinking of the open box with all the uneaten sweets and can't concentrate on anything. Last week, under such circumstances, I sneaked the box into the stationery cupboard and ate eleven – I counted – eleven chocolates in under five seconds. That really worried me. I do have some abandonment issues from my childhood and I wonder if I should see an addiction counsellor.*

Fran, Newcastle

A. I am sick to the back teeth of all this addiction stuff. If you're not addicted to shoes, you're addicted to drink and if you're not addicted to drink you're addicted to Pringles. In my day, Fran, you didn't have 'issues' (unless it was of *Woman's Way* magazine) or twelve-step programmes or 'co-dependence' (whatever that is when it's at home). Nowadays you want to be addicted to everything and it's only because it's fashionable. Not so long ago it was fashionable for you girls to be lesbians and before that it was vegetarians. Chocolate is lovely, everyone knows that. Only a 'weirdo' doesn't love it. We have a tin in our house with a great selection in it, and

I myself enjoy a fun-sized Twix with my cup of coffee every morning, and most days after lunch Mr Walsh and I share a KitKat. (Not the chunky kind, the old-fashioned, four-finger ones. I actually bought them for Helen; she was in bed with a throat infection and asked me to get her KitKats when I went to Dunnes. However, being Helen, she didn't specify that it was actually KitKat Chunkies she wanted and when I arrived home with the non-chunky variety, she nearly ate the head off me. It was so bad that Mr Walsh got back into the car and drove around till he found the chunky ones. Since then we have been working our way through the non-chunky ones and very nice they are too.)

Under

*I*t's so peaceful down here. Muffled and calm, and empty, empty, empty. No one but me. Countless fathoms of empty air above me is another world, the one I came from. I'm not going back.

Not that that's stopping them. My husband, my parents, my sister and my friends are determined to make me come round. Someone told them that people in a coma respond to stimulation, that hearing is the last sense to go, that music and conversation and the voices of my loved ones might haul me up from the depths.

They have me fecking well badgered.

They're nearly in competition over it, showing up at my hospital room, day and night, telling me the deathly dull minutiae of their day, from the dreams they had last night to how many red lights they broke on their way to work this morning, determined that they will be the first one to reach me. Or, worse still, playing music that they insist is my favourite but so isn't. It's the stuff *they* like. They can't help it; it's the rule; it's why people always buy presents for others that they'd like themselves.

The way Chris, my husband, insists I like Coldplay. I don't. He's the one who likes them, but persists in buying their CDs for me. But I see no need to disillusion him, it's only a small thing. The music I really love (seventies disco, for the record) is in my car because driving around on my own is the only time I can be myself.

My dad, mum and sister Orla have just arrived. Orla launches into a complicated account of a blow-drying disaster at the hairdressing salon she runs, where some woman said she was going to sue them for giving her whiplash of the eye with her fringe. Then Dad and Mum give me a blow-by-blow account of a film they've just been to see. I have a strange, sad little feeling that they only went so they'd have something to talk to me about – half-confirmed when Dad suddenly sighs, 'Is there any point to this? Do you think she hears us at all?'

Yes, Dad, I can hear you more than you'd think. It's coming from far away, like from a distant galaxy, but I can still hear you.

'We'll try a bit of James Last,' he suggests. 'She loves that.'

You mean, you love it, Dad.

'We used to dance to it every Christmas,' he says. 'Me and her. She loved it.'

Dad, I was six then. It's nearly thirty years ago.

A muzaky version of 'Waterloo' fills the room. Must be the Abba medley.

Christ, if they're wanting me to return to reality, they're going the wrong way about it.

Gratefully I slip below the surface, down, down, down, down, towards the fathomless bottom. It's so deeply restful here, like lying for a week on a beach on a perfect tropical island, with nothing to worry me, nothing to fear. Feeling nothing, nothing, nothing.

Chris, my husband, is here a lot. He sits very close to me and cries, Coldplay whining quietly in the background. He always smells nice and while he's here he triumphs over the decay and death of the hospital air. He talks incessantly, in a desperate voice. Today, he's saying, 'Laura, remember the first time we met? On the flight to Frankfurt? And I wanted to sit by the window to see the Alps, and you wouldn't give up your seat? I thought you were the feistiest woman I'd ever met. And you said no matter how feisty I thought you were, you were still going to sit beside the window.'

Yes, Chris, I remember.

'And remember when you took me shopping for my interview suit, and you got me into all kinds of stuff I'd never have worn before? We had such a laugh.'

Yes, Chris, I remember.

'Please come back, Laura, oh please come back.' And then – I presume no one else is around – he whispers right into my ear, 'I'm so sorry, Laura, I love you so much, I'm so very, very sorry. I'll make it up to you, just please come back. I'll do whatever you want.'

You could knock off the Coldplay for a while, I think.

But it doesn't matter. I'm going nowhere. I like it down here.

I get lots of visitors. Some I'm more aware of than others. The girls from work came and tried to create the atmosphere of the office by bringing countless bars of chocolate and arguing heatedly about how milk chocolate was so much nicer than dark chocolate – a big chorus of 'Barf! Ooh, *dark* chocolate – puke! I'd rather go without – almost!' broke out.

Lots of laughter at this but it was happening a long way away. I can't always control how conscious I am, I come to and fade out again like a badly tuned radio. Or maybe I just wasn't interested this time. Maybe I was afraid they'd start talking about work stuff. Because I so did not want to know. In many ways, this has been like a little holiday for me. Nicer than a holiday, actually, because the only person down here is me.

With a fright, I'm jolted out of my dark nothingness. My room seems to have filled up with irate cockneys. Several of them shouting angrily: someone has slept with someone else, and the someone else thought the first person loved them but now they're going to effing kill them. Shouty voices and horrible aggression – what's going on? This business to stimulate me has gone too far! I want them out of my room.

My bed is shaking. Now what's happening? A cockney-related earthquake?

'What on EARTH is going on here?' The voice of authority. Some sort of nurse, I'd be bound. 'Mrs Coy and Orla Coy, get OUT of Laura's bed immediately.'

More bed-shaking and my mum's mortified voice. 'Sorry, sister, we were trying to recreate watching *EastEnders* at home. When Laura comes over, we watch it snuggled up on the couch.'

'But she's critically ill! Her head must not be moved! And you could have dislodged one of her tubes, that's the tubes that are keeping her alive, Mrs Coy.'

I'm not sticking around for this. I sink back down, wafting

slowly like a feather, waiting to be subsumed by dark comforting nothingness.

But something must have gone wrong when they invaded my bed because I'm not suspended in the balm of nothingness, I'm standing beside a river. This is new.

'Laura, Laura, over here, Laura!'

On the far bank is a collection of people, young and old, and they're smiling and beckoning energetically. Who the hell are they? As I keep looking, some start to seem familiar; they look like my dad, who is prone to roundy-facedness and high colour. Cousins of mine, they must be. And there's more. There's Aunty Irene, Mum's sister, who died when I was a baby; I recognize her from photos. And there are other Mum lookalikes. I am related to these people.

The whole tableau is strangely familiar. It looks . . . actually . . . it looks exactly like a family wedding. They are all happy and red-faced as if they've just been flinging themselves around some manky ballroom in their wedding finery to 'Let's Twist Again' and 'Sweet Caroline'. Any minute now it'll be time for the rubbery chicken. I shudder.

And then I clock Old Granny Mac, grim and upright in a hard-backed chair. In her hand is her blackthorn stick, the one she used to hit me and Orla on the ankles with when we were young. Well, fuck that, I'm not going someplace where someone else can hit me.

'Get in the raft, Laura,' they call. 'It's there, behind the rushes.'

I take a look. The raft is a gammy, leaky-looking thing, more like a pallet; there aren't even sides to it. No way am I getting on. I might drown. Although from the looks of things, it seems I'm already dead.

'No!' I say loudly and it seems to boom in the sky overhead. 'I'm not going.'

A clamour of 'But you have to, it's your time. Your time is up!' reaches me from the other bank.

'I don't give a flying fuck,' I say, 'I'm not going.'

Family above me, family down here. I'm trapped.

'. . . heart-rate stabilizing . . .'

'We nearly lost her that time.'

'She's a fighter, this one.'

'Oh yes? Might explain all those old bruises on her then.'

Fiona's been here before, but I've only barely been aware of her. This time I can hear her clearly.

'Laura,' she's beseeching, 'don't die, Laura, just don't die and it'll be okay. I will help you fix it.'

I can *feel* her desperation. She's suspected for ages. She hasn't actually said anything but there have been a lot of meaningful looks and coded suggestions. I should have told her, but I haven't. Haven't been able to. Even though she's my best friend. Because it's too shaming, you know?

Chris is back. The nice smell and the low, intense voice is beside me. 'Laura, remember the time I was looking out into the garden and I said, "Laura, look at the beautiful red poppy"? But it wasn't a poppy at all, it was just a chipsticks bag. But because I wasn't wearing glasses, I thought it was a poppy. Remember how we laughed?'

Yes, Chris, I remember. And I remember what happened next.

*

389

Next person to show up is my bossman, Brian the sweat-meister. Chris thanks him for coming. Apparently I'm very conscientious at work; if anything would get through to me, it would be the reminder of how many people I was letting down, while having the temerity to be lying in bed with a life-threatening head injury.

'You sure it's okay to talk to her about work?' Brian asks and a chorus of voices assures him it is the Very Best Thing for me.

A bulky, sweaty presence arrives at my bedside and Brian is not comfortable, not one bit, with talking to the closed face of a woman deep in a coma. He'd never make a children's television presenter; they have to have convincingly vivacious conversations with carrots and flaps of felt and all kinds of inanimate stuff.

Hold her hand, someone urges him. So – gingerly – he does. I'm liking plenty of this coma stuff, but having sluicey bosses, who take all the credit for your work, hold your hand, is a little too much.

'Hello, Laura, I don't, er, know if you can hear me. If you can, I'd like to tell you that all the gang at work misses you and is wishing you a speedy recovery.' *Lifted straight from some crappy greeting card.* 'And let me see . . . um . . . Janet has hit her target weight on Weight Watchers and . . . and . . . oh you'll love this! You know that new young fella, bit of an eejit . . . anyway didn't he walk into the car park the other morning, just after a car had gone through, and he'd forgotten about the barrier – which had gone up to let the car in obviously – and next thing it came belting down on top of the young fella's head! Broke his nose and cracked his skull. Ah sure, as we're all saying, it can only be an improvement!'

Thanks for that, Brian. Telling a woman in a critical condition with a head injury about someone else getting clunked. No wonder they no longer let you anywhere near the clients.

'So, ah, Laura. As you know the launch date for Acideeze – sure of course you know – you set it up! Well, time marches on and we're all depending on you, Laura. You're the best we have, Laura, no one charms those doctors like you do. The others are doing their best, pulling all the showcases together, but we need *you*. Come back, Laura!'

I sense the others in the room are impressed with his bravura plea. That will surely have me lepping out of the bed and into my worksuit, they are thinking.

But behind my blank face I am doing a bit of thinking myself. Hmm, let me consider this now, Brian. So what are you offering me? Going back to work with a broken head and working my arse off on the launch of some new stomach antacid, which if it's a success you'll take all the credit for and if it's a bomb, I'll get the blame? Or staying here where it's restful and peaceful most of the time except when you show up to badger me? Let me just have a little think . . .

You're on your own, bud.

Chris is back at my side. 'Laura, remember the weekend we had in Galway and we saw the dolphins? Remember, there were loads of them, maybe twenty, playing with each other, jumping and diving, like they were putting on a show for us. Such a glorious day and we had the whole beach to ourselves.

Do you remember, Laura? We felt like we'd been personally chosen for a little miracle.'

I remember, Chris, course I remember. Mind you, I remember better what happened next. Remember driving back to the guest house, we accidentally went the wrong way and somehow it was my fault and you swung your arm almost casually across my face, delivering such a blow to my nose and mouth, that blood spurted over the dashboard? Remember that, Chris? Because I do. I had to tell the people in the guest house I'd slipped climbing the rocks. Remember that? And they marvelled at how unlucky I was, how only the day before I'd had that accident on the sailing boat that made my eye close up.

You'd never believe it to look at me, not even when I'm patterned with cuts and bruises. I wear high heels, I'm bossy at work and my hair is always nice (except when clumps of it have been torn out). I manage to explain away my injuries on a sporty lifestyle which people buy because the truth would be so shocking. And, of course, everyone loves Chris. (Well, *nearly* everyone; I think Fiona has her doubts.) They say what a sweetheart he is. So devoted to me. So devoted that if I'm home ten minutes late, he dashes my face against the wall, or punches me in the kidneys, or dislocates my shoulder.

Looking from the outside in, I should have left a long time ago. But the first time he hit me it was a one-off, a unique aberration. He was in the horrors, crying, begging for forgiveness. The second time was also a one-off. As was the third. And the fourth. At some stage the series of isolated incidents stopped being a series of isolated incidents and just became normal life. But I didn't want to see that.

I was too ashamed. Not just by the humiliation of being smacked and punched by the man I loved but because I had made such a big mistake. I'm a smart woman, I should have known. And once I'd known I should have legged it.

It complicated things that I loved him. Or had loved him. And, shallow as this may sound, I'd invested a lot of time and trouble in him being The One; seeing how wrong I'd been was hard to suck up. Especially because we sometimes had our good days. Even now. There were times when he was like the person I'd first met. But I wasn't. My stomach was always a walnut of nerves, wound tight with anxiety, wondering what would happen to tip his mood. A telemarketer calling when he was having his dinner? A button missing from his shirt? Fiona ringing me?

The more he hit me, the less sure of myself I became. At times he almost had me convinced it was what I deserved.

I used to lie awake at night, my head racing, wondering if there was any way out of the trap. Perhaps he'd grow out of it and eventually stop? But even I could see he was getting worse, as he got away with more and more stuff. Go to the police? But they wouldn't help if I didn't press charges. And I couldn't do that. It would make my mistake, my shame, so horribly public and tawdry.

I could leave him, of course. Well, I'd tried that, hadn't I? And look where it had got me. Him going ballistic and flinging me down the stairs and fracturing my skull.

Down here, in the silence, everything seems calm and logical. Sometimes all you need is a little time out to see these things clearly. It's a bit like being on retreat. (Not that I've ever been on one, but I like the sound of them. Just not enough to submit to a weekend without telly and double-ply loo roll.)

Imagine, if I die, he'll have murdered me. He'll have done what he's threatened to do so many times. Although I never really believed him. In fact, I don't think he did either. He might have scared even himself with how badly he's injured me this time. Bottom line is, if I die, he'll be guilty of murder. But I'm the only witness. So if I die, he's in the clear.

But if I don't die . . . ? Well, it's obvious: I will leave him. Even press charges. Why not? You can't go round hitting people and flinging them down flights of stairs. It's just not on.

But I might be too late, because down here something is changing . . . The darkness is filling up with white light. Not just ordinary white light, but super-intense, as though it's being backlit with cleverly concealed halogen bulbs, the type they have in boutique hotels. And the light is forming itself into a shape – a roundy tunnel, with a pulsating circle of fluorescent white light at its end. Suffused with well-being and serenity I am compelled to walk towards it. It's exactly like the stories in the *National Enquirer* from those near-death merchants!

I'm dying! Other than a small tinge of regret that I won't get to fix Chris, I'm, actually, excited.

I keep on walking towards the white light, which throbs hypnotically at me. And then . . . surely I'm imagining it . . . is the light fading a little . . . are the walls of the tunnel becoming more insubstantial? Yes, they are. They definitely are. Going, going, fast. Now there are only wisps, like dry ice; now they're entirely gone, the whiteness replaced with familiar darkness.

'Hey, what's going on?' my head calls.

'It's not your time,' a voice booms.

'But I'm all set. I liked the feeling. Bring it on.'

'It's not your time.'

'Well, make your bloody mind up!'

A pause. Have I gone too far? Then the boomy voice, sounding a little sheepish, murmurs, 'Sorry. Administrative error.'

I wait a little while, to see if the white light returns. Nothing. Nada. Rien. For countless hours, I eddy about in the silent nothingness, and for the first time since I came down here, I'm a little . . . well . . . *bored*. I watch carefully, alert to any signs that the light might return, any little chinks at all in the darkness. But there's nothing; it won't be back.

Well, I decide, if you're not going to let me die, I might as well live.

I take a deep breath and dive towards the surface. I'm coming up from under.

Previously unpublished.